CW00347156

A Falklands
Family at War

A Falklands Family at War

Diaries of the 1982 Conflict

Neville and Valerie Bennett

Edited by
Rachel Simons

Pen & Sword
MILITARY

AN IMPRINT OF PEN & SWORD BOOKS LTD
YORKSHIRE – PHILADELPHIA

First published in Great Britain in 2021 by
PEN & SWORD MILITARY
an imprint of Pen & Sword Books Ltd
Yorkshire – Philadelphia

ISBN 978-1-39901-023-8

Typeset by Concept, Huddersfield, West Yorkshire, HD4 5JL.
Printed and bound by CPI Group (UK) Ltd, Croydon, CR0 4YY

Pen & Sword Books Ltd incorporates the Imprints of Aviation, Atlas, Family
History, Fiction, Maritime, Military, Discovery, Politics, History, Archaeology,
Select, Wharncliffe Local History, Wharncliffe True Crime, Military Classics,
Wharncliffe Transport, Leo Cooper, The Praetorian Press, Remember When,
White Owl, Seaforth Publishing and Frontline Books.

For a complete list of Pen & Sword titles please contact
PEN & SWORD BOOKS LTD
47 Church Street, Barnsley, South Yorkshire, S70 2AS, England
E-mail: enquiries@pen-and-sword.co.uk
Website: www.pen-and-sword.co.uk
or
PEN & SWORD BOOKS
1950 Lawrence Rd, Havertown, PA 19083, USA
E-mail: uspen-and-sword@casematepublishers.com
Website: www.penandswordbooks.com

Contents

List of Plates

Timeline

7 March 1982 – An Argentine Hercules aircraft filled with military personnel makes an unexpected landing at Stanley airport.

19 March 1982 – The Argentine flag is raised over South Georgia, a British island 800 miles to the southeast of the Falkland Islands.

21 March 1982 – HMS *Endurance* leaves Stanley harbour in the early morning carrying twenty-two Royal Marines, headed for South Georgia.

28 March 1982 – Heartfelt entry in Valerie's diary: 'Argentina sends naval reinforcements to S. Georgia. *Endurance* there on her tod – all alone.'

29 March 1982 – 6.30pm. RRS *John Biscoe* arrives in Stanley harbour with the new detachment of Royal Marines. She leaves late evening, headed for Germany.

1 April 1982 – His Excellency the Governor, Rex Hunt, announces to the residents of the Falkland Islands that an Argentine invasion is expected early the following morning. Appropriate preparations made with resources available to defend our islands and homes.

2 April 1982 – Argentine forces invade the Falkland Islands.

5 April 1982 – The first Task Force ships leave Britain for the Falklands.

7 April 1982 – General Mario Menéndez sworn in as Argentine Governor of the Falkland Islands.

12 April 1982 – The British announce a 200-mile exclusion zone around the islands.

22 April 1982 – Argentine President General Leopoldo Galtieri visits the Falkland Islands.

25 April 1982 – British forces recapture South Georgia.

27 April 1982 – A group of civilians from Stanley is taken prisoner and held at Fox Bay. This group included Dr Daniel Haines, the senior medical officer, and his family. The group will be held there until the liberation of the islands. Overnight blackout and curfew to be observed in Stanley, 6.00pm–6.00am.

1 May 1982 – RAF Vulcan bomber raid on Stanley airport, followed by Harrier raids on Stanley and Goose Green. No fewer than 115 civilians taken captive and held under harsh conditions in the community hall at Goose Green; they will remain there until the liberation of Goose Green at the end of the month.

14/15 May 1982 – British special forces attack an Argentine base at Pebble Island, destroying eleven enemy aircraft.

21 May 1982 – British forces begin landing at San Carlos.

28 May 1982 – British forces retake Goose Green.

29 May 1982 – Nightly curfew in Stanley extended to run from 4.00pm to 8.30am. Blackout continues to be a requirement.

14 June 1982 – British forces arrive in Stanley. General Mario Menendez, the leader of the Argentine troops in the Falklands, surrenders.

25 June 1982 – His Excellency the Governor, Rex Hunt, returns to Stanley.

Main Characters in the Diaries

Valerie Elizabeth Bennett, MBE SRN SCM – 3 May 1936–8 June 1986. Nursing sister and midwife, qualified at the Royal Devon & Exeter Hospital, England. Acting Matron of the King Edward VII Memorial Hospital during the war.

Neville Kenneth Bennett – 14 October 1937– Dental technician and fireman. Acting Superintendent of Stanley Fire Service during the war.

Stanley Bennett – Neville's father.

Uncle Harold – Harold Bennett, younger brother of Stanley Bennett. Registrar General of the Falkland Islands until retirement on 31 March 1982.

Isobel Bennett – Daughter of Neville and Valerie, aged 13 in 1982.

Rachel Bennett – Daughter of Neville and Valerie, aged 11 in 1982.

Malcolm Binnie – Dockyard foreman. Lifelong friend of Neville.

Pat McPhee – Assistant Superintendent of Stanley Fire Service.

Dr Alison Bleaney – Senior medical officer during the war.

Argentines

'Bloomer' – Lieutenant Colonel Carlos Bloomer-Reeve.

'Dowling' – Major Patricio Dowling of the Argentine Army.

'Hussey' – Captain Melbourne Hussey of the Argentine Navy.

Admiral Busser – Naval commander of the Argentine invasion of the Falkland Islands.

Colonel Dorrego 'the colonel' – Argentine head of public works during the occupation. Dorrego was a colonel in the Argentine Army.

Alfonso Quinones – The fire chief of Comodoro Rivadavia, a city in southern Argentina.

Captain Gafoglio – Naval Intelligence officer, based in Gilbert House, Dockyard.

Captain Paganini – One of Colonel Dorrego's engineers

Dr Mario – Argentine civilian doctor.

General Menendez – Commander of the Argentine forces in the Falkland Islands.

Corporal George – The colonel's driver and bodyguard, and the office messenger; proud carrier of an Uzi.

Lieutenant Colonel Gamen – Argentine Airlines (LADE) representative in the Falklands.

Foreword

by Professor Tony Pollard

Many books on the Falklands War, or Falklands/Malvinas Conflict as it is officially known, have appeared in the almost forty years since it was fought. The conflict marked a watershed in the nature of military writing, with the full arrival of what I call the 'squaddie memoir' giving voice to those of lower rank, who actually did the fighting, as opposed to those in senior positions who up until then were more likely to put pen to paper. Many aspects of the war at sea, on land and in the air have been covered, and no doubt the fortieth anniversary will see more books appear. These will probably include the personal recollections of veterans, many of whom are still young enough to have reasonable memories of the events of 1982. There will also, no doubt, be more secondary works, which, given the passage of time, are now readily classifiable as works of military history. To me, as a university-based historian and conflict archaeologist, who both studies and teaches the conflict, all of these new ventures into print will be welcomed. One aspect missing, however, is the Argentine perspective, with fewer works on the conflict written in Argentina and not many of these translated into English. It is hoped that the fortieth anniversary might mark a change here, but it is not the only gap that needs filling.

On 2 April 1982 the Falklands were invaded by Argentine forces, and from that moment on, until the surrender on 14 June, the islanders were to live under military occupation. For most of us it is impossible to imagine what this experience must be like, and it is here that civilian, not military, voices play a vital role in fleshing out the record. There have been very few published memoirs by islanders; the first of them was the diary of John Smith, who is mentioned in the present volume, which appeared in 1984 as *74 Days: An Islander's Diary of the Falklands Occupation*. This was later joined by several works by Graham Bound, who at the time of the invasion was the editor of the island's newspaper, *Penguin News*. These include *Falkland Islanders at War* (2002), and *Fortress Falklands: Life Under Siege in Britain's Last Outpost* (2012). The present volume will therefore make an important contribution in presenting another islander perspective on the invasion and the occupation and conflict that followed.

It is, however, an important work in its own right, presenting as it does the experiences of not one person but a family of four.

I have kept a diary for years, and endeavour in it to record my activities on any given day. Writing it up every evening has become a habit, with a growing number of volumes providing me with an *aide-mémoire* of tasks accomplished, meetings attended and places visited. For anyone else it would make for a most tedious read, and indeed there are times when I wonder why I bother. Ironically, when exciting things are happening, the entries are sparser than normal and at times missing altogether, for the simple reason that I have been distracted, but I also might feel that the photographs taken during these periods will stand as record enough. Fortunately, none of this is true of the present volume.

The diary entries contained within these pages are packed with fascinating insights into life under Argentine occupation, commencing just before the arrival of the invasion and extending to well beyond the surrender, which took place 74 days after Amtrak troop carriers made landfall on beaches to the north of Stanley. We are indebted to Valerie Bennett, who was made MBE for her service as a nurse in Stanley during the occupation, and her husband Neville, who as an all-round handyman helped to keep the town running and served as a volunteer fireman, for recognising the historical gravity of the days they were living through and never failing to provide some record of the day's events. This is not a work that has been composed in retrospect, where hindsight will be coloured by knowledge of liberation; it grew on a daily basis during a time when war crept ever closer as British forces landed to the west and fought their way to Stanley. This, in addition to the constraints of occupation, shifting relationships with occupying forces and regular air raids, which at times occurred frighteningly close to the town, provided the incredible backdrop to daily life, which included all the requirements of raising a family.

It is the voice of that family which is heard here, and this volume has been edited by Rachel Simons, the youngest of Valerie and Neville Bennett's two daughters, who was ten years old at the time of the invasion and, as the diary entries record, celebrated her eleventh birthday just a few weeks into the occupation (her sister, Isobel, is mentioned in the diaries). Rachel has provided useful footnotes and in places added her own recollections. At times, these additional comments add striking imagery and colour to the accounts, such as when she recalls the smell of grease on an Uzi submachine gun which an Argentine soldier casually tossed onto the kitchen table. Movingly, Rachel also recalls whiling away time by building and decorating doll's houses, creating miniature spaces in which she could find some sanctuary from harsh reality. These brief additions to the text help to get across the trauma generated by insecurity, upheaval and uncertainty, to the point that one comes closer to understanding why it was not just some combatants who went on to develop what we now know as PTSD.

This is more than the story of a family at war, though, and for this reader the trickling in of news of British progress following the landings on 21 May was fascinating to follow. At times these snippets of news appear to have been nothing more than rumours, and as such could be half-truths or just plain wrong. For instance, the tragic and confused incident on 28 May, when three British paratroopers were killed while seeking an Argentine surrender on seeing a white flag, comes through in the diary entry for 31 May as the death of seventeen Royal Marines after the Argentine defenders of Goose Green had shown a white flag (the total British death toll for the battle was actually sixteen men from 2 Para, one Royal Engineer and one Royal Marine helicopter pilot).

Observations on the activities of Argentine forces in Stanley during the occupation and their reaction to the pressures applied by terrestrial combat to the west and multiple air raids represent important new insights into the conflict, from a perspective only available to those in Stanley at the time. The Argentines are painted fairly here, with some of them shown to behave as decently as circumstances would allow and others doing little to earn respect, and the confirmation that booby traps were set around Stanley just prior to surrender is certainly one manifestation of the latter.

To go into any more detail here would risk spoiling the reader's experience, and so it just remains to be said that this volume will be accompanying this reader on his next visit to the islands, and while in Stanley one destination will be the junction of John Street and Barrack Street, where the diary entry of 5 May records two holes containing 40-gallon drums, with banked earth creating a firing position. Could it be that there is some archaeological trace of this feature still visible?

Tony Pollard

Professor of Conflict History and Archaeology,
University of Glasgow, Glasgow.
February 2021

REFERENCES

Bound, G. (2002), *Falkland Islanders at War* (Pen & Sword).
Bound, G. (2012), *Fortress Falklands: Life Under Siege in Britain's Last Outpost* (Pen & Sword).
Smith, J. (1984), *74 Days: An Islander's Diary of the Falklands Occupation* (Century).

Preface

This is the story of the Falklands war from our end of the street. Our house was 2 Drury Street, in the middle of Stanley, the main town in the Falklands Islands. It is the story of the 74-day war told through the eyes of local residents.

We were a family of four, plus one cat, ten hens and a rooster. Mum was the senior nursing sister, the Matron, in the hospital. Dad was the chief fireman. Isobel was 13 and I had my 11th birthday during the war.

During those dark days mum and dad both kept daily diaries, noting down their activities and observations of events going on around them. Until I opened it early in 2020, mum's diary had remained in a storage box, unopened except for the occasional glance by dad. In 1986 dad bought an electric typewriter, typed up his diaries and gave a few copies to friends, with the hope of one day publishing them.

During the first Covid lockdown of 2020, I took their diaries and blogged them on the parallel days through the months of April to July. It was an emotional journey. Mum sadly had died in 1986. Seeing her beautiful handwriting again and reading her perspective on events was very special and surprisingly reassuring. I'm at a similar age now to hers back then, and through reading her diaries I have been able to meet my mum as an adult. Those daily blogs were a huge success; our logs show us that at their peak of popularity there were several thousand readers each day in an astounding ninety-one countries. Time and time again we were asked to publish these diaries in book form, so here we are!

Dad is Neville Bennett, and his ancestors were amongst the first settlers on the islands. Born in Stanley on 14 October 1937, he completed an apprenticeship as a dental technician, making false teeth, crowns, bridges, braces, etc., in Stanley. At the age of 20 he worked his six-week passage to England onboard RRS *Shackleton* as galley crew – and still remembers peeling 213 potatoes a day! Having completed his studies, dad returned to the Falklands with his City & Guilds of London Certificate in Dental Technology and started work as a dental technician at the hospital in Stanley.

Mum was Valerie Bennett; she was born and grew up in Taunton, Somerset. She met dad on her first day working as a midwife and nursing sister in the hospital in Stanley. Mum had trained in the Royal Devon & Exeter Hospital; in 1957 she qualified and was awarded England's 'Nurse of the Year'. Mum worked locally for a few years after qualifying, but then, fancying a change, she applied for a job in the Falklands.

Dad's diaries reveal, in great and fascinating detail, life in occupied Stanley and his work as a heating maintenance man in many Argentine-commandeered properties. Every day he was in contact and conversation with the 'Argies', and he included some of these conversations in his diaries, weaving in his own brand of humour.

Mum's diary is in more of a medical note format. She calmly reports on her role leading the nursing staff of a small, isolated hospital in the middle of a war. She writes of the struggles with the Argentines, of delivering babies and being a mum trying to run a home with limited supplies and a failing washing machine. To respect medical confidentiality, mum's diaries only use the initials of her patients. Despite the daily pressures, mum took the time to notice the weather and always included a daily summary.

The islanders' war story has rarely been told. It is my privilege and honour to present to you our story, from our end of the street.

Rachel Simons
November 2020

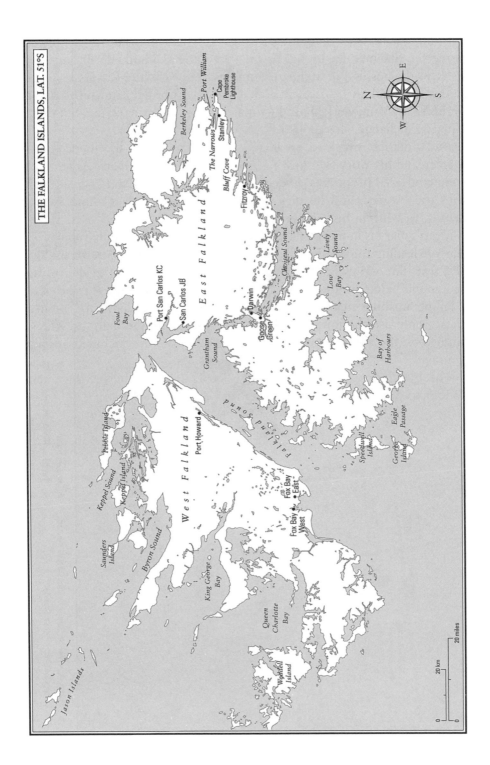

THE FALKLAND ISLANDS, LAT. 51°S

N
W E
S

Jason Islands

Saunders Island

Pebble Island

Keppel Sound
Keppel Island

Byron Sound

West Falkland

Port Howard

King George Bay

Queen Charlotte Bay

Weddell Island

Foul Bay

Berkeley Sound

Port William
Cape Pembroke Lighthouse
The Narrows
Stanley

Port San Carlos KC
San Carlos JB

East Falkland

Bluff Cove
Fitzroy

Grantham Sound

Darwin
Goose Green

Choiseul Sound

Lively Sound

Low Bay

Bay of Harbours

Falkland Sound

Fox Bay East
Fox Bay West

Speedwell Island
George Island
Eagle Passage

0   20 km
0   20 miles

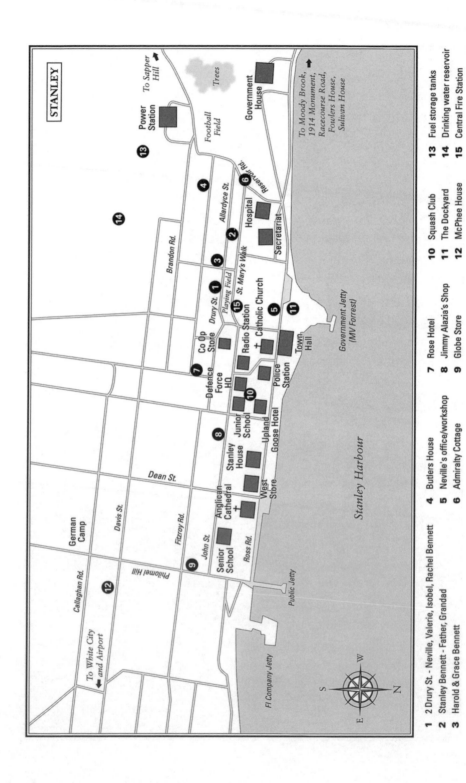

STANLEY

To Sapper Hill

Trees

Power Station

Football Field

Government House

To Moody Brook,
1914 Monument,
Racecourse Road,
Fowlers House,
Sulivan House

13

14

Reservoir Rd.

4

Brandon Rd.

Allardyce St.

Hospital

Secretariat

2

3

Drury St.

Playing Field

15

St. Mary's Walk

Co Op Store

1

Catholic Church

5

11

7

Radio Station

Defence Force HQ

Town Hall

10

Government Jetty
(MV Forrest)

Police Station

8

Junior School

Upland Goose Hotel

Stanley House

Dean St.

West Store

Anglican Cathedral

German Camp

Davis St.

John St.

Fitzroy Rd.

Ross Rd.

Senior School

Philomel Hill

Callaghan Rd.

9

12

Stanley Harbour

To White City
and Airport

Public Jetty

Fl Company Jetty

N
E   W
S

1   2 Drury St. - Neville, Valerie, Isobel, Rachel Bennett
2   Stanley Bennett - Father, Grandad
3   Harold & Grace Bennett

4   Butlers House
5   Neville's office/workshop
6   Admiralty Cottage

7   Rose Hotel
8   Jimmy Alazia's Shop
9   Globe Store

10 Squash Club
11 The Dockyard
12 McPhee House

13 Fuel storage tanks
14 Drinking water reservoir
15 Central Fire Station

'Invasion Day'

by Rachel Simons

There go our boys

Creeping. Dropping. Signalling. Stopping.
Gun bearing, black clothed strangers invade our town.

Creeping. Dropping. Signalling. Stopping.
Green beret wearing friends defend our homes.

Concern-silenced parents stare at the radio in hope of
hearing hope.

Concern-subdued youngsters drift from room to room
searching for distraction.

Cat sleeps on.

White flag carrying Matron Mum summoned to hospital.
Cautiously walking through recently silenced street battle zone.
Much work awaits our very own Florence.

Rattling. Squealing. Crunching. Grinding.
Tanklike monsters growl along our gentle streets.

Sky: noisily filled with unfamiliar craft.
Heads: filled with unfamiliar feelings. Fear and Shock.

Poultry need feeding.
All present and accounted for, hens hungrily peck and gobble,
oblivious to the invading madness.

Lifeless. Facedown in the roadside gulley, one mother's
precious son won't return home.

Royal Marine prisoners. Family friends.
Inwardly defiant. Standing proud. Herded away.
Sister cries. Dad sighs 'there go our boys'.

MARCH 1982

Sunday, 7 March 1982

Valerie's diary

7am–3pm (hospital shift).

Pleasant 1st thing, wind freshened from n/w and overcast by 3.00pm. Gale force wind all evening, 50–60 knots.

Very quiet at the hospital. Two patients and six residents.

Finished knitting back of Isobel's rose-pink top.

Emergency landing by an Argentine plane, losing fuel, luckily nothing serious.

Plenty of vegetables around after the horticultural show.

Polish yacht anchors off public jetty.

Neville's diary

A very windy day even by Falkland Islands standards. I was called out to Stanley airport with two fire crews. The Civil Aviation Authority had received what we believed to almost be a 'May Day' call from the Captain of an Argentine Air force Hercules C130 transport plane with fuel problems. Apparently, he was losing fuel and had only a few minutes flying time left. Despite a 50–60 mph wind from the northwest a successful landing was made.

When the plane pulled onto the apron in front of the control tower and airport offices, about thirty Argentine military men jumped out, all bearing side arms. The Argentine fuel depot man arrived with the couplings for refuelling.

That was when a couple of minor snags sort of crept in. The plane was forty or so yards away from the fuel point, when the Captain, with very clever use of the reverse thrust of the propellers, zigzagged the plane to the desired position.

And snag number two: the Argentine airline aircraft which usually refuelled here were Fokker F27 or F28. The connections would be a little different in size to those for a Hercules.

That was eventually sorted out. Meanwhile, the passengers were having a look round the control tower and offices and having a natter with the resident Argentine ground staff. These were in the Islands to maintain the link with Lineas Aereas del Estado, the Argentine state airline (LADE). This was our only contact by air with the outside world by an agreement made in 1971 or so.

The LADE staff consisted of a Vice Comodoro (Lieutenant Colonel), an office manager and a radio operator. A local person was employed as driver and general factotum.

After the pantomime with the fuel pipes, the delivery of fuel to the Herc began. Normal practice was that when an aircraft was refuelling, two members of the fire service stood by with suitable extinguishing equipment. I had a look into the hull of the plane. There were parachutes placed round the sides and two large fuel tanks in the forward part of the hold. There was none of the baggage that one would have expected to see belonging to men who had been relieved from an Antarctic base. There was moisture dripping from the wing surface, but it didn't smell of fuel. I noticed that there were refuelling drogues in pods on the underside of the wings. Having a quick glance at the control panel by the fuel entry point, I noticed that the needles were all hard-over to the right, usually indicating full. Perhaps they couldn't transfer fuel in flight from the supernumerary tanks to the in-use tanks.

All the time this was happening the Royal Marine contingent had been deployed round the perimeter of the Airport, one had managed to take a few snaps of the interior of the Herc'. The passengers all returned to their places, the Aircraft took off again at 6.30pm, no problem at all, straight up and away to the northwest.

As we were driving back up the road to Stanley I saw that the water in the harbour was lifting and steaming with the force of the wind, an indication of a very high wind indeed.

APRIL 1982

Thursday, 1 April 1982

Valerie's diary

Day off.

Warmer this morning, dull, light s/w wind.

I was called into the hospital at 6.15pm.

Possible confrontation with the Argentines to-night, all medical staff are on standby.

Neville's diary

Early in the evening, I was helping prepare the family meal. I heard the sound of aircraft engines. That's odd I thought, a bit late in the day for a medical flight. I nipped into the front room to look out of the window. The Islander aircraft of the Falkland Islands Government Air Service (FIGAS) was flying unusually low from the east. Stanley Airport and the Islander hangar were at the east end of the harbour, looks like it had come from there. The plane swung round and landed at the racecourse, west of Government House. Why was that then? It had never landed there before.

7.20pm Brian Summers, Superintendent of Stanley Fire Service, knocked on my door. He handed me a bunch of keys and told me that I would have full responsibility for the Fire Service until further notice as he would be rather busy for a while with a Morse key in one hand and a self-loading rifle [SLR] in the other.

7.30pm His Excellency the Governor, Mr Rex Hunt[1], came on the Box,[2] asking everyone to remain calm as there was a distinct possibility of a skirmish on the beach at Yorke Bay[3] sometime during the night or early in the morning and it could be a bit noisy.

The penny drops – that's why the Islander aircraft was brought up to town for shelter.

Valerie, acting Matron of the King Edward VII Memorial hospital, had been called over to a meeting earlier in the evening and had returned in a rather distressed state. It transpired that none of her staff were trained in the care of gun-shot wounds, bomb blast and other warlike damage to the human frame. She well knew that there were several ladies in the town in an advanced state of pregnancy and what would all this excitement do for them?

---

1. His Excellency the Governor was Her Majesty the Queen's representative in the Falkland Islands.
2. Local term for a cable rediffusion system in the town permanently on. The farms outside Stanley, locally known as the Camp, relied on radio.
3. 4½ miles from Stanley on the airport road.

I phoned Pat, the Assistant Supt Fire Service. I told him what Brian had said. Together we checked the fire appliances, which were sited at various places around the town.

3 Godiva trailer pumps,
1 lightweight portable pump on a trailer,
1 × 250 gallon water bowser.[4]
1 × hose laying truck, which was a Canadian Ford of 1940 vintage.
3 × Land Rover Firefly vehicles with a 100 gallon water tank.

Each firefly was carrying an assortment of extinguishers, regular fire-fighting equipment, chimney fire kit and drain cleaning rods.

The larger of the 3, registration plate F55, was garaged in the Central Fire Station on St Mary's walk.

Fireflys registered 212 and 399 were garaged at the top of the town in a garage in Callaghan Road.

399 was also equipped with airport specific equipment.

We checked the breathing apparatus sets, put some spare air cylinders and spare charges for the extinguishers on the trucks, put out some extra fuel cans and went home.

I compiled a list of men who were in the town and not connected to the Falklands Islands Defence Force [FIDF] or the Police Force. I phoned them all and got 36 blokes willing to turn out to designated stations if called. I warned them that they might have to dodge some bullets. They were all willing to risk that.

I began to consider what we would be up against. A town of some 1,200 people who mainly lived in wooden buildings, although there were some stone and brick structures in the town. At the east end of the houses was the Argentine fuel depot consisting of 50 or so cylindrical tanks of 1,000 to 1,500-gallon capacity. These contained petrol for local use and JP-1, the fuel for the LADE F-28 jet planes that came across from Argentina each week. I didn't know how much fuel they had in stock. A bit late in the day to start asking those sorts of questions. If that lot got hit by a mortar bomb or any incendiary device, we might as well write the lot off and any houses for quite a way round.

On the hill to the southwest of the town, behind the power station, were two enormous tanks containing diesel oil. This was for the generation of electricity and general use for the Government such as heating of public buildings and fuel for vehicles. These tanks were 40 ft high and 36 ft in diameter, one being full and the other half empty.

---

4. Water tank on wheels.

In the flat area below these tanks, behind the power station were two ready use tanks for supply to the power station. Being only 18 ft high they didn't pose such a problem, and because of their position were not so vulnerable as the two on top of the hill.

Further up the hill is an area called Dairy Paddock with some springs and swampy land which all drains down past the oil tanks and the power station. This is called the Government Stream and it flows into Stanley Harbour. The nurses' home sits on the edge of this stream and the hospital is just across the road. Oh, dearie me, if anything hits those tanks and ignites the oil there could be a problem. Fingers crossed and keep a loo-roll handy.

The Falkland Islands Broadcasting Station (FIBS) was to stay open and on air all night, giving information regarding any situation which may arise. The station usually closed down at 10.30pm with the national anthem.

Our two daughters, aged 10 and 13, were in bed. We had told them there might be something unusual happening and there could be a bit of noise during the night. If they heard any shooting they were to keep down as low as possible.

At 9.45pm the phone rang. My immediate reaction was to wonder what disaster had happened. Pat had had a call from the telephone exchange to say that a report had come in of smoke and visible flames at the rear of Government House. He would call for me in Firefly 212 which was kept on Callaghan Road just behind his home. We approached Government House quietly along Ross Road, using the rotating light only in case the siren caused a bit of panic. We entered the courtyard behind the main building and saw two 40-gallon petrol drums, which is the standard Falklands rubbish bin, well alight. A very large man in a white sweater who I had never seen before, was feeding papers into the flames.

I asked him what he was doing.

'Have a beer mate,' he replied, 'we're burning classified documents from the communications centre in the Governor's office.'

He thrust a couple of cans of Brown Ale into our hands.

I explained that the usual procedure was to ring the exchange and tell the operator before lighting a bonfire after dark, and it may have been prudent to do so at this time.

'Bugger off mate; we've got other things on our mind tonight.'

I then noticed a pair of SLRs leaning up against the fence as well as other military bits. Things were tending to get serious after all.

Another phone call on arrival home, it was Andy Mac. The Royal Marine garrison[5] was due to change-over at this time and the people of the town took [in] members of the old detachment as guests for a few days until they were shipped out. Over the year we had formed a friendship with Andy MacDonald. On the phone Andy said that he wouldn't be able to get down for the night as they were expecting a bit of a party. I wished him luck and said we would see him later.

Friday, 2 April 1982

Valerie's diary
Disturbed night.
1st Shots heard 5.00am ish. The invasion is on.
Argentine warships in Port William. Planes on the strip.
Troops around Government House and Stanley.
Very confused in the hospital.
Argies and guns in the hospital. Disconcerting.

Neville's diary
I didn't sleep very much last night; I don't think Valerie did either. We had both gone to bed half-dressed just in case the call came.

The radio could be heard quietly coming from the kitchen through the open doors. The night dragged on.

Oh well! Let's have another listen to the Box. Rex Hunt was saying that there was still nothing doing and to keep calm.

The staff on duty in the broadcasting studio were playing records. 'Strangers in the Night' seemed to come on quite often.

I made a cup of tea on the gas hob. The kitchen was quite cool as I had turned off the oil-fired Rayburn cooker, just in case.

Back to bed for some more sleeplessness.

I wonder what the Marines[6] are up to, something nasty no doubt.

WHAT THE HELL WAS THAT?

Quickly out to the kitchen, Rex Hunt was saying that a boat had come in through the narrows and was firing on Government House ... no it

---

5. Forty Royal Marines of Naval Party 8901 were stationed for year-long tours at Moody Brook barracks. This was located at the west end of Stanley harbour.
6. As it was detachment change-over time, there were almost double the usual forty Royal Marines of Naval Party 8901 stationed in Stanley. A number of them had been taken to South Georgia onboard HMS *Endurance* to deal with the Argentine invasion of that British island. Almost seventy Royal Marines were left in Stanley, positioned to defend the town for as long as possible against the Argentine invaders.

wasn't ... something had blown up in The Narrows,[7] anyway it was a big explosion.

I must have dropped off to sleep after all. I started up to a loud thump and the sound of a lot of small arms fire at around 5am.

I wondered if there had been any Argies lurking round at Government House when we had been there a few hours previous. Anyway, the Marines and the FIDF[8] would soon sort them out as there could only be a handful or two as a token force.

The Box was quite busy, reports of a large force landing at Yorke Bay.

An exchange of fire, the invading force moving up to the Airport.

Sounds of explosions and small arm and automatic weapon fire from the west end of the harbour at Moody Brook where the Royal Marine barracks are situated.[9]

Rex Hunt was on the Box again saying that Government House was under fire from various types of weapons, and that he was ok and sitting under his desk with a 9mm pistol.

I could hear footsteps and voices on the hill alongside the house. I went quickly and quietly upstairs to look out of the west window.

In the early morning light, I could make out the forms of six or seven Marines, crouching down at the corner, using my uncle's house and the pillarbox as cover. They were firing continuously at the trees at the back of Government House, or where the trees would be if there was enough light to see them by. One tall 'Bootie' with a General-Purpose Machine Gun was blazing away to the westwards and getting some answering fire. He was complaining he had put 'so many rounds into the bastard but the f***ing idiot didn't know when to give in'.

Surprising what a bit of tension would do, the 'lads' were not given to using foul language on the street in Stanley. They moved off down the hill over the fence into Malvina Paddock and onto the front road.[10]

Rex Hunt on the Box again: someone had tried to put a hand grenade in through the west porch door of Government House and they had been dealt with quite firmly.

---

7. The Narrows are the entrance to Stanley harbour, an inlet 7 miles long and over a mile across at its widest point, which has the town of Stanley along much of the south side.
8. Falkland Islands Defence Force.
9. Added by N.B. in 1986: We were told later that the Argies had gone into the 'Brook' in classical style, tossing hand grenades in through the doorways following with bursts of small arms fire. Did they think the Booties [Royal Marines] were going to be there sitting playing cards waiting for them to burst in like a western film?
10. Ross Road.

That was the only fatality the Argentines admitted to.

More shooting and explosions. The radio announcer came on again, this time to say that the Argies had cleared away all the obstructions on Stanley airport and a large number of tracked Armoured Personnel Carriers [APCs] were on their way up to the town. A comment came from Government House that bullets were hitting the roof and walls like hailstones. I wondered how the reports were reaching the studio, they must have had observation posts all around the town.

Some were calling on the phone from their homes into the studio: Tom Davies and Alistair Greaves on Davis Street East by the Common Gate. Two houses had been hit by mortar bombs. No fire resulting although there was some damage. Tom couldn't say much more as his roof had collapsed on him and he could hear running water as the water supply tank in the loft space had been hit by bullets.

The APCs[11] had reached the town. Rex Hunt said they had 'bloody big cannons' and you couldn't fight against those with just small arms, a lot of damage would be done to property and severe loss of civilian life could be the result.

I knew the FIDF was out with the Marines, so perhaps it was just a couple of handfuls of us against a lot of 'them' instead of the other way around as I had a originally thought; 'they' were certainly serious – and had met some very serious, albeit small in number, opposition.

A strange voice came on the Box, heard faintly over the top of the studio broadcasting. He said that he could hear the studio and wanted to get a message to the head of the Government and to use the broadcasting studio to relay messages. His message was that the Falklands forces should surrender and avoid more bloodshed. Whose blood was being shed, I wondered. The announcer said there were armed men in the studio. We could hear him saying 'Get that gun out of my back and I will talk to you.'

A new voice came on the air: 'Peoples are advised to stay in their houses and to surrender, we have a lot of armed men in the town.'

Things happened quite rapidly then. The caller was the leader of the invading force on a ship in Port William. A conversation between the ship and Government House was conducted through the studio, [and] a cease-fire was arranged.

Hector Gilobert, who had previously been the Vice Comodoro in charge of the Argentine fuel depot and LADE airline link, was in the

---

11. These were LVPT7 Amtrack Armoured Personnel Carriers. They had a crew of three and the capacity to carry up to twenty-five armed personnel.

Islands. He appeared on the front road bearing a white flag and arranged the surrender of the British Forces in the Islands.

The Royal Marines and FIDF had been up against 6,000 plus troops. There seemed to be a fair amount of noisy chatter coming over the air on the Box. I suppose the Argies[12] were in their usual fashion 'quietly' organising things and arguing who was going to be in charge. One of the overnight presenters was complaining bitterly, 'The bastards are swiping all my fags. Why don't you get some of your own?'

The other presenter was trying to get some sense into the disorder. He said that a contact had been made with the Argentine communications. If people had to go off their property for any good reason, the should ring him first and then he would contact the Argy forces and they would ok the trip. Fine.

Our phone rang, 'Would Valerie please get over to the hospital as soon as she could as there is a bit of an emergency.'

I rang the telephone exchange and asked to be put through to the broadcasting studio. Wonderful: 'they' even know how to work the Stanley telephone switchboard. Still, I expect Hilda Perry and the girls would be there to make sure that things went ok.

The producer in the studio said he would broadcast to the forces that Valerie would be walking along St Marys Walk to the hospital on official medical business.

I said cheerio to Valerie at the door. She went through the front gate, crossed the playing field, went onto St Marys Walk and then turned towards the hospital. Two armed men fell in a few yards behind her with rifles at the ready. An escort I presumed. I thought they were pretty quick off the mark rounding up an escort that fast.[13]

Rachel remembers ...

My most painful invasion day memory is watching mum bravely, boldly walking away from home carrying her white flag.

To make her flag, dad had got a white pillowcase from the airing cupboard and tied it to a spare broom handle. I stood in the front room window and watched as she went through the gate, across the playing field

---

12. Argentines.

13. Speaking of this some years later Valerie said she hadn't been aware of these men and if she had seen them, she might have had a nasty turn there and then. I also found out that they weren't an escort but a couple of soldiers having a look round and probably 'souveniring'. It did look a bit worrying, though, the acting matron of the hospital with a white flag over her shoulder followed by two armed men.

and out of sight towards the hospital. Just an hour or so before that the playing field and street had been the site of fighting between the Royal Marines and the invaders. It felt to me that the noise of the bullets was still in the air. We didn't know what mum would face at the hospital or if we would ever see her again.

Neville's diary continues ...
The sun came out and promised a warm day, a thing that didn't usually happen for tourists. Oh dear! Not an omen.

I thought it was time to check up on the situation regarding the Fire Service. I rang the telephone exchange, normally the source of all information. An Argy answered. I asked him what they had done about the incidence of fires in the town. His reply was that they had stopped shooting. I said not that sort of fire but houses and other buildings burning.

'Who has lit a fire?'

'No one.'

'No problem.'

Click, the line went dead.

I had a look out through the front porch and saw that Gerald Cheek was being escorted home to the Police Cottages by two armed men. He seemed to be minus a fair bit of his FIDF uniform.

Another announcement on the Box. What it boiled down to was that there were a couple of ways of getting yourself shot: (1) disrespect of the Argentine Flag, and (2) disrespect of any member of the Argentine Forces.

It carried on: The Argentine forces had repossessed the Islas Malvinas, the Islas Malvinas were now under the control of the armed forces of the Republica Argentina.

By the look of the masts and funnels coming into sight out in Port William,[14] this was not something got up on the spur of the moment. A lot of organising had gone into this invasion attempt against 70–80 minimally armed men. The day wore on, the sun was shining, and armed Argentine soldiers patrolled the streets.

I spoke to my 70-year-old father on the phone, he was ok, he had a few beers and enough food.

There were plenty of aircraft movements, all sorts of helicopters, Chinooks, Pumas, HU 1's. The 'Observer's Book of Aircraft' was referred to very often.

Some of the APCs were to be seen moving down the other side of the harbour. One appeared to be in some sort of difficulty, I think it had shed

---

14. The outer harbour, accessed from Stanley harbour through The Narrows.

a track. One of the helicopters goes over to look at it, all fixed and they move off again towards the naval fuel depot with its tanks of diesel and other stores.

They went up the hill towards the caretaker's house. The sound of gun fire came over the water. What were they doing? Were there some 'Booties' hanging around there? Were Hector and Millie Anderson inside? No one came out and no bodies were carried out. Just pure bloody-mindedness. Vandalism. How far round the Islands had the Argies got, were there armed men on all the farms?

The voice on the Box was still urging people not to go out but stay on their own property unless there was urgency about going out.

There were six young armed men in a patrol going up and down our street; they looked very tired and very thirsty. I had a good idea that they had been seasick not too long before, and seasickness is a good way of getting dehydrated.

Camouflaged vehicles started to appear on the road. A couple of Land Rovers and some Mercedes with soft tops like a Land Rover and a small Volkswagen 4 × 4. That would be ok for fishing trips when they had all gone home. They had taken the doors off the Moody Brook Land Rovers and were joyriding in them, all seemed on a 'High'.

At about 5.30pm the Governor's Car, a burgundy coloured London taxi, passed along St Mary's Walk, with the Governor Rex Hunt, his wife Mrs Hunt and someone else inside. The Governor was wearing his official uniform, big feathered hat and all. Behind the car came two rubber-wheeled amphibious personnel carriers[15] with the Royal Marines in them. All were in uniform except for one chap standing up in the front in a navy-blue boiler suit. Where they were being taken, we didn't know. We hoped they would be treated fairly, even though they had tried to take out the whole of the Argentine forces. Still, that is what wearing the Green Beret is all about.[16]

Rachel remembers ...

I was standing beside Dad, watching the two LVTP7 Amtracks shooting at Hector and Millie's house and the surrounding rocks. I was surprised by

---

15. These were LARC-V (Lighter, Amphibious Resupply, Cargo, 5 ton): aluminium-hulled amphibious cargo vehicles capable of transporting 5 tons. They are not arm-oured, and look like boats with wheels.

16. We were told later that Rex Hunt, Mrs Hunt, their son Tony, all the Marines and their wives had been taken to a neutral port for repatriation to England. We only believed that when we heard from the BBC that they had all arrived home in the UK safely.

the noise and amount of shots being fired. It seemed way too much for one stone house.

Then, watching the Royal Marines leaving, being driven along St Mary's Walk, was a hugely sad moment. Dad just sighed and said, 'there go our boys' and we felt so very alone and unprotected.

Neville's diary continues ...
On the Box they were asking for information as to the whereabouts of seven Royal Marines who were unaccounted for. Anyone knowing where these dangerous men were must inform the military. If they were given up immediately, no harm would come to the person hiding them. This message was repeated quite often during the evening.

I had a look out through the front window and saw some military policemen walking past with white writing on their helmets and armbands. They had got that wrong, PM? Shouldn't it be MP? Oh no! In Spanish things are a bit back to front so they say Policía Militaria. I suppose we will have to become fluent in Espanish or even Spanglish.

I turned on the radio to listen to the outside world. London was fairly non-committal as they didn't have the full story. USA hardly mentioned the affair at all, and Moscow didn't say a word.

Valerie was still at the hospital, we hoped to see her in the morning.

Another bit on the Box, some of their troops came on air to lament their comrade who had been killed at Government House. They ended up in tears, they wanted to rename Ross Road after him.

So ended a quite traumatic day: having one's home invaded, the established representative of the head of state being deported, and being confined to one's own home by the people who said they had come to liberate us from British oppression. I think that they had wanted us to have been down on the beach waving banners and shouting 'Viva'. What a silly idea, we don't even get excited about a church bazaar.

Saturday, 3 April 1982

Valerie's diary
Woke in nurses' accommodation.
Armoured trucks all over the place. Seems calm everywhere.
Delivered Sandra Villalon's baby girl.

Neville's diary
Started off dull and foggy with quite a fresh breeze from the northwest. Valerie was still at the hospital, she had intended to spend the night there, sleeping in the nurses' quarters.

I looked out through the front windows and looked again: there were armoured personnel carriers parked all along St Mary's walk and on into John Street. Parked at the side of the road and on the grass verges. Armed men were wandering round looking rather lost and dejected, not the conquering heroes of yesterday.

Isobel and Rachel had slept well and were busying themselves round the house, I advised them not to go outside the property until the atmosphere had calmed down and the tension had gone.

My 70-year-old father had been alone in his house since Thursday. I went the few hundred yards along the road to see him, he was in good health although a little frazzled, and his temper was not exactly the best.

'Come and look at this, boy,' he led me into the front room and pointed out through the west facing window. 'The so & so's have taken down the Governor's flag and replaced it with that monstrosity of a blue and white thing, I'm going to look out of this window each day until the proper flag is put up again.' Wow, I hadn't seen him so wrought up before.

His house hadn't suffered any damage, but on looking at his peat shed and old wash house 20 yards away, I found quite a lot of hits from rifle fire from east and west. That was probably the Marines I had watched the previous day giving and receiving a few blasts.

He needed a few items of shopping, he said Jimmy's shop would be open, off I went and got his bits and some things for ourselves.

It was rather disconcerting to see so many armed men on the street. So shortly before it was usually only possible to see one or two Marines out and about at a time, and then always unarmed. A parade on the Queen's Birthday or Remembrance Day with Royal Marines and Falkland Islands Defence Force marching together made quite a sight with about seventy-five men in uniform and, if a Royal Navy ship was in, a few more.

Passing alongside the playing field on the way home there was a strong smell of urine, I guessed that all the men from the APCs had used the green as a toilet overnight.

There was a yacht in the harbour flying the Czechoslovakian flag, another 'round the worlder'. He had called in for some fresh water and a stretch of the legs a few days before. The lone sailor was going around shaking hands with local people on the street and apologising for what had happened and expressing his sympathy. I guess Eastern Europeans know a little about military rule.

Arriving back at my father's house he mentioned that the flag hadn't been put back yet, he thought the Argies had done the wrong thing this time and would suffer for it.

I said I would go over to the hospital and see Valerie and he wasn't to do anything daft and to keep his head down if any shooting started again.

'Don't worry about that, lad,' he said. 'I did a bit of training with the West Yorks[17] in the Second World War, if you hear a bullet crackle it's close but ok. It's the one you don't hear that gets you.'

I walked along St Mary's Walk towards the hospital. Approaching from the direction of Government House there were two naval officers, a seaman and a marine of the Argentine forces. I stopped them and asked if anyone spoke English. The younger officer said yes, a little, the more senior said he did and how could he help. I asked what provision had been made for firefighting in the case of any mishaps with cooking, etc, had they brought a fire service with them. They exchanged embarrassed looks and admitted to having forgotten that point. I explained I had been asked (or volunteered) to have charge of the Stanley Fire Service and asked if we would be able to operate freely. He took my name and phone number saying I would be contacted later.

I found Valerie in good health if not in good temper. She kept on muttering about soldiers with great big boots and nasty guns wandering round in her hospital. On the previous day the medic from the 'Brook'[18] had come back to help if necessary. She said that he looked as if he needed a bath and set out to get it ready for him. One of the other lot had different ideas about that and stopped the move to the bathroom with his gun, and said that the bloke was a prisoner of war. Nothing of note had happened. She went on to say that some Argy doctors had been in the operating theatre the day before, without success, and she would be happier when they all went home. She was quite willing to help them on their way.

The staff of the hospital at that time consisted of: the Senior Medical Officer (SMO) Daniel Haines and his wife Hilary, also medically qualified; Dr Alison Bleaney; and Dr Mary Elphinstone, a recent arrival as locum for one of the doctors who was on leave in the UK for a couple of months. Alongside Valerie there were two nursing sisters: Bronwyn Williams and Karen Timberlake. Also, six locally trained nurses. There were the usual domestic staff, cooks and kitchen staff, laundry ladies and cleaners; a radiographer/lab technician; one dental surgeon and nurse; a clerk/storekeeper; and two caretakers who doubled as gardeners, handymen and porters as well as driving the ambulance.

---

17. The 11th Battalion, West Yorkshire Regiment was stationed in the Falkland Islands during the Second World War.
18. Moody Brook Royal Marines barracks.

The doctors held a clinic daily by radio/telephone (RT) for all outside Stanley, they accepted emergency calls over the RT on weekends, the Royal Marine radio operator at Moody Brook also maintained a listening watch. Each farm has a medical cabinet, the manager or his wife being authorised by the doctor to issue the medication as prescribed over the air during the consultation. Medications not contained in the cabinet were flown out to the farm if a landing was scheduled or dropped with the mail next day, weather permitting.

I returned home to await the call regarding the fire service. It was lunch time for the visiting troops, they were having a cook-up in the back of their APCs and issuing stuff from cardboard boxes with a cloverleaf brand on them.

There were a few small children close by with their parents who had been having a quiet drink sitting on the grassy bank of the playing field. The boiled sweets common to all ration packs were offered to the children, permission of the parents having been sought first.

All seemed relaxed until an officer stood up and screamed for everyone to stand still. He leaped down from his vehicle and very gingerly walked across the grass for a few yards and picked up something about the size of a penguin egg.[19] It was a hand-grenade. The children and the adults were escorted off the playing field. The officer ran off in the direction of the FIDF headquarters. He came back in quite a short time, ordered all the men off the APCs; he said that the grenade wasn't one of theirs. They formed a search line and walked up and down the green a couple of times and pronounced the area free from any other explosive items. There were many tufts of grass which could have hidden anything of that size. Some-one must have dropped it in the excitement of Friday morning.

The phone call came at 2.30pm. Would I go to the Town Hall at 4.30pm and ask for a Lieutenant Colonel Alegeria? Thank you.

Valerie arrived home at 3.30pm and immediately started taking photos through the front windows of the troops and the vehicles parked along St Mary's Walk. I said that it would be better if she didn't do that, as the men were still a bit edgy.

I arrived at the Town Hall and was met by the navy commander I had seen in the morning. He was talking to some of the Polish seamen who had jumped ship a few months before and were seeking asylum. He took me upstairs to the refreshment room. Several residents were there arranging for permits to leave the Islands. There were also foreign press men milling

---

19. 7cm long, 5.5cm wide.

about and loads of armed guards. The room had been set up with tables placed in rows where people were being interviewed. As we made our way across to Alegeria, a more elderly gentleman in combat clothes with a lot of stars etc on his shoulders came up to me, embraced me like a long-lost son. He then shook my hand and wished me luck for the future. As he went out through the door all the Argies stood up and saluted. I asked who he was, and the reply came, Admiral Busser the Commander of the invasion operation.

Alegeria was a small man with a ready smile and a good command of English. I explained who I was and the circumstances for my being there. I said that I was concerned about the safety of the town which was constructed almost totally of timber. He said that he had noticed the wooden houses and it was quite a fire hazard. After detailing the types of appliances we had and the other equipment, I told him that I wanted to go and check on any damage which may have happened during the fighting. Would he issue me with a pass or an identification card to show any guards as might be necessary? He said that they weren't prepared for the issuing of identification cards at the moment, but it wasn't needed as the Islands were Argentine, but I was still British. 'When you have examined the machinery come back and tell me what you want to do about things.'

I left the Town Hall and headed eastwards towards the FIC[20] jetty complex where we had a trailer pump housed. Several of the foreign press questioned me about the situation and said they had facilities to report in the newspapers of the world. They didn't use a recorder or take notes so when I eventually read their reports my name was wrong, and my comments were not as I had said; I thought I had given quite a good comment on the short-sightedness of politicians.

As I neared the pump shed, I met the Argy seaman again, the one from near the hospital. Again, his headwear caught my eye. He was wearing a British or Royal Navy flat-top type hat, not the American style hat. I never found out why either. I said to him that part of the Fire Service duties was to provide cover at the airport for the twice weekly scheduled flights from Comodoro Rivadavia and I didn't think we would be going down there anymore.

'No,' he said, 'there would be other arrangements made about that.'

There was a bloke with a rifle by the warehouse, so I told him I was going into the shed and start an engine which may make a bit of noise.

'No problem, sir, carries on.'

---

20. Falkland Islands Company.

The door fastening didn't appear to have been tampered with. None of our sheds were locked, just hooked closed so that whoever was first on the scene could get ready for the off.

I then walked up Philomel Hill to the cluster of Nissen huts known as the German Camp on Callaghan Road. On the way I checked a couple of red painted boxes on the roadside which housed a hydrant standpipe, a hydrant key and a length of hose and a branch. In the main hut were our two Firefly Land Rovers (registrations 212 and F399), a 250-gallon towable water bowser, also a lightweight portable pump, this is a pump which four good sized blokes can pick up and carry, mounted on a trailer.

Oh dear! The shed was riddled with bullet holes, just like a colander, and the shiny new F399 had suffered a few hits.

I looked under the bonnet at the engine but saw no damage. I turned the key and the motor ran as smooth as ever. The older vehicle 212 only had a couple of bullet holes in the body, but the hose reel had suffered quite a bit. The rubber hose had been cut in a few places, that would definitely have to have a bit of tender loving care and attention before being of any use on a call out. We had another hut in the camp where I had stored a dozen 30-gallon foam trolley extinguishers which were due for shipment to the farms which had a landing strip for the Islander aircraft. There was also a number of containers of Light Water, this was a concentrate used to make the foam solution for the trolley jobs. All was ok in that shed.

I walked back to the Town Hall, checking hydrant boxes along the way. I called into the Central Station which was about 300 yards from my home. This building had large sliding double doors and housed two vehicles: the pride and joy of the Fire Service, a six-cylinder Land Rover Firefly plus a hose laying truck and two trailer pumps. All was ok there. The rover started on the button, the engine was so smooth it was almost inaudible. The hose truck, a 1940s Canadian Ford which had arrived in the Islands by mistake years ago, had hose racks in the back and a couple of long ladders on the roof; it also carried the salvage and demolition gear. That started first swing of the handle and the two pumps sounded beautiful. I pulled the doors to, stepped back and had a look at the building. I had spent some time, since taking on the job of Fire Service handyman, repairing the corrugated iron roof and walls and giving it all a coat of paint. I still had the guttering and name board to replace.

The Town Hall was just down the hill, so I went back to have a word with the chappy about Firefly 212 being out of action for the time.

On all the street corners were heaps of empty 7.62 mm cartridge cases[21] where the boys had been busy Friday morning.

Alegeria asked what the procedure was regarding informing the members that 212 was not serviceable. I said that the usual thing here is to have an announcement read over the local broadcast system. He asked how that was arranged. I explained the procedure and pointed out that a member of the broadcasting staff is out there talking to that redheaded man at the table by the door. The redhead was wearing a grey woollen sweater and khaki trousers.

I asked who he was, Alegeria replied: 'Oh that's Major Dowling.'

The name didn't mean anything. Not then.

We went out to the table where they sat. I said to the broadcaster would they put a message on the Box to the effect that Firefly 212 was out of order and not to be used until further notice.

Dowling said that the people of Stanley were in a war situation and should be treated as such and would be under curfew and have a blackout.

Alegeria said that it was not necessary to be like that, and that people like the fire service members would need to move round freely even at night.

Dowling jumped to his feet getting a bit steamed up, waving his fists and shouting: 'I am Major Patricio Dowling of the Argentine Army. I am half Irish and have the temper to go with the red hair, don't mess with me, this is military matters.'

Alegeria said quietly: 'Come with me, Major.'

They disappeared into the kitchen of the refreshment room and shut the door. They came out a few minutes later, Dowling still in a rage and Alegeria all smiles. 'I won again' he said.

Dowling with very bad grace said, 'People can meet and must go to pubs, there will not be a curfew and no blackout.'

I said, 'Thank you Major, you are the first person to tell me I must go to pubs.'

'I mean may go to pubs,' he said.

Valerie had supper all ready when I got home, but we made time to have a G&T, just to be civilised, before we started to eat. We talked about our day, she was a lot happier, she had delivered a baby. An Argentine Doctor had poked his nose round the delivery room door and said, 'That is a nice Argentine baby, the first one.'

---

21. Military rifle bullets – presumably from the Royal Marines of NP 8901, 'the boys', as the cartridges were piled in heaps where the Royal Marines had been seen fighting.

She replied, 'No it is not, the baby is born in the Falkland Islands and the parents are Chilean.'

That ended that little episode.

After our meal we went into the front room and looked out through the window at the harbour; it was a pleasant evening. We could see a lot of ships' lights out in Port William. The APCs were being brought down the harbour to the mother ship which was alongside the FIC jetty. Some aircraft were flying about. I hadn't realised all the APCs were amphibious.

We listened to the local announcements on the Box; they had put in the one about the Firefly so that was ok. There was a message from Dennis the senior plumber in Public Works, he'd had to repair a water main burst on John Street in a bit of a hurry; this water leak had only become visible after the APCs had been shifted. The message read: 'would drivers of heavy vehicles please be careful where they park.'

Not much to do. I tried to read but couldn't concentrate so I put on my headphones and listened to the short-wave radio. Valerie did some knitting and the girls did a bit of homework and generally amused themselves until their bedtime.

Sunday, 4 April 1982

Valerie's diary
Overcast first thing. Rain with a cold, light s/w wind. Blue patches of sky by 1.00pm.
UK are sending their fleet down, at last. None of us want the bloodshed there'll be.
Unsettled but quiet in hospital. We're busy filling up pill pots and preparing as many medical supplies as we can, getting ready for evacuation to Camp.[22]

Neville's diary
The four of us had had a good night's sleep. I fed the cat while Valerie got the breakfast ready. I had toast while the others had cereals (the most expensive breakfast food in the Islands due to freight rates).

Valerie gave me a set of house keys that she had been given the day before. Some of the Marines were married to local girls and had been taken away on Friday evening. The keys had been passed to Valerie with the message: 'could Neville see to the stove and gas, etc. at Rod and Lil's house on James Street?'

---

22. Camp is the local word for the farms/settlements outside Stanley.

Rod and Lil Napier lived on West Point Island. They had a house in town too. Their daughter was one of the wives who had left in a hurry with her Marine husband; they had been using Rod and Lil's town house. I usually serviced the stove for them, so that posed no problem. The house was at the east end of the town. I set off walking with my bag of tools just in case there had been any mishaps to the property.

Valerie put a roast of meat in the oven for lunch as I left, that would be ready about one o'clock. There were a few people about, on their way to church as per usual, not a lot of traffic, in fact a normal Sunday morning.

Then something not so normal happened. An Argy stopped me and asked, 'Where is the nearest coffee bar?'

I replied, 'We don't have such a thing here.'

He said, 'I don't believe you and you're subversive.'

His hand moved towards his pistol. With that another Argy came up to us and apologized and sorted the other one out.

Phew. That was nearly a nasty one.

Rod and Lil's house didn't look as if anyone had broken in. I turned off the oil to the stove and let that go out. Turned off the gas bottles, which were supplying some room heaters, and disconnected them. I made sure all the lights were off and there was no perishable food stuffs about. Shut off the water at the mains, locked the doors and started off back home. Just another job for a friend.

Walking home again there appeared to be more traffic on the road, quite a few local 'rovers'[23] were dashing about, one driver stopped by me and said he would be taking his wife and two small children out to one of the farms, he thought that they may be safer out there for the time being.

The day was improving, the clouds were breaking up and it was getting a bit warmer. Lunch wasn't ready for a while, so I took the opportunity to go along the road to see my father. He was ok, but in need of some beers. He didn't feel able to go along the road himself in the present circumstances. He asked would I go for him?

The Rose Hotel, not far along the road, was licensed to sell takeaway drinks, and being our 'local' I went over there and bought his requirements. I decided to make use of 'Glory Hour' while I was there. The pubs are open for one hour only on a Sunday, this leads to some fast and furious drinking. The public bar was packed elbow to elbow, not a chance of falling over even if you wanted to. The gossip was going at full strength, everyone had a tale to tell. Apparently, the Argies had photos of all the

---

23. Land Rovers.

FIDF members and were able to identify them and where they lived. That just goes to show that not all people who turned up on tourist boats with cameras and binoculars were bona fide tourists.

Six Royal Marines had given themselves up and were awaiting shipment out. The Argies were upset that the seventh would not surrender or come in. The name they were broadcasting was taken from some list or another and was actually the initials of a Royal Marine radio call sign that had been put on the end of the list. There was no seventh Royal Marine.

I delivered father's goodies and went home for lunch. The Argies were still prattling on over the Box about this and that, and above all not to upset the military etc.

Lunch over, we sat in the sunny front room and drank our coffee watching the world go by, well, our little bit of it. We wouldn't be able to take our Sunday stroll that day.

Sunday strolls in our family could be anything up to 10 miles in duration, very often accompanied by a fishing rod or two and perhaps a shotgun so we could have a change in our diet. We could wander along the seashore or up in the hills around the town without any harm coming to us. Before we had the children and were newlywed, I had a rather large motor bike, a Triumph 650cc, with reduction gears which meant we could really go cross country on it, Valerie enjoyed that. She also became quite adept at fishing.

The fine weather had brought out the troops. The Argies were not carrying rifles any more. They were just bunches of lads ambling about and smiling at anyone, these were different troops dressed in green drab colour not the grey of the invading force which were their marines. So, these are the garrison troops. Where are they going to live? There's millions of them, well a few thousand, and loads of transport planes flying in all the time. The children said they looked like greenfly swarming all round.

The neighbours, Neil and Mary Jennings, came in for a drink, a natter and to put the world to rights, as we often did. Another friend came in to say that the .22 rifle I had loaned him had been taken by the Argy marines on Saturday. They were collecting arms house to house and had given him a chitty[24] for it. I hope I would see it again.[25]

Tuppence, our small black cat, couldn't understand what all these different people were doing on the roads, they were not the ones he was

---

24. Receipt.
25. Both of Neville's guns were returned to him after the Liberation. However, his ammunition was not.

accustomed to having a chat with, and all those noisy things in the sky, he had never seen those before.

The Falkland Islands Executive Council[26] had met during the day to establish what was going to happen. The Government Chief Secretary[27] was going to be deported and the Argies were going to put in their own Governor. People could, if they wished, have a passage to England, but they could remain in the Islands and be quite safe. They were liberated from Colonial Imperialism.

Blimey.

On Sundays at 6pm, the BBC broadcast a programme to the Falklands.[28] We tuned the radio in to listen direct in case the visitors didn't allow us to hear the repeat over the local Box after the Church Service. The frequency was crystal clear, no static, no interference whatsoever. Peter King, the presenter, began by saying how sorry he was that we had been invaded, but he was happy to be able to inform us that a task force had been assembled and was on the way to our rescue. WOW!

The rest of the half hour was filled completely with messages of good wishes. Some that were phoned in were a bit tearful, but what could you expect being so far apart and really remote.

Thinking back over the last couple of days we really had been lucky, neither civilian nor any British military persons had been killed or wounded.

Monday, 5 April 1982

Valerie's diary

7am–3pm.

Light n/w wind. Sunny spells. Warm.

Rumour has it that the phones are being tapped and taped.[29]

Busy again making evacuation preparations at the hospital. I spent much time in the dispensary filling up pill pots.

Seems to be a bit of a panic in town, people getting passports in order and taking money out of their accounts at the Secretariat.[30]

---

26. The Falklands Islands Executive Council is the policy-making body of the Government of the Falkland Islands, advising the governor.
27. The Chief Secretary was Mr Dick Baker, assistant to the governor and taking on the role in his absence.
28. This programme was called 'Calling the Falklands'.
29. Listened in to and recorded.
30. Local government offices.

Neville's diary

Mondays are not the best of days; some people say they should be cancelled. This one should be quite interesting.

Valerie got up at 6.00 and made tea as she was due on duty at 7.00am. Off she went fully prepared to do battle with any chaos which may have crept in. I expected her to return about 3.30pm.

Turn-to time for me in my regular job of Handyman to the Fire Service was at 7.30am until 12 noon and then 1.00pm until 4.30pm. I had an office/workshop in the Public Works Department[31] [PWD] base at the dockyard. I was responsible to the Superintendent of the PWD. My duties were the maintenance of all firefighting equipment such as hoses and handheld domestic extinguishers. All properties belonging to the Government, domestic or business, had extinguishers supplied. I had the dry powder charges, foam and CO_2 cartridges for refilling purposes stored in my office. The compressor for recharging the breathing sets was taken up to the Central Station on Thursday night for convenience. The mechanical side of the maintenance of the pumps and engines, as such, was in the hands of the Plant and Transport Authority (PATA), a Quango of the Falkland Islands Government and the Ministry of Overseas Development.

There weren't many blokes on the road headed for work, a few 'green-flies'[32] walking round. I went in search of the Yard Foreman, Malcolm, an old friend from school days. Malcolm said there was no use to turn-to as everything was back-to-front and would take a bit of sorting, everyone was being sent home.

There was no school, so the children busied themselves round the house cleaning and bed making.

I fed the hens and the cat and decided to look at food supplies. In our deep freezer we had a fair bit of frozen meat: beef and mutton, some fish (mullet and trout) which we had caught, some wild geese I had shot too. Peas, beans, strawberries and raspberries from our garden all frozen down nicely. We had home grown potatoes, cabbage, cauliflower, parsnips, turnips and some carrots. I had bought in some extra potatoes as we didn't have enough ground to plant enough for the year.

There were eight laying hens and a rooster up in the hen run. I could always knock them on the head if the need arose. There should still be food available in the stores. The supply ship hadn't been, it was due shortly to bring supplies [and] take away the wool clip.

---

31. Public Works Department (PWD) – the government works.
32. Our family name for Argentine soldiers.

I kicked my heels around a bit and did some fidgeting, decided to go over and have a chat with Father. He was full of beans.

'They haven't taken down that flag yet' was his greeting.

We had a good natter; he told me of his wishes if anything should happen to him. We decided that a good thing would be to keep on smiling, anyway it takes fewer muscles to smile than it does to frown or scowl . . .

I walked back home. There was a large section of fence lying on the playing green. The driver of a tracked APC had tried to get his vehicle along our road which was wide enough for two Rovers to pass with difficulty, he couldn't negotiate the bend. Harry Ford in 6 Drury Street had managed to wave him to stop before his front porch was demolished too. The driver reversed out but unfortunately had gone over the kerb through the fence and almost capsized the thing, no damage to the crew or passengers. Monstrous great machine, it's a wonder they get them to float.

Whoops! There goes the telephone; it was the operator in the exchange:

'There is a chimney fire in the home of Len Reive, on James Street.'

'Thank you.'

'Do you want me to set off the siren?'

'No thanks, it might start a panic if the Argies see half the male population running along the roads. Would you please ring John Smith's and Jem Bayliss?'

'Will do.'

I ran across the green, opened the fire station doors and started the motor on the Firefly. By that time John Smith[33] with his two sons, Jem Bayliss[34] and Richard Caine (a fellow teacher staying with him) had arrived. The Fireflies are equipped with chimney brushes, rods, scrapers and asbestos blankets to cope with chimney fires. Obviously, we had ladders on the trucks too.

With the occasional bleep of the siren, I drove down John Street at a reasonable speed under the circumstances – bearing in mind that the speed limit is 20 miles per hour.

Would you believe it there was an Argy strutting down the middle of the road as if he owned it? Now, a petrol driven six-cylinder Land Rover is a pretty quiet-running machine. And if you are wearing a tin hat pulled down over your ears you can't hear it. So, I (unsportingly) let rip with the siren, he broke several Olympic records getting off the road!

---

33. Author of *74 Days*. Another Falklands war diary.
34. Headmaster of the Senior School.

The building, as are many of the homes in Stanley, was a bungalow with a flattish roof extension at the back, thus no difficulties in getting a ladder onto the main roof to the chimney in the centre of the ridge. The fire was in the kitchen chimney as usual, the most used in the house. The range burned peat. It was well alight; Len was through the house with a neighbour as the kitchen was full of smoke. I got the mirror on a stick to look up the chimney, a pair of pliers, a screwdriver, a soot rake and asbestos blanket from the truck. I drew out the coals from the fire into a steel bucket and had them put outside. I spread the asbestos blanket over the top of the range. Removed the stove pipe, had a quick look up the flue and on the plate at the bottom of the chimney. Just a mass of red lumps of fallen loose soot, I raked all that into empty 5-gallon peat buckets.

Meanwhile the lads had got onto the roof.

We had a problem; the chimney was a double flue, one for the front room, and the other the one we were dealing with. The chimney itself was just over 3 feet above the ridge and the salt glaze pots another 3 feet on top of that. The flashing round the bases of the pots was well crumbled with age, so the pots were lifted off and laid on the roof out of harm's way. The chaps attempted to sweep the chimney with a steel wire brush which was 9 inches in diameter, as was the flue, but with the build-up of soot a 6-inch brush had to be used in the beginning, anyway we got it all out and let it cool down a while. Len would have been able to use the hot coals which were removed from the stove in the first place to relight it. He apologised for not being in a position to offer us a cup of tea, but 'would we accept a wee dram to wash the soot down?'

'Yes please, whisky applied internally is a good antidote for soot and smoke.'

After wiping down the rods we packed up the truck and headed off home for a good scrub.

I had a phone call from Harry Bonner, acting Superintendent of the PWD. He asked if I would be willing to go to work for the PWD doing my usual job for the same pay and hours for the duration, as it was a necessary part of the community. I couldn't see any harm in that, and it would be an income for the home. If I turned this down where would I be if nothing else was presented, we could be in dire straits. Ok, turn-to at 7.30am as usual.

Valerie came home at 3.45pm. She was a little depressed. She had been organising medical supplies for the Camp and packaging up dressings etc in case there was an evacuation if things hotted up with the Task Force being assembled. At the hospital they were concerned that there could be street fighting which could be dodgy for the people remaining in Stanley.

We discussed our immediate future and decided to remain at our jobs while they lasted. People were leaving the Islands by courtesy of the Argentine Air Force. We asked the children what they wanted to do, would they like to go out to one of the farms or go to England and stay with their Grandmother. No, they said, 'We will stay with you cos we might miss the shooting.'

[Rachel interprets this as 'we don't want to be separated from you if there is street fighting'.]

Tuesday, 6 April 1982

Valerie's diary
3pm–11pm.
Started off overcast and drizzle from the n/w but cleared by 9.30am ish. Sunny spells.
Me and Rachel did some shopping, very quiet everywhere, armed guards in evidence. Jenny's letter went out with a F.I. stamp!
More troops and weapons coming over from Comodoro.[35]
Gale force winds late night.

Neville's diary
Nothing happened during the night to startle us. I went off to work in time to turn-to at 7.30am. Valerie was due to go on duty at 3.00pm which meant that we would have a cooked lunch and a cold light supper in the evening. Quite a few men had turned-to, not all of them the regular work force. These men had arrived looking for employment as their normal job for one reason or another was not open to them. They were given work as they had skills to offer which would contribute to the general running of the Public Works operation.

The Public Works Department in the Falklands is quite a complex affair. It is responsible for the maintenance of Government House, Secretariat, hospital, the Town Hall and both schools. The Water Filtration and Fire Service as well as roads and the Funeral Direction Services all came under the umbrella of the PWD. There is also a lot of Government-owned housing rented out. This all had to be repaired and maintained.

The PWD with all its various offices, workshops and supply depots is based in what is known as the Government Dockyard, a block of land along the north side of Ross Road and bounded by the harbour to the

---

35. Comodoro Rivadavia. A city in southern Argentina.

north. Stanley harbour is about 7 miles long, cigar shaped, with Stanley about in the middle of the south side. The dockyard has a jetty which is 'T'-shaped jutting out into the harbour and rests on the remains of a stranded wrecked ship called the 'Margaret Rose'. The FI Government's vessel MV Forrest moors at the Government jetty.

I got a lift to the German Camp on Callaghan Road to pick up Firefly 212 and then drove it down to the dockyard to my office. I ran the hose off the reel and found that it was punctured in two places by bullets. I cut out the damaged parts and repaired it by inserting a piece of copper tube and securing this with jubilee hose clips. I started the motor and engaged the pump but no matter how I revved the engine the water only trickled out. I shut everything down, took off the pistol grip nozzle and shook out a piece of shrapnel, it all worked ok then.

Beside my office was a big wooden packing crate; the large extinguishers for the Camp airstrips had arrived in it a few weeks before. I decided to dismantle this crate completely and store the pieces of wood in my office/workshop, even if I had to nail them to the ceiling. I managed to get all but some of the reinforced base apart. The base had disappeared from outside my workshop by the next morning. Some visitor was probably using it for a roof to his dug-out or to keep warm. So, anything not nailed down will be removed, aha. The town's people were locking their doors now.

12.00. Lunch time. One of the lads took 212 back up the hill as it was on his way home. All fire appliances had to be returned to their sites when not in use.

Valerie had been down the road to the West Store[36] for some shopping. She had topped up the larder with some reserves, dried milk, dried onion and some tinned fruit.

1.00 back to work.

The hospital has a heating and hot water system supplied by a pair of oil-fired furnaces. The supply tank for the diesel oil burned in the furnaces was situated under the main building adjacent to the stoke-hole in the space originally intended for peat storage. With the coming of oil as a more economic fuel, the peat system was done away with and the large fuel tank needed was put in the space but no thought was given to safety.

I asked Malcolm for a driver, a flat truck and a couple of hands to help shift two of the 30 gallon foam extinguishers from the store shed in the

36. Stanley's largest shop, by modern UK standards a small supermarket, with a very wide range of goods from food to clothing, footwear, childrens' toys and tools for property and vehicle maintenance.

dockyard to the hospital. They would be better than nothing if an incident did happen to start a fire. They might just be enough to contain the burning oil if it came to that.

We had recently taken delivery of some new red neoprene-coated hoses with instantaneous, push-fit, connections – thus making the old and mostly perished rubber-lined canvas hoses redundant. I had several lengths of these hoses in the office. I cut them into 6-foot lengths, filled them with sand and riveted the ends tightly shut. I took them up to the hospital too, they could be used as a dam across the doorways if the oil tank leaked.

I had been working on some signs for our various sheds used for appliances and equipment. I thought it may be best to take the ones on which the paint had dried and put them on the appropriate buildings to stake out our 'territory', especially with all these troops coming into town. They would be grabbing anything which appeared to be unused to billet them in, that is if we weren't chucked out of our homes.

I knocked off at 4.30pm, went home [and] had a cup of tea. Then walked over to see my father and we had a natter, nothing new on that front.

The children and I listened to the radio, local broadcast. There was the usual guff about not giving a Churchill salute to the Argentine flag nor to any member of the Argentine forces. Doing so would result in dire consequences.

Tomorrow was going to be the day of days: the Argentine Governor was going to be sworn in.

All the people of Puerto Argentino (Stanley), Gran Malvina and Soledad (East and West Falklands) are invited to witness this historic occasion. Nice of them to ask us.

Valerie came home shortly after 11pm. She had had a busy day trying to run a normal service at the hospital and still packaging stuff in case an evacuation to the Camp happened.

Wednesday, 7 April 1982
Valerie's diary
Very strong winds. 80 knots recorded on Weddell Island.
The Argentine youngsters are cold and hungry.
New Government is sworn in.

Neville's diary
Cold windy morning with some blustery showers. Valerie had gone off to the hospital for 7am.

There was a lot of Argy activity in the LADE[37] end of the building, men putting up aerials and sticking earth wires into the ground. I hope they don't hit a water main. I continued to work on the new sign for the Central Station, all wood with a moulding round the edge. I was painting it red with yellow lettering, that being the paint I had in hand. The previous sign was ancient blue and white enamel, most of which had flaked off and rusted over the years.

Malcolm came quietly into the office. I really must have a word with him about his appearing quietly, I might be moonlighting!

'Do you know anything about clocks?' his opening question for the day. I decided to play this cool and safe. 'No.'

'Good, here's a key, nip over to the Town Hall and wind up the clock.'

'That hasn't gone since they put it up.'

'Not that one, the one in the court room.'

'That's up the creek as well.'

'Go over and put the key in the bally thing and make it look good.'

'Who is over there anyway?'

'Some of "them" getting ready for the swearing in.'

'Shall I comb my hair?'

'Ha ha.'

'Will I get an invite to the ceremony?'

'If you are unlucky.'

The Court and Council Chamber of the Town Hall is at the eastern end of the building and on the right as you enter, opposite the library. The table had been removed as had the coat of arms, the royal portraits and other pieces one might find in a Council Chamber. The witness box and dock for court purposes were still in the room. The lino on the floor shone like a mirror, there must have been a lot of 'greenflies' on jankers.[38]

A well-fed officer met me at the door. 'Ah, you will fix the clock'?'

'No, I shall wind it and see if it works.'

Someone brought a step ladder. The clock was fully wound, probably had been so for several years. The clock was on a shelf and fastened to the wall. I couldn't see how to get it down and give it a good shake. We called it quits, a can of WD40 might have helped. The officer departed.

A young chap attracted my attention and gave me to understand that he had broken a light bulb and would I replace it for him. That took about

---

37. The Argentine Airlines' office was situated in the same building as Neville's workshop/office.

38. Military punishment.

two minutes, but each time I moved someone was there with a cloth to polish out the marks left by my boots on the immaculate floor. I took the key back to the office; I think it was the wrong one any way. Time to go for lunch.

There is a sump at the back of the Town Hall. (This is one of the few buildings in Stanley having the north side called the back.) This large underground tank catches rainwater from the roof, giving a source of fresh water to test fire appliances – otherwise we might have to use expensive drinking water from the system.

Malcolm asked me to take a Firefly over to the Town Hall and using water from this sump clean the area outside the entrance to the Hall. He said it was a bit mucky. I presumed he must have had orders from above. He was quite right, there was a mountain of fag ends and other rubbish strewn all over the place. There were soft drink and beer cans jammed in the drain covers. All was in need of a bit of high-pressure hosing. I started up the engine and began to pump. The largish officer came out to see what was happening. I explained to him. He replied 'very good, but finish now as they are on the way'. A large puddle had accumulated in the doorway.

2.30pm. All guard of honour troops stood to attention. Looked smart ... and waited.

2.45pm. Still waiting.

3.00pm. The officer said they are on their way now, always late, same every time.

The military all went into the court room. Speeches and singing (must have been their national anthem), then cheering and the sound of hand clapping came out through the window.

I could hear motors revving up and moving off in a hurry. The bigwig who had talked with me earlier came out rolling the flag round a staff like a lance.

'Thank you very much, you may continue. Thank goodness that's over,' he said.

Valerie was at home with a cup of tea waiting. The weather was still cold with blustery showers. She said that Weddell Island had reported an 80-knot wind, the troops looked cold and hungry. Be best to lock up the hens tonight if that's the case.

The speech by the newly sworn-in governor, General Menendez, was broadcast over the Box along with lots of 'edicts', mostly the same things as before. A new one was that any person, military or civilian, accused of stealing would be tried fairly in front of the military court.

The Islands had had a military governor before, the first recorded one was Captain Farmer in 1779. But that was different, he was British.

A fine night for sitting in front of the fire.

Thursday, 8 April 1982

Valerie's diary
3pm–11pm.
Still strong winds from N/W, dry.
Sounds as if we're 4 days from a war.
Went up to see Grace McPhee with the girls. Not many strangers around town.
Blockade around the Falklands by 0400 GMT on Monday.

Neville's diary
Maundy Thursday. I wondered where the Queen would be giving out the coins this year.

My father had always taken the afternoon off work on this Thursday. He would go off and catch some fish for the traditional Good Friday fish meal. We had some fish in the deep-freeze and he was quite welcome to share it with us.

I usually tested all the fire appliances on a Friday, whether they had been used or not. Being Good Friday and a public holiday tomorrow, I decided to do the checks today instead. No one got inquisitive whilst I did the rounds, which took all morning, and involved walking down to the east end pump, then up to the German Camp and back via the Central Station. Under normal circumstances I would have taken the 'Fly' from Central Station, but perhaps it was prudent not to at this time. All were still in order: fuel and water levels correct. The hand cranking of the old Ford truck raised a bit of a sweat.

The German Camp is a collection of Nissen Huts[39] directly to the south of the town on Callaghan Road. They were originally built as a camp for the Royal Artillery during the Second World War. Having fallen into a state of disrepair, they were refurbished to house a party of Germans who had come out to work on rebuilding roads etc in 1955. The huts were now used for storage except for one double hut used as a dwelling.

The lunchtime news from the BBC said that there was to be a blockade round the islands as of 0400 Monday, this would be midnight Sunday to us as our time was 4 hours behind GMT.

39. Half-cylindrical buildings made of corrugated steel.

Valerie had been out for a walk with the two girls and they'd called in on an old friend, Grace McPhee, up on Davis Street. This could also be classed as a district nurse visit as Grace was housebound. She had an excellent view from her kitchen window of the harbour, Port William and the airport. Valerie said that there was a great deal of activity and movement going on in both areas. Stuff coming off ships and aircraft landing and taking off.

People were still able to leave the Islands by Argy aircraft. The Secretariat was issuing passports.

Valerie was due to go on duty at 3pm until 11pm. We had our cooked meal together at midday.

For the remainder of the day I worked in the office trying to sort out bits and pieces of paperwork, equipment manuals, and lists of personnel etc. Some things wouldn't possibly be used again, such as the diagrams of emergency practices for the F27 and F28 aircraft which had been used by LADE.

I spent a while looking again at the firefighting manuals, recent fire reports, and the street plans of Stanley with the hydrants marked on them. There was also a booklet of instructions on how to rescue the aircrew from several types of crashed fighter planes, how to open the cockpit with a fire axe and to immobilize the ejector seat, what not to touch etc, better study this one in case things did warm up a bit.

Still, there is a Task Force on the way, and talks are ongoing between Argentina and the United Nations. It would soon be all over and they could go home and leave us with the serious business of getting on with our own lives our own way.

After work and a cup of tea I walked over to see Father and spent a while nattering to him. I went over to the 'Rose' for a pre-supper drink. After the meal I worked outside tidying the garden for a while. The nights were certainly drawing in now. Wonder what the 'greenflies' will do if it belts down with snow?

Friday, 9 April 1982

Valerie's diary
7am–3pm.
Good Friday.
Light n/w wind all day.
Preparations/meetings going on for the eventuality of an evacuation or street fighting with multiple casualties. I attended various meetings to that end.

The Islander aircraft flew out of town for ? – much speculation. Were they bringing in the councillors from the West?[40]

Neville showed the hospital staff how to use fire extinguishers, which we won't use anyhow – the fire brigade will.

Seems as if Argie top brass fly home for dinner each night.

Neville's diary

Good Friday.

Valerie went on duty at 7am.

Quite a fine morning. I busied myself about the house.

I heard the Islander aircraft take off and head in a westerly direction. Perhaps they were taking it over to 'the other side'[41] as a trophy. Or there could even be a medical emergency.

I had been asked to go over to the hospital to give a demonstration to the staff on how to use the fire extinguishers that were placed at strategic points in the building.

The hospital was built in two parts: the older section was constructed of timber, and covered with a corrugated iron roof, insulated with felt between the iron and roof boards. A typical Falkland Island construction, wood and iron being more economic to import than fragile, heavy, bricks and slate. It wouldn't stand a chance if hit by an incendiary device. The newer Churchill Memorial wing had been constructed of cement blocks, made on the site, with wooden roof rafters and clad with rubberoid felt tiles. Completed in 1953 in time to open for the coronation. The old wing was used as a geriatric ward and sheltered accommodation. The acute patients and maternity facilities were in the Churchill wing, as were the administration offices, outpatient clinic, dental department, x-ray department, operating theatre, kitchens and staff dining room. The laundry and furnace room were under the main wards. On-site accommodation for the nursing staff was over the old end in private rooms converted from loft space. The sisters and matron had private flats in the building across the road known as Admiralty Cottage. The Doctors lived away from the hospital but close enough to get in rapidly for emergencies.

If there was an incident, the staff would be too busy evacuating the patients to use an extinguisher and would rely on the fire service. It was a request made to me and I had fulfilled it. I had better check on hand lanterns and batteries and make sure they were in place and kept so.

---

40. West Falkland is locally referred to as 'the West'.
41. Argentina was locally referred to as 'the other side'.

Valerie said they had been having meetings in the hospital to discuss the eventuality of open warfare and were preparing themselves accordingly.

I started looking around the garden and peat shed for bits and pieces which I could use for building up a barricade at the back of the house so that any inadvertent bullets would have the sting taken out of them. I piled up some old chimney bricks, lengths of timber, and some assorted lumps of iron at the back of the wash house. My thinking was that if anyone came over the hill shooting, the girls would be sheltered if they slept on the bedroom floor. I also piled up a bit of junk in the gateway at the top of the garden to prevent it from being used as a thoroughfare or shortcut. Anyone seriously intent on using the garden as a short cut could jump over the fence anyway.

Rachel remembers ...
Having barricades built up at the back of the house frightened me. It all seemed so out of place in our usually peaceful home.

Saturday, 10 April 1982

Valerie's diary
Day off.
Light s/w wind, much colder. Sunny spells am, overcast by lunchtime.
Hilary, Daniel and their 3 children came to lunch.
General Hague[42], USA, to hold talks with Argentines in Buenos Aires.
We seem to have been adopted by Misty, Tina's cat.

Neville's diary
Saturday morning I worked in the Dockyard more or less to show the flag and to keep occupied. Had a word with Malcolm and suggested that we started a rumour that the Gurkhas were coming to chase out the invaders.

'Don't be silly, they would think a Gurkha was something to eat,' he said.

We chewed the fat for a while and concluded that things were getting a mite serious.

Valerie had invited the Senior Medical Officer, Dr Haines and his wife, also Dr Haines, plus their children for lunch. This made quite a change to the usual conversation, the two doctors had spent some time in Africa and had run into a spot of trouble before.

In the evening news from the BBC, it was said that General Haig had started off to meet with the Military Junta in Buenos Aires (BA). He

---

42. Alexander Haig, US Secretary of State.

would, after talking with Galtieri and his mates, go off to London and talk to Mrs Thatcher (bless Her). No doubt he would be banging his head against a brick wall in BA, but at least he was trying ... (Very). Didn't appear to be many others in the world doing anything for us.

Anyways, keep on with the smiling and at frequent intervals.

Sunday, 11 April 1982

Valerie's diary
Day off.
Overcast. Light S/W wind, dry.
Another meeting sorting out the current military situation and preparing for the worst.
I met with Ron and Nij Buckett to organise care of the oldies living at home.
The Fire Chief from Comodoro called in to see Neville.
No Argentine boats around in the harbour any more.
Have to feed Snoopy, Duane and Aarron's cat.[43]

Neville's diary
Easter Day. Valerie had today off but was called over to the hospital to a meeting with Ron and Nij Buckett; they had kindly taken it on themselves to do a welfare job with the elderly folk in the town in conjunction with the local Red Cross.

As the cargo vessel had not arrived there weren't any Easter eggs in the stores. Mrs Ashworth the wife of the dairyman made some chocolate eggs for her own children and brought some up for our two girls. Malcolm made his milk deliveries to customers in a former military Land Rover. He was told by the Argentine authorities to paint an identifying mark on the doors. So, being a good Yorkshireman, of course he painted the White Rose on the door panels, and they stayed there right through the occupation.

I walked over to have a chat with Father and a glass of beer. He was still on about the fact that the flag had not been replaced at Government House, and it was about time that it was.

In the evening we listened to the 'Calling the Falklands' from the BBC on the radio, still more messages from friends and relatives in the UK. The most important message this time was at the start of the programme: 'Hello me dears, this is your usual host Peter King, now pin back your lug

---

43. The Stewart family, Phyllis, Duane and Aarron were neighbours at 1 Drury Street. They had left Stanley and moved out to the Camp for the duration of the war.

'oles and listen. You know who the Booties are, and the Para's, well they are coming out to see you, and there will also be the Jock Guards with their broken bottles to fight on the beaches, the Taff Guards will be there to sing them to death and of course various other blokes and those lovely little gentlemen from Nepal, well I hope that makes you happy.'

Wowee just fancy that, might be advisable to keep the head down.

After supper we had a couple of visitors, Brian Summers, who had VOLUNTEERED me for the job of looking after the Fire Brigade, [and] with him was a bloke I had never seen before. Brian introduced him as Alfonso Quinones. The fire chief of Comodoro Rivadavia, he had a really gravelly voice. He was very interesting to talk to. He had trained in America with an oil company and Comodoro is an oil town, that would explain how he had the position of Chief and also the voice. We nattered on for quite a while. Brian said we would have to watch Alfonso or he would be shipping all the things he liked over to Comodoro. He was impressed with what little equipment we had and especially our hoses with instantaneous couplings; all theirs were screw fittings and used considerable time running out hoses at an incident.

After they had been gone a while, there was a phone call from Brian asking me to meet him at the Central Station. There was a fire reported at the rear of Dr Haines' property. We drove up there past the monument without the siren or rotating lamp. Arriving at the scene we found a fire in a rubbish drum. In itself not too much of a hazard, but it was right next to the diesel tank for the cooker and central heating. We soon put the fire out rather than letting it burn out.

That was the end of quite an exciting weekend, we would be back to work in the morning as we didn't get Easter Monday off.

Our next door neighbour, Mary,[44] who was a member of the Executive Council as well as being the General Secretary of the Falkland Islands General Employees Union, had decided it could be prudent to go out to one of the farms because of her position politically in the Islands. She took her mother, daughter and niece with her. The idea was to get to Goose Green where her brother was the skipper of one of the inter-island vessels. She hoped that they could get across the Falkland Sound and then cross the West Island to the far west and then on to West Point Island and stay with Rod and Lily Napier.

Neil, her husband, would stay in the town to work and look after the house and their cat, Sooty.

---

44. Neil and Mary Jennings lived at 3 Drury Street.

Again, I was volunteered for something: to take charge of the affairs of the General Employees Union and keep an eye on the offices which were just along the road from my workshop. At the previous year's Annual General meeting I had been elected to the executive committee. The Chairman of the Union had also thought it to be wise to go out to one of the farms and away from the limelight.

Valerie now had some more feline charges to care for: Misty, Mary's niece's cat and Snoopy belonging to Phyllis next door, on the other side. Phyllis had gone off to Green Patch with her two sons to stay with her sister. Valerie already had Tuppence our own cat and I think Sooty already had his nose in the food dish in our kitchen.

With our neighbours from both sides having now left, this meant that our usually busy Drury Street now only had the following residents:

No. 1 empty,

No. 2 us,

No. 3 Neil,

No. 4 empty (the owners lived in the camp),

No. 5 Ramon with his wife and family,

No. 6 empty,

No. 7 John Smith and family,

No. 8 Rudy, Camilla and their daughter Katrina (the same age group as our two),

No. 9 Jem Bayliss and Richard Cain, two teachers who had remained in the Islands,

No. 10 empty.

Talk about a skeleton crew. I wonder how many more would leave.

Rachel remembers . . .

Stanley was filling up with Argentine military and emptying of civilians. As a small community we all knew everyone. We knew who lived in which house, where everyone worked. Now there were hundreds of unfamiliar faces everywhere and the people we knew were missing. There was nothing about this that felt good.

Monday, 12 April 1982

Valerie's diary

Day off.

Dull. Overcast. Light s/w wind.

Rachel went to school at the Peatfields' home. They collected her and brought her back.

It's official: the Falklands are a war zone as of 0400 hrs.

Started doing a pile of washing[45] but something wrong with the machine so ended up at the hospital with the girls doing some.

Early night, must have been the excess of gin in the system!

Neville's diary

Off to work hi ho. We didn't have Easter Monday off in the Islands any more because of a dispute from some years ago between the Government, the General Employees Union (the Union), the stevedores in the jetty gang[46], and the FIC.

I had a chat with Malcolm about the Union affairs and office. We decided that as I had been elected Vice Chairman of the Union this year, I should retain the keys and see what developed.

I did some work in my office and tidied away the wood I had saved from the packing crate, disguising it as a ceiling.

I then went up to the German Camp and collected the Firefly we garaged there which belonged to the Airport. I gave it a run round as well as a good check over because of the bullet holes which it had received on the morning of the 2nd. I'd parked it outside my office and had gone in to get some tools when I heard the sound of vehicle doors being opened and slammed shut. I thought it a bit of a cheek – someone messing about with the truck – so I went out to see what was on. I was confronted by, of all people, Lieutenant Colonel Gamen[47] and a corporal of the Argies. When I asked what this was all about, the corporal tried to open his holster to draw his pistol. The Lieutenant Colonel said that this vehicle belonged to the Airport, and he was taking it to the Airport where I was to show this man how to operate the machinery.

I asked why they hadn't brought any fire equipment with them but was met with more fiddling with the holster and instructed 'You will show him.' Discretion being the better part of valour, I politely asked the bloke if he could speak English, but from his reply I deduced he could not.

I went into my usual lecture on how to operate the pump, telling him that the engine must be running, and that the clutch pedal must be pushed down before engaging the pump and then put the motor into third gear, thus engaging the power take-off.

I went round to the control panel and showed them how to raise a vacuum for the suction and how to use the hose reel and couple up the

---

45. Valerie was using a twin-tub washing machine.
46. Dock workers who loaded and unloaded ships.
47. Argentine Airlines (LADE) representative in the Falklands.

standard hoses, explaining that there was a water tank at the airport to refill the water tank on the machine. They both gave me the nod to say understood, (perhaps they didn't want to admit not understanding a silly local?) before they drove off looking quite proud. I think our Firefly was to be used by the Gallant Gamen as a personal runabout. I was feeling a bit miffed about it, so I contacted the fire chap from Comodoro Rivadavia. He said there wasn't much he could do about it, as they were military, and they held the upper hand. I thought he was here to help us. I decided there and then not to take any fire truck out unless it was for an emergency or a genuine fire – what the eye doesn't see the heart doesn't grieve about (or want).

Home for lunch, the news said the blockade was in place and so far there hadn't been any action. There were still the aircraft movements every ten minutes, with people still able to leave, and troops being brought in. Ships had appeared in Port William and were offloading a lot of containers and vehicles. The children on our street were a little worried as they had seen trucks with slatted sides driving round the roads. They thought they were the same as the ones the Nazis used to take prisoners to the camps in the war in Europe. They had seen these trucks in the war comics they read. It took a bit of talking to calm them down.

Back to work to face another shock: Harry Bonner, the acting Superintendent of the PWD, asked me who had the keys to the Union office. When I told him that I did, he said someone wanted to see me in the office at two o'clock. I told Malcolm, also a member of the Union executive committee, who said there wasn't much we could do if the Argies wanted to commandeer the building. I duly presented myself at two. Quite soon Harry walked in with a rather stockily built man in a uniform with some stars on his chest (they didn't seem to go in for shoulder pips).

Harry said: 'This is Colonel Dorrego.'

The little chap (Dorrego) said: 'You are in charge of this building?'

Me: 'Yes.'

Colonel Dorrego: 'Ah, good.'

Me: 'This building is privately owned by the Union in these Islands.'

Colonel: 'It is not Public Works building?'

Me: 'No.'

Colonel: 'I am taking charge of Public Works, and I will occupy this building. It will be looked after and not destroyed by anyone, and when we leave it will be returned to you in the same condition as it is now.'

Me: 'Do I have any option?'

Colonel: 'No. You have exactly two hours to organise your stuff; you may take it away or you may leave it where it is, it will be safe.'

Me: 'I think Colonel, for the sake of the two of us, I shall put everything in the cupboards and lock them.'

Colonel: 'As you wish.'

He fastened his holster and departed with Harry. They really like fiddling with their holsters; perhaps they should have worry beads.

I rushed out to find Malcolm, as some decisions I could make myself but this I wanted a witness for. The room at the east end of the building had been rented out to a chap who produced the local newspaper, [and] I feared that there may be some of his literature lying about. There also could be some of the papers from Mary Jennings' Government work in the cupboards. Malcolm arrived with some old sacks and said he would return with a truck, and that we could go down to the incinerator at the rubbish tip to have the lot destroyed. I didn't do much sorting; anything obviously Union work I put in the cupboards, all else went in the bags. I got some hasps and staples and fitted them to the cupboard doors and put locks on them, keeping the keys myself. Not a high security job but all I could manage in the time; if anyone was intent on getting into the cupboards they would do so anyway. Just have to see what my blind trust leads to.

Malcolm arrived with the truck and off we went to the tip. Mr Perry, the man in charge of the incinerator, said there would be no problem burning our bags. He'd already had several requests of a similar nature from others. I wonder how much of our historical papers went up in smoke that day. We drove back up into town and I popped into the Union building and had a scout round to check if I had missed anything. I left the picture of Her Majesty the Queen on the wall, closed the door and handed the keys in to Harry.

I had spoken to Valerie regarding the security at the hospital, especially at night when the staff was reduced in number. We agreed that there would be some mileage in having an extra person in the building overnight just to do an occasional patrol checking various bits. I said I would ask some of the younger lads in the fire service if they would do this job. Jeremy and Martin Smith and Robert McAskill said they would be only too happy to help out and take it in turns to stand watch.

Rachel had been to the home of Mr and Mrs Peatfield on Racecourse Road for some school lessons. Mr Peatfield was her class teacher and had taken the step of collecting his pupils each morning and taking them to their home for schoolwork. Whether this was contrary to the Argentine

'Edicts' or not would remain to be seen. Isobel was doing her best to study alone at home.

When I arrived home from work, I found there had been a bit of a disaster. Valerie had been doing the washing; the pump on the (beastly) machine had failed. It wasn't exactly a new machine but dash it there was no need for it to be subversive. Valerie walked over to the hospital and – pulling a bit of rank – used the laundry facility there. After all, why can't the Matron do a spot check on the equipment?

Rachel remembers ...
I enjoyed having school at the Peatfields' home. Being with friends again and the familiarity of school lessons was comforting. It was a good time for sharing experiences and some informal debriefing.

Being driven to 'school' in the Peatfields' blue Mini was an interesting but threatening experience. Every day there was something new to see, the Argentines had vehicles, weapons and troops everywhere. Street corners, open spaces, vacated buildings were all being taken over by our invaders. Fences were broken, grass torn up and the roads themselves were becoming very potholed. We were frightened by what we saw.

Tuesday, 13 April 1982

Valerie's diary
Day off.
Cold, dry, light n/w wind.
Mr Haig is having extra talks in London as complications, didn't say what, at the Buenos Aires end.
R/T[48] is now only to be used for medical purposes.
Veronica Fowler has a baby boy, Daniel.
Me and Rachel went to see Grace McPhee. Most depressing to see so much military activity from their window.
A couple of families, Johnny Goodwin's and Tim Halliday's, have moved out of their houses.
Neville moved the Firefly and fire equipment out of the garages in the German camp.

---

48. Radio/telephone, a short-wave radio system for talking with each of the farms and settlements outside Stanley. At the time it was Stanley's only permitted form of communication with the rest of the islands and the only way the rest of the islands could officially communicate with Stanley. Now the Argentines had decided it would only be for medical use.

Neville's diary

I charged up some more spare fire extinguishers and took some of them up to the hospital as well as a crowbar, a large axe and a breathing set. The three boys from the fire brigade who had stood in for security duty were experienced in the use of these bits of gear, maybe they would get a five-minute head start if anything nasty did happen.

[Valerie had lectured all the staff regarding keeping the fire door, which was between the two parts of the hospital, shut. This was a thick wooden door specially made to fit the very large frame. This door would retard any rapid advance of smoke and/or flames from the old wooden end. But later she had difficulty in making the Argies understand it was not a joke when she kept slamming the door. This followed spraying a good measure of aerosol deodorant down the corridor which covered the smell of decaying flesh from trench foot and their other wounds. She was often heard to say 'exterminate' in a Dalek-type of voice while spraying. They did eventually catch on that Matron wouldn't shout at them if they shut the door.]

I worked in the office for a while during the morning. Alfonso came in and I told him what I had done with regard to the equipment I had put in the hospital. He agreed that it probably was the best thing to have done especially if things did hot up.

Malcolm came in and asked me if I would take one of his men and go up to Davis Street in a Firefly and tend to a blocked drain. The larger of the two Flies, garaged in the Central Station, was equipped with the necessary rods and devices for clearing drains. Alfonso declined to join us in this alternative fire service action. I think someone had sent him down to see what I had been doing wandering round with fire equipment, an axe and a crowbar so early in the morning.

Off me and young Ned Stewart went. We lifted some drain covers on the road, found the offending spot and determined the flow direction. We connected up the rods and tried to push the muck along the pipe. There was a small amount of movement but not enough to get a flow going, so we resorted to the big gun. We connected a 2½-inch hose to the pump, jammed the end into the drain with my foot and gently applied pressure to blow everything back and see if we could find the cause of the blockage. Might have been a bit daft on reflection, you didn't know what might have been dropped down the drains on the night of the invasion.

Ned, being young and not too experienced at handling the pump, got a little throttle happy and increased the pressure a bit too rapidly. The lengths of hose we used on these jobs were not new and were made up from cut-down damaged lengths. Of course, the joint blew apart, otherwise it might have lifted me off my feet. However, without us noticing, the son of the house with the offending drain had sat himself on the nearest fencepost to observe the goings on. I don't know if it was the shock from the noise of the joint blowing off, or if he was knocked off the fence by a jet of water, but anyway he ended up in a puddle of spillage from the drain. His mum wasn't any too pleased about it either. Still it goes to prove that drain cleaning is not a spectator sport! The blockage was caused, as in many cases, by a fizzy drink can having been introduced into the drain somewhere along the line.

While we were cleaning the rods etc, the airport Firefly drew up with three men in the front. One was the chap who had taken it away. He started pointing and jabbering at me and pointing to the Fly I was using. I couldn't understand what he was saying so I told him to go to Government House and ask for Alfonso and that he wasn't going to get another truck from us.

The lunchtime news said that Mr Haig was in London for extra talks, and there had been complications at the Buenos Aires end; it didn't say what the complications were, but one could guess.

The local news items were that the radio/telephone service was to be used for medical calls and emergencies only. According to 'them', Eileen the operator had been a little naughty and spoken to someone called 'Red Plum'[49] who had wished us all good luck and would see us again shortly.

Veronica Fowler had given birth to a baby boy in the hospital, Daniel.

The Argentines had fully taken over the broadcasting studio on John Street in Stanley and sent over a bloke from Buenos Aires to run the show.

I did some swotting up in the office and had another roll call on the spares we had in stock for the extinguishers; it would be some time before we got any replacements from the UK. I knew the Central Store carried a limited number of spares which would have to be used in an emergency.

The families living on the extreme outskirts of the southern boundaries of the town had been ordered to leave their homes and move down into town. This meant some houses were getting a bit crowded. I would have to check on fire extinguishers as part of the service and hope common

---

49. On 2 April HMS *Endurance* ('Red Plum') had called the RT station on their radio and had a short conversation with radio operator Eileen Vidal. We were listening in too. She had given a brief report on the situation in Stanley and had encouraged them, for the sake of their own safety, to stay away. They had wished her and us all good luck and promised to return soon. Which they did.

sense prevails. They had all been told that it could be dangerous to remain on the perimeter of the town; someone obviously was using belt and braces logic.

The meteorological office and adjacent buildings used by the Grasslands Trial Unit and Veterinary Officer had been taken over by the Argies. These buildings were on a high point at the rear of the town. One bright lad had constructed a machine-gun nest for himself on top of the diesel shed using bags of fertiliser.

Guns had been set up on Sapper Hill and things had been going on in Dairy Paddock – which was behind the big fuel tanks at the power station.

Valerie and Rachel had been up to see Grace on Davis Street. The three McPhees had not yet been asked to move out of their house. Valerie said it was quite depressing to see the amount of stuff which came onto the FIC jetty in large shipping containers. More troops were arriving at the airport daily.

People taking passengers to the airport to depart on a flight said that there were mountains of crates of ammunition stacked up – they were certainly making an effort to settle in.

I went over to have a natter with Father. He was still in good spirits but not happy about going out on the roads as he wouldn't be able to move fast enough to get into shelter if there should be an attack. We would have to ensure that his shopping was attended to.

When I got back home my old friend Jumbo Witney arrived. He was in quite a state. When he had taken a few deep breaths and calmed down a bit he said the 'B*****s' are shifting the Fly in the German Camp as well as other gear. I got into his Rover and we went up the hill at a fast rate of knots.

There weren't many soldiers in evidence, perhaps a dozen. So what was causing the fuss?

An officer came up to the vehicle and said his name was Lieutenant Joe Louis Blanquette, and I was to keep my colleague quiet or there could be trouble. He said that he spoke perfect English but his men didn't and he asked what did we want.

I told him I was the Chief of the Fire Department and asked what had been happening to my equipment without authority.

'Ah sir, I have placed your machine in a safe shelter as we need the building it was in. Come, I will show you.'

We walked over to the shelter usually used by the road repairers, there was the Fly backed in under the roof.

'I am a good driver and have taken the keys for security. You may come and ask for them when you need the machine,' he said.

To which I replied 'NO. I take the keys now and the machine.'

'Come into the house and I will talk to you.'

This house was the home of Chris Spall, a deeply religious man, a vegetarian, with whom I had worked in the Central Store for a while. He wasn't very pleased at having his home invaded by a very loud-voiced Argentine officer demanding coffee.

'How goes it Chris?', I asked.

'They have broken into my store shed and taken all my dried fruit and vegetables and all my honey.'

Chris, at some great expense to himself, had imported a queen bee and some workers. He had started a hive which had been quite successful, having produced 90lb of honey. He was saving this honey to feed back to the bees over the winter.

Blanquette began telling me what a glorious thing the liberation was and that he would personally look after the fire machine, but it was only a toy.

'It happens to be one of a group of machines which, used properly, is quite efficient. We haven't had any problems in the town until now and we are going to keep it that way. I will take the keys now and the tank and pump from the shed also.'

He threw the keys on the table and grudgingly said, 'Take them.'

We went out and towards the Nissen Hut where our stuff was stored; someone shouted at him and he seemed to grovel. 'Si mi Capitano. Si. Si,' all smiles.

He led the way, Jumbo heaved open one of the double doors.

Blimey!!!! So that's where they had been hiding: Blanquette had shut the soldiers in. There seemed to be hundreds of smiling faces, all youngsters, and wanting to practise their English at the same time.

I said, 'Come on chaps, give us a hand to hitch up these two machines and we will be away.'

'Okay Senor.'

Blanquette roared at them and they froze. He then told the lads in Spanish to help, which they did. To help them he kicked their small solid fuel cookers out of the way. That was the end of the day's rations for some.

One lad asked me if there were washing facilities and a shower. Another asked if there was drinking water. As far as I knew the water only went to the home of Chris and the other end of his double Nissen hut, so I said no.

We manhandled the pump and water bowser out to the Fly and hitched the pump to that. We hitched the bowser to Jumbo's Rover. He was still hopping mad. His house was opposite the Camp and he used a garage behind the site of the Camp. The Argie troops had demolished part of his garage and strewn some of the contents over the area. It almost got to a snarling match between him and Blanquette. A small officer, with colonel pips on his front, stepped in between them and told Blanquette to go away. He asked Jumbo to calmly tell him what the problem was.

'The Bastards have broken down my garage. I know it's not in a good state, but they shouldn't do that to private property anyway.'

'I quite agree sir, please give me your name and address. I will see that you are compensated.'

'Thank you, that will be ok.'

We got in the trucks and drove away before any more shenanigans happened. We took the appliances down to the drive in front of the hospital and parked them there. I checked the water and fuel levels all round, nothing needed to be done there.

We decided to go over to the Rose Hotel for a beer for medicinal purposes. Jumbo was still muttering on about the 'Purple, Green and Blue Bastards'. Dear old Mrs Johnson, the Landlady, and a strict disciplinarian didn't even tell him to mind his language. That's a first.

When I returned home, I telephoned the number where I knew I could contact Alfonso and told him the story in full detail. His answer to that was 'They are military.' This made it quite clear which way the wind was to blow.

Straight away I re-allocated fire personnel to the new equipment locations and informed them of the changes and the reason.

This is getting serious.

Wednesday, 14 April 1982

Valerie's diary
3pm – 11pm
The glass[50] has dropped ++. Overcast and heavy rain/sleet from s/w by 11.00 hrs.
Bought Rachel some new shoes £21.85 from the West Store.
The 2 kittens, Misty and Snoopy, are great friends now and are larking around the house.

---

50. Barometer.

Neville's diary

The early cold rain had turned to sleet by midday.

The Argies were all milling round in the dockyard, some were huddled together for shelter and tucking into corners where they could. I worked in the office stowing away useful sized pieces of wood. The workshop ended up with about three false ceilings in places.

Valerie had taken Rachel down to the shops and bought her a new pair of shoes, £21.85. Probably the usual inflated price. 'It's the freight charges you know.' Potato crisps and cornflakes are millionaire food 'due to the freight charges'. Well, 9,000 miles by sea and £100 per cubic metre, plus the handling charges at both ends of the journey and don't forget the profit margin!

The kittens, Misty and Snoopy, had been making themselves at home skylarking about the house, watched by Tuppence with a disdainful look on his face. Even at 8 years old he wasn't above bashing a ping pong ball about, as long as he thought no one was watching.

There was nothing to get alarmed about on the news at mid-day, nothing to relieve the tension and uncertainty either. The Task Force was on its way.

The opposition was building up, and there were guns and ammunition being moved through the town.

I went back to work at 1pm, Valerie was due to go on duty at 3pm.

Rudy came in to look for bits and pieces for the spare portable fire pump which was showing signs of its age. Tender loving care was needed.

I made a sawhorse as there wasn't anything to prop wood on while ripping it by hand, [and] I would have had to get a chit from the PWD office for anything to be done in the carpenters' shop. This took quite a while as I had never considered the calculations for the angles of the legs to be cut to splay them enough to be rigid. However, I used the tried and tested method of 'rule of thumb' – a bit off there and a bit off there, and it didn't wobble. I'd have to make another one even if it was just to sit on for 'smoko'.[51]

Poor little Argies, all cold and hunched up in their thin cotton uniforms. They had PVC ponchos with hoods which gave them a good bit of fight experience – that is they had to fight like the dickens to keep the things from wrapping round their heads in the Falklands wind. They were about as useful to the lads as a crinoline skirt.

---

51. Morning coffee break.

Nothing new on the evening news, usual messages from 'Calling the Falklands', some cryptic and others blatantly clear. There were messages of good luck from people who had never been to the Islands like Spike Milligan.

Anyway, a good night for hot rum by the fire and hope the phone does not ring. The children were busy doing things and keeping amused.

Thursday, 15 April 1982

Valerie's diary
7am–3pm.
Cold and overcast from s/w during the night.
I discharged Veronica and Daniel, mother and baby, from hospital.
GT to has gone to Comodoro, Argentina for medical treatment.

Neville's diary
Valerie was up and about first as she was due on duty at 7am.
As I left the house, I gave a shout to the girls to stir themselves. I received the usual 'Yeah Dad' then heard the beds creak as they turned over and went back to sleep.

I checked into the office and then walked up to the hospital, just a few hundred yards or so, and checked that 212 was where I had left it last night. Everything appeared to be in order, the engine started first push of the button. But the two 'Pony' transceivers had disappeared as well as the 6-volt hand lantern. Both were quite vital parts of the equipment. I reported to Alfonso about the missing items, and, yes, got the familiar reply. Probably he wasn't taken any notice of as he was a civilian too. Blimey, was he ever going to be able to do something for us?

The rest of the day was spent in the office. I had the sign to finish, and other little maintenance jobs in hand.

Valerie came off duty at 3.30pm and there was a cup of tea waiting for me when I got indoors.

We went over to Father's together. Sometimes she popped in to see him on her way home from the hospital. He was ok, wanted to know the latest gossip and news.

While waiting for the supper to be cooked, I whiled away the time by looking at the world go by from the front porch windows.

Something going on here I thought, half a dozen HU 1 helicopters flying down the harbour at 6–8 feet above the water. They had their cargo doors open and it was possible to see through the body of the machines. I discreetly got a pair of binoculars and looked at the 'Hueys'.

There was what appeared to be a heap of large grey plastic bags in each machine. They went out through The Narrows and came back again after a few minutes empty. I suppose they had time to fly as far as the Islands in Port William. They made the journey perhaps three times each that evening. They had come from the direction of the beaver hangar[52] but that was out of sight behind Sullivan House so I couldn't see exactly where they had lifted off from.

Friday, 16 April 1982

Valerie's diary
7am–3pm.
Light s/w wind, sunny spells. Bit nippy first thing in the morning. Wind freshened during the afternoon.
More anti-aircraft guns are going up onto Sapper's Hill and the surrounding area.
Buenos Aires *Herald* reporters have been visiting the hospital.
Neville is worried about ammunition being moved along the FIC jetty. Bloomer-Reeve wants a Firefly there.

Neville's diary
Usual Friday routines for me. All the fire appliances were in correct order, nothing further had been removed. The engines all started ok, even 212 though it had stood outside for the best part of a week. I must get Rudy to check the anti-freeze and put a bit extra in that one if it is going to stay out in the open for a while.

There were a few guns being hauled through the town and up Sapper Hill. I saw a couple of twin barrelled things on four wheels and a very large single barrelled gun being towed by a large Mercedes lorry. Also, a lot of other trucks carrying what looked like cases of ammunition and some heavy calibre shells. It could be dodgy hauling that through the town. I suppose that if questions were asked the answer would be: 'They are military and there is nothing we can do about it.'

I was called up to the Secretariat building by Vice Comodoro Carlos Bloomer-Reeve ('Bloomer'). He had been in the Falklands during 1974–75 as the representative in the LADE office. His English was perfect, he was

---

52. Property of the Falklands Islands Government Air Service (FIGAS), two de Havilland Canadian DHC-2 Beaver floatplanes were kept in a hangar at the side of the harbour on Ross Road West, beyond the final houses. Both were damaged beyond repair during the war.

able to translate spontaneously even humour from Spanish to English and vice versa. I asked after his family.

'Last time I saw them they were ok thank you.'

'Bloomer' had been given 24 hours to get from West Germany, where he had a position in the Argentine Embassy, to the Falklands – and wasn't all that thrilled about it. He was to replace the Falkland Islands Government Chief Secretary (Dick Baker), and even occupied his office.

He asked me about the fire service and what I had to do with it.

I told him the position as it stood there and then. He wanted to know how we would stand if there were to be air raids. I said that we were willing to come out. But that by the time we got up and running the raid would be over anyway, so we could get on with whatever we had to do. Don't forget we have to draw water from the harbour to extinguish fires. He said that he remembered that, and it was a good job as there was likely to be a water shortage. The filtration plant was hard pushed to keep up with the demand now that there were so many more people in the town.

He requested that I prepared a list of the names of all the members and have another chat with him.

I said 'the blokes wouldn't come out if there was any street fighting in the town ...'

'Why not?' he asked.

I replied: 'We think that could be classed as dangerous, so is an air raid, but there is a difference.'

He went on to say: 'If there is going to be any street fighting in Stanley, we have lost anyway.'

That must have been the end of the pleasantries. He next said that he wanted a fire appliance on the FIC jetty and the men to run it 24 hours a day.

'Why would you need that?' I asked.

'We are bringing ashore explosives as well as other combustible materials. If a fire were to start, it could cause a big bang and do some serious damage.'

I replied: 'You can have a pump but none of our men to run it. You have a man here from Comodoro Rivadavia who is a firefighting expert. He can train some of your men to run the appliance.'

'Uh! Well! He has had to go back and report,' said Bloomer.

'Ok, we will wait for him to train your men on his return,' I replied, indignant.

'All right, but I want fire protection on that jetty.'

I then left the office and went back to the PWD. As it was Friday, I collected my pay, it was close to knock-off time, so I went home.

Saturday, 17 April 1982

Valerie's diary
3pm–11pm.
Overcast and dry first thing. Sunny spells from s/w.
The Polish seaman, in hospital with appendicitis and psoas abscess, went to Buenos Aires for further treatment.
A few Americans evacuated.
GB comes in from Goose Green by helicopter with a fractured collar bone.

Neville's diary
The weekend. We had a bit of a lay in, and the girls weren't very keen on early rising anyway. We strolled over to Father's house and had a beer and a natter with him. He very often had a spell of reminiscing of his childhood and youth – 'When I was a lad, my boy' etc. From some of the tales he told I think my Dad, his older brother and their mates were a right bunch of tearaways. Not that they did any wilful damage or any hooliganism, high spirits seemed the appropriate way of describing their activities.

In the early and mid-1920s most people in Stanley had their own cows for milk. Some had a bull too. These animals were free to roam the common land, which was over the back of the hill to the south of the town. One of the lads' Saturday afternoon pastimes was to walk over the common. When they found one of the bulls asleep in the sun, a coin was tossed to see whose turn it was to ride the bull. They would quietly get on the back of the animal, wake it up by violently digging the neck with both thumbs, then sit tight for as long as they could!

He used to relate other tales of daring-do which I looked on as really adventurous. But when you have a go at similar things yourself, you immediately become an 'irresponsible careless youth' and 'you should know better' and 'you have worried your parents sick'.

There was a time when James and I went to Gipsy Cove. There was a shag's[53] nest on a rock out in the water, this bird had never successfully raised her chicks in the three years we had observed her. I decided that to deter the birds the eggs should be taken. The only way I could see was to jump out on to the rock, about 4 feet, then scramble down headfirst to the

---

53. Rock cormorant.

nest which was in the shade all day – hence the chicks perishing. Once there, I put the eggs in my mouth and climbed back up feet first. This accomplished I looked at James – he had his hands over his eyes. 'Couldn't stand it Nev, if I heard a splash, I'd leg it back to town and let your parents know.' The eggs were boiled there and then in a tin over a campfire and were excellent.

Now that I am a parent, I know what Father meant.

At the Secretariat I had a bit of a natter with 'Bloomer'. Alfonso wasn't back yet. We discussed what would be needed at the jetty with regards to fire safety while they were unloading ammunition. I could get fire extinguishing foam concentrate, but we were short of foam making branches. I would have to see what was hidden in the dim dark recesses of the various sheds we had equipment stored in. There were many lengths of rubber lined canvas hoses stored in the German Camp, together with some of the new light water concentrate and a lot of the older protein concentrates.

Valerie went off to duty for 3pm. She would sleep in the hospital overnight as she was on call, returning home at 3pm Sunday.

I did some tidying up in the garden, straightening up some fence battens, a nail here and another there. I collected up leaves and vegetable tops for the compost heap. I considered having a bonfire but decided against as I didn't want a lot of smoke blowing around. I would have to think about it though as we didn't know when, or if, the rubbish bins would be emptied on a regular basis.

At about 4.30pm I looked down towards the harbour and there, billowing over the fence between Mrs Luxton's house and Cable Cottage, was loads of smoke. I also noticed that there were clouds of black smoke pouring out of the chimney at Cable Cottage. That wasn't right as it was an oil-fired Rayburn in the kitchen which should never produce smoke unless something drastic had … oh shit!

I sprinted across the green to the fire station, calling to John Smith and his sons who just happened to be outside their house. We drove down the alleyway beside Cable Cottage and saw that the one lot of smoke was coming from a rubbish drum and tended by two young 'greenflies'. The Argies must have taken over the house and put some soldiers in it. The house had been standing empty, so no one was displaced.

I looked through the open kitchen window and observed that the hot plate on top of the stove was red hot and glowing, smoke was oozing from all the joints and flames were visible in the ash pit. That wasn't proper. I nipped along to the front door and walked in, calling out 'Hello? Anyone here?'

I went into the kitchen, opened the sliding damper in the smoke box, gently opened the fire box door and had a look in. There was a mass of flames all red and yellow, instead of the required blue flames three to four inches above the deflector plate. Burning fuel was spilling over the burner rings into the bottom of the stove. I switched off the fuel supply and waited for the flames to die down.

With that, in walked quite a large burly man with colonel's pips and a parachute emblem on his shirt. He carried on his belt a dagger with a brass hilt and knuckle bow.

I must have been a shock for him as we didn't have a uniform, just ordinary clothes on and a safety hat with 'Nev' written on it in green fluorescent Day Glo paint.

He asked, 'Who are you?'

'I am the fire officer. You have a dangerous situation here. I have switched the cooker off, and I will inform the proper department who will repair the stove. Too much fuel has been coming through, it must remain off until they arrive. I am not worried about you and your men, but there is a nice elderly lady over the road, and I wouldn't like anything to happen to her house. I will now use your telephone.'

'Yes, she is rather a nice person. Please use the phone.'

I rang Dennis Place, the senior government plumber. That department was responsible for maintaining all cookers and heating appliances in government houses. I told him what had happened and what measures I had taken.

The officer was Lieutenant Colonel Hilger, supplies officer to 'them'.

The fire in the bin was harmless, the two boys had been ordered to clean up the yard at the back of the house, had pulled up some grass tufts and put them in the bin with some cardboard boxes. Just a lot of smeech, they did have an extinguisher to hand anyway.

We put the Fly away and went off home. I went over to the Rose for a drink and to hear the latest.

Quite a pleasant evening.

On the way home I debated with me how best to cook the hindquarter mutton chops I had taken out of the freezer to thaw out. The result being I would cook them on the 'Asado'[54] or barbeque in the garden. There was a light south-westerly breeze which would carry the smell of wood smoke and cooking meat down over the town and the hungry, homesick 'green-flies'. We enjoyed the chops and chips and didn't get any visitors.

---

54. 'Asado' is a South American expression also used in the Islands.

Sunday, 18 April 1982

Valerie's diary

Molly Perry died at 2.30am. RIP.

I found out what the recently painted pink mortuary looked like.

Fine first thing but wind freshened and strengthened from n/w.

Plenty of troop movement over Sappers Hill.

Water supplies are getting short.

Dr Mary Elphinstone came to supper after church. We spent a pleasant few hours together.

Neville's diary

Usual Sunday chores: feed hens, get some veg, shout to wake the girls. They would normally have gone to Sunday school in the Tabernacle but without a resident minister there wouldn't be any services in that church. All members of the congregation were invited to the Cathedral to join the services there.

I wandered over to see Father, all ok on that front. Then went over to the hospital and have a look in. Valerie was ok but I fancied something was bothering her.

'Come on,' I said. 'What's up?'

'Well, you know that before all this started, I had the mortuary painted out?'

'Yes.'

'Well, one of the old dears died in the night. I took her body out to "Rose Cottage" and do you know that someone has put a bullet right through the wall. It has ricocheted right round in the building and gone out through the skylight. Ruined all the paintwork. I'll have to get it re-done and I'm not sure if there is space in the hospital budget for it.'

I thought then that perhaps we <u>were</u> safer in a wooden house.

She said that she had invited Dr Mary over for supper after the church service. I suggested a gosling from the freezer which would be quite nice and tender. And I would get a bottle of wine from the 'Rose' and a few beers also.

The children were preparing a light lunch. I went along the road and spent a happy hour gassing away. When time was called, I looked out of the windows. Outside was the Sergeant of Military Police, not a tall man but he had a sort of look of authority about him. We thought that maybe he had turned up in case there had been too much drink taken and a rough-house might ensue. He drew his pistol (automatic .45), checked that it was loaded and returned it to his holster. That didn't look too healthy. Someone made a move to leave. Mrs Johnson said hang on, give him a few minutes. We waited. He stood there smiling. After a few more minutes Carlos, one of the locals, finished up his drink and said 'Oh! Hell, it's me he's after. I'll go out and see what he wants.'

They moved off in a friendly fashion, but you can never tell with a policeman, especially when he smiles like that. We all left for home wondering what 'they' thought Carlos had been up to.

The wind got up a bit in the afternoon but not unpleasantly so. Wizz [Isobel] and I decided that we should change the colour scheme of the front fence and gate. It was currently pale blue with a white gate in the middle, coincidentally the colours of the Argentine flag. Searching through my shed we gathered all the paint we could find and mixed two or three-part cans of paint and came up with a 'yeuchy' green. We painted all afternoon.

Blimey!!! What's this?

Six armoured cars carrying quite a large calibre gun drove by, just a couple of feet away from where we were painting. They had narrow wheels. Wouldn't get far over the peat with them.

Dr Mary came in after church. Mary said that the service had ended with the singing of 'Land of Hope and Glory' as the National Anthem had been banned from public use.

She stayed and chatted with Valerie for a long time. Close on midnight she decided that it might be a good idea to go home. The wind had got up quite strong, although dry. I said that due to the hour I would accompany her over to the Dr's flat in Admiralty Cottage. Going along the road, we came up behind a patrol of 'greenflies' armed to the teeth and pussy-footing it in the middle of the road. The strong northwest wind prevented them from hearing us. None of them looked round, good job too, we just might have been taking the mick out of them and they could have got a bit miffed.

Monday, 19 April 1982

Valerie's diary
3pm–11pm.
Weather continues to be favourable for the 'tourists'.
Sunny, warm spells, light n/w wind.

Neville's diary
I arrived in the office at the usual time of 7.30am.
There were Argies bustling about up and down the road as if they had been established in the various places for a long time.

At 8am on the dot, there sounded the tones of a silver bugle from the direction of Government House. All traffic screeched to a standstill. All personnel stood to attention, faced west and saluted while the 'tune' was played. Must have been the hoisting of the flag.

They had tried to have an Argentine flag outside St Mary's Roman Catholic Church, but the Monsignor said not likely, and put up his own diocesan flag. The flagpole outside the Secretariat had had a very large Argentine flag flying from it. On a particularly windy day, that flagpole snapped, and the flag was carried away down the harbour by the high wind.

I was idly minding my own business again when the dulcet tones of a familiar voice behind me said: 'Congratulations.'

'What for this time'?

'Seeing that you are accepted by the Argies as the Fire Officer, you have now been appointed official cleaner and maintainer of all oil-fired heating and cooking appliances installed in any Government building.'

'Oh shit! I hate that job. It's filthy, dirty, and all that diesel and carbon plays havoc with my hands. It's going to be difficult to get overalls clean with the water shortage.'

'Look at it this way,' said Malcolm, 'you will have access to all sorts of places, and you might hear all sorts of funny things.'

'No option?'

'No. Dennis has spoken to the Colonel and he approves.'

The Colonel, being of their Engineers, was in charge of the Dockyard.

'When do I start?'

'Right now. Get your stuff together and go up to Cable Cottage. You put the stove out after the fire there on Saturday. Go up and sort it out and protect Government property. The plumbers can't manage jobs like this with all the problems at the filtration plant, and the water line repairs caused by heavy trucks going through the road surface. Besides, you have an extensive knowledge of these things.'

I pointed out: 'You've got some of my tools at your place.'

'No, they are all here and I called in to your home and collected the rest from your shed too,' said he, producing my tool bag from behind his back. Scheming so and so.

'Ok, I'll go up after breakfast.'

'Yes, but don't take too long. They get a bit anxious once they have issued a request."

So, after a couple of jam sarnies and a mug of coffee from the thermos, off I went.

I knocked on the open front door and walked in, there were two lads washing dishes with water from an electric kettle.

'Hello, I've come to repair the stove.' In a friendly fashion.

That was met with sagging jaws and blank stares.

'I, me (pointing to my chest) repair Rayburn,' indicating the cooker.

'Bueno, Senor.'

Well, there'd be neither risqué stories nor propounding the theory of evolution here.

The stove burner was still out. I removed the hot plate; it was thick with soot and oily smuts. I gave the boys to understand that they should remove the clothes from the airing line over the stove. I then started to dismantle the stove pipe soot trap and smoke box. They were also clogged up with sooty cobwebby muck. I took all these bits out to the dustbin and gave them a good brushing to remove all the deposits of carbon etc. I then started to dismantle the fire box. A voice said: 'What are you doing here again?'

I replied, 'Morning Colonel, did you volunteer for the Army'?'

'Yes.'

'I have been given this job to do, it's very dirty and not very nice. The house will be safe, and you will have the facility to cook and heat water, and I didn't volunteer for this.'

He laughed.

I continued: 'I have the same system in my own home and have been trained to clean and maintain that one and others.'

'Good. Are you a Falklander?'

'Yes.'

He was almost speaking in my ear, sort of confidentially.

'Have you children'?'

'Yes, two.'

'Are they suffering from us being here?'

'Not yet.'

'They are not at school?'

'No, but they study at home."

'Soon all will be settled, and they will be back to normal.'

He went away and another of them came into the kitchen and in the same half-whispered manner asked the same questions. They were obviously keen to have a go at talking to this captive Falklander. Others also appeared but seemed a bit shy or couldn't speak enough English. I thought it prudent not to air the few words of Spanish I know.

I removed the burner unit and gave it a good clean. There was a build-up of carbon all the way into the oil feed pipe; it's a wonder there had been a flame at all, let alone too much fuel being burned. I put it all back together and recalibrated the fuel flow. I would have to wait for 20 minutes now to make sure the fuel level was maintained.

While waiting, one of the lads passed me a cup of black coffee, very tasty, must have been officer's rations not just the ordinary instant stuff.

Now was the moment to be brave. I inserted new asbestos and then lit the thing. Instead of shutting the fire box door, I used a special inspection door with a mica window in the centre, so I could observe the behaviour of the flame which would take a little while longer than usual as the stove was cold.

I took out my tobacco pouch and papers to roll a smoke. A cigarette appeared over my shoulder, a Jockey Club brand. I thanked the lad, my Capstan tobacco and Rizla papers would not have tasted too good having rolled it with all the muck on my hands.

I peered into the fire box through the window and saw that the flame was blue and a few inches above the burner. The regulator was at maximum, the hot plate felt warm to touch. I took off my inspection door and closed the proper one tightly.

With a little difficulty, I explained to the lads about the switch and that the top would get hot rapidly now, but the water in the cylinder would take a while to heat as it was starting from cold.

I looked at my watch, nearly midday. That was nearly three and a half hours at Cable Cottage. I walked up the alley to home to get the dirt off my hands and face.

I got a wonderful warm welcome: 'And how many stoves have you cleaned this morning? You smell!'

'Only one, Dear.'

'Put your boiler suit on the fence until after lunch. I'M NOT HAVING THAT IN THE HOUSE.'

'No, dear.'

Valerie said: 'I thought there was something up when I saw Malcolm go into your shed this morning. He had the cheek to tap on the window and call out Coo-ee.'

'Yes, dear.'

Back to work. Malcolm was waiting for me.

'How did you get on?'

I told him all the nitty gritty' and how long it had taken to clean and re-assemble the burner unit.

'I thought you might have a bit of a problem with that one, the previous occupant thought they could maintain it themselves. Come on then, get in the truck and I'll give you a lift up the road to John Fergusson's[55] house. Same problem there. His wife is alone with the children. John went away just before the invasion to check on some grassland trials he had set up in Peru or Bolivia on the way to the UK for some leave. I think his Mrs is waiting to get away to meet him in England.'

I replied: 'I'm in enough hot water already at home because of this boiler suit. I'll have to take home some hand cleaner to get the muck off, then wash it in a bucket. If I go near the washing machine, I could be in very deep you-know-what.'

'As you know the Dockyard is now a military establishment and if you take anything from the military it is classed as sabotage and the penalty for sabotage is execution. But the hand cleaner will be deemed as a necessary and authorised removal.'

After a few Anglo-Saxon terms of non-endearment, we arrived at the house on Ross Road West.

I prepared myself to do battle with the next lot of carbonised remains of a by-product of crude oil. This stove was a different kettle of fish, having been maintained by the plumbers, just a routine clean and polish.

Tuesday, 20 April 1982

Valerie's diary
7am–3pm.
Strong n/w wind and rain squalls, cleared by the evening.
Very quiet in the hospital.
Talks still going on between London, Buenos Aires and Washington.
We've been told on the Box to be ready for air raids and to start preparing blackouts. Charming!

Neville's diary
Nothing alarming happened in the first five minutes of being at work. Then Len McGill, the government chief clerk, came in with a Union agreement in his hand. At the Falkland Islands General Employees Union,

---

55. John Fergusson was the team leader of the Grasslands Trials Unit (GTU). They had their headquarters in the old Met Station at the start of Eliza Cove Road, at the south of the town. Alistair Greaves and Tom Davies (mentioned on 2 April) were part of his team, as was a veterinary surgeon, and some assistants to help. They were researching into how the pasturage in the Falklands could be improved, thus producing better wool and a better sheep for mutton.

we had negotiated to completion this agreement with the Stanley Employers in January–February this year, with a slight kerfuffle on the way.

'Morning Len, what's up then?'

'The Colonel brought this in. Said he had found it in the office and asked what it was all about. I told him it is the wages agreement between Falkland Islands Government, the Falkland Island Company and the General Employees Union applicable to all members in Stanley.'

I wondered if the document had been placed strategically by someone helpful, or if he really had found it.

Len said that the Colonel had replied that it is an excellent document, and you will pay all the men by this, no more and no less.

'That's what it's all about, Len.'

'Yes. He also wants a roll-call every morning, so we don't have any freeloaders making a convenience of us.'

'That keeps our noses clean then.'

'Yep.'

I had a lean on the gate while I was having my breakfast.

A new system had started; all passengers for a flight out had to assemble at the Town Hall instead of making their own way to the Airport. Well, we would have to see what 'they' came up with next.

I continued to scour the office for bits and pieces of fire equipment to put down on the jetty when we got a pump sorted out for there. I really couldn't let one of the town pumps go no matter how vital Bloomer said it was.

I went up to the Central Station, [and] on top of the spare fuel cupboard I found a very antique foam generating set. This was a backpack kit which included a 5-gallon tank of foam compound. I don't think 'they' would have anyone strong enough to carry that lot. It would work with a siphon tube into a drum of foam too. Anyway, if the Argentine ammunition on the jetty did catch alight there wouldn't be enough time to do anything about it. Only one option remained: I would have to go up to the Secretariat and ask about getting pieces from Moody Brook and inquire when thingamajig Alfonso was coming back.

I walked up to the Secretariat to see the man. I had to show my official pass to get in the building. All I did was flash my Falkland Islands driving licence at the bloke on guard duty and walk in.

I met Bloomer. He said that Alfonso wasn't coming back, and he would make inquiries regarding equipment from 'the Brook'. He stressed that I was to get something down on to that jetty pretty quick.

I then told him I wanted to have a meeting of all persons available for firefighting duties. Quite a lot of people had gone away; either out of the Islands or to camp and I wanted to know where I stood with manpower. Public meetings were prohibited by edict, but I would like to have everyone to my house when convenient. He said that would be in order, and as the next day was a public holiday that would be a good time to meet. Blimey! They were giving us a public holiday for the Queen's birthday.

Later, Malcolm asked me if I would go to the home of Harry Bonner and have a look at his oil burner as it was giving a bit of bother. He would run me up to where Harry and his wife Doreen were living on Davis Street. Harry was the acting superintendent of the PWD.

Doreen[56] and I were at school together, so we had a good old chat about times past. I used to sit beside her younger sister Hazel in class; their parents had a small farm, Mullet Creek Farm, to the south of Sapper Hill and Mount William. The farm consisted of a house, cow shed and stable. Further away on the track was the woolshed used for shearing in the season and storing the pressed wool until collected for shipment. They had 2,000–3,000 sheep.

Doreen wasn't too happy in the house on Davis Street, as it was quite close to the danger zone and the Argies had dug in at the top of the garden. I got the stove sorted out and left them to it.

The lunch time news said that the talks were still going on and everyone was saying no.

One of the local announcements was that the traditional public holiday on 21st April would be observed by the people of the islands. It was not compulsory to do so, and the day should be celebrated in a quiet manner. So that was it: no parade by the FIDF and Royal Marines, no twenty-one gun salute from Victory Green, and I don't suppose anyone would be crawling home in the gutter after 'Glory Hour' with loyal toasts in the bar.

Tom Perry, the General Foreman in the PWD, collected me and my gear and took me up to a house in Racecourse Road to sort out the cooker. The tenants, some teachers, had evacuated to England leaving the house vacant. The Colonel had said that it was to be occupied by Argentine officers. Tom had cleared out and stored the possessions left behind by the departing people, leaving just the Government furniture.

The cooker was very dirty and well out of adjustment. Oh dear, more muck on the boiler suit. The level of fuel in the tank was fairly low too but

---

56. Doreen Bonner was one of the three civilian ladies sadly killed on 11 June.

that was not any of my concern. Let the new occupants deal with that, they had more manpower than we did.

Bloomer had told me that we in the fire service should have armbands to identify us. The bands were to have the word 'Bombero', which means fireman, written on them. I got some yards of elastic and white material. The children got out the sewing machine and set to making the arm bands, using permanent markers to handwrite the word on.

The announcement regarding the public holiday for HM the Queen was repeated in the evening and the announcement about the Fire Brigade meeting in our house was read out too. Also announced was that people must be prepared for air raids and blackouts and that the Argentine forces would be training and practising with their guns, firing out to sea.

Wednesday, 21 April 1982

Valerie's diary
Day off.
Queen's Birthday, public holiday.
Hail squalls during last night.
Fire Brigade meeting in our house.
Party in Admiralty Cottages [the single doctors and nursing sisters' accommodation] for Queen's birthday – no counter revolution by the natives!
Lots of smoke from one of the Tussock Islands off Yorke Bay in Port William.

Neville's diary
Planned lay-in disturbed by a phone call. All it does is ring and cause anxiety.

Harry Bonner. 'Got some trouble with the cooker old son, it's gone out.'

'It was ok yesterday. I'll come up.'

'Well, we've moved to No. 4 Ross Road West. It was too much for Doreen at Rincon Cottage on the hill, now we shall be away from the activity.'

'Righto, I'll pop up presently, but I've got a meeting at 11am.'

I got some breakfast on the go and thought to myself 'Oh dearee me!! More muck on the boiler suit!' I might get a chance to clean it some-time – I think it cringes each time I pick up my tool bag.

During the cleaning I just had to accept Doreen's invitation to have a glass of something, (a) To keep my tonsils clear & (b) (More important) a Loyal Toast.

'Good on yer, Ma'am. Happy Birthday!'

Harry, Doreen and I heard some loud bangs and some thumps outside. Wondering what it was all about we had a look out. To the northeast we could see some aircraft flying round Port William and diving towards Yorke Bay, probably at the Tussock Islands. A large black oily cloud billowed well up into the sky before it was flattened by the breeze. It must have been quite hot stuff. No doubt 'they' wouldn't tell us the truth if asked what's going on.

The stove was going ok, it hadn't been all that dirty, just hadn't been alight for a while and was lit from cold. These oil conversions of peat burning stoves are not high tech and are just a little fussy.

We had a good turnout for the meeting, thirty-six members in all arrived. Isobel and Rachel had done wonders with the 'Bombero' armband production. I advised all members to carry one at all times and to put it on when the usual siren was sounded: a long or continuous note would indicate a fire. If there was an air raid there would be a long wavering tone and then the all clear would be a steady note. This could be confusing; I think there were a lot of us going round with crossed fingers.

I warned the younger lads not to go pushing their luck in the name of the Fire Brigade, or they would come off second best. Especially if they went round the town speeding on their motor bikes or in Rovers.

We decided on the best way to re-allocate the drivers and mates now that the equipment that used to be on the German Camp was down at the hospital. As Gerald Cheek lived nearest the hospital, he would be driver of 212 and the previous crew would fill in on other jobs until they had their vehicle back. The members all said they had no fears of turning out in a war situation, but didn't relish the thought of getting mixed up in street fighting. I told the meeting that I had already spoken to Bloomer on that score and repeated that he had told me there wouldn't be any street fighting in Stanley. I also informed everyone there was to be a fire drill tomorrow at 1pm, no siren would be sounded. We were to meet at the site of the old watering jetty below the hospital. We would practise hose laying, use of the pumps and put some water in the old reservoir in front of Admiralty Cottage. We would also try out the Breathing Apparatus (BA) crew with the guidance of Owen and Brian. By this time, it was lunch so off they rushed for theirs, or for whatever you do from 12 noon – 1pm on the Queen's birthday.

At 3pm we went over to the Matron's flat in Admiralty Cottage for a party, there also just happened to be invited the senior member of the Council and therefore the Governor's representative. The usual Loyal

toasts were proposed and drunk. This according to 'their' edicts consti-
tuted an illegal assembly, but who cared. Tradition demanded the gathering normally be held in Government House. We agreed to meet weekly to
repeat the medicine until such times as things returned to normal.

The 'Calling the Falklands' programme was full of live recorded
messages from absent loved ones, accompanied by hiccoughs and sobs.
There seemed to be more of the interference experienced during that previous programme. The presenter said that they knew we were experiencing
difficulty in reception so have extended the frequencies they broadcast on
and would also broadcast more times a week. Rex Hunt had a stirring
message for us too.

Other news: America announced that the Task Force had split up and
part of the force was heading for South Georgia. BLABBERMOUTHS.

There used to be a weekly record programme on the Box, presented by
someone from the public who had records they liked to share with others,
or chosen from the thousands in the studio. The veterinary officer, Steve
Whitley, was to be the presenter on this occasion. He displayed his sledge-
hammer subtlety. The first record was dedicated to 'that lovely lady
Elizabeth Windsor', others to 'Maggie', 'Sandy'(Admiral Woodward) and
'Andrew'[57], see you soon, to absent friends and those soon to be friends.
The choice of music left no one in any doubt as to what we were celebrating: Land of Hope and Glory, The Yeomen of England and many
other stirring ditties.

I suppose that was the nearest anyone had come to a little local insur-
rection.

Quite a good day all in all under the circumstances.

Rachel remembers . . .
One of the teachers, Mrs Stewart, had invited a group of children to her
home for a party. It was officially to celebrate her niece's 12th birthday.
We all knew it was also to honour the Queen too. We all stood out on
Ross Road West and watched as Argentine Pucara planes, with their
distinctive engine sound, swooped low and dropped some bombs onto the
Tussock Islands out in Port William, the outer harbour. The islands were
burning furiously, first with big billows of black smoke and then settling
down with white smoke. We were all, naturally, very concerned about
what on earth was going on. We could only speculate and cling to the
reassurances from our lovely teacher.

---

57. Margaret Thatcher, Admiral Woodward (commander of the Task Force) and Prince
    Andrew.

Thursday, 22 April 1982

Valerie's diary

Day off.

Dull, overcast first thing, then sunny and spring like from the n/w.

Went shopping during the morning with the girls. Getting ready for Rachel's birthday party on Saturday.

The girls have swapped bedrooms. Isobel is now upstairs.

Car bomb in Paris. Killed one person, injured many more. France and Syria now at loggerheads.

President Galtieri is here for the day.

Neville's diary

Valerie was on a day off; she said that she would take the girls down the shops and get some goodies for Rachel's birthday party, which we planned to have on Saturday. Most of Rachel's friends were away to the camp or England. Some had been away since before the invasion. There were still enough children about to have a good thrash. There wouldn't be many things to buy as the three-monthly charter boat from UK hadn't arrived back before the invasion. We didn't know if it was floating about in the Atlantic waiting or if it had been prevented from leaving the UK. Hopefully there would be something to buy for Rachel as she reaches the ripe old age of 11 years.

I did some rushing about checking pumps and vehicles etc ready for the drill at 1pm. After a quick lunch, during which there was a decided atmosphere between mother and daughters – there usually was after a joint shopping expedition, Valerie sent the children outside to feed the hens so we could have a chat on our own. Christmas and birthday presents are usually kept top secret until the time of presentation. She told me, in the absence of the two terrors, what she had managed to get so far in the way of presents and dainties for the party. I thought she had done marvellously well under the circumstances. The Argentine forces were not permitted by their own Edicts to go into the shops. They didn't have much money anyway but would have played havoc with our supplies of goods on the shelves – especially the sweets and biscuits, not to mention the 'spirituous liquors'.

We had a quick listen to the overseas news: Hooray! Francis Pym had gone over to the USA for talks with the Reagan Administration. This is surely progress towards peace.

A car bomb had blown up in Paris killing and maiming some innocent people.

The local news said that some chap called Galtieri had flown over on a visit for the day. So that's why the big show.

1pm

Waiting on the sea wall where the Government Stream runs under the wall where the old watering jetty used to be.

At a low tide some of the pilings can still be seen. This jetty was used in the old days when ships had no water making facility and couldn't carry enough water. There used to be a couple of water barges in Stanley harbour to service the ships. These barges were filled at the jetty by water piped from the reservoir in front of Admiralty Cottage. This was in turn fed by a reservoir further up the hill by Bonners Paddock next to Dairy Paddock.

We were going to attempt to fill this lower reservoir this afternoon. In the past there had been talk of turning this reservoir into a swimming pool, but this idea had met with a lot of opposition.

The day had improved, bright and sunny, warmish and the only cloud on the day was blue, white and blue hanging from Government House flagpole.

All the members of the fire brigade turned out. The trucks had their appropriate drivers. Hoses were laid, suctions thrown into the harbour, good job the tide was still high enough.

Many of the Argies couldn't understand why the water disappeared from the 'lake' twice a day and came back. Not at the same time each day either. Their Navy probably did, but there weren't many of those about, and the Navy wouldn't talk to the Army, the Army wouldn't talk to the Air Force and vice versa.

Well, everything worked ok. The pumps pulled water out of the harbour and pushed it through the hoses. The remaining radios worked. All was going smoothly except for one little thing: the shut off valves in the reservoir had rusted open and when the water reached the level of the outlet it ran back into the harbour. Nevertheless, it was a good exercise.

Perhaps El Presidente was watching, there were a lot of soldiers assembled over on the football field, he was probably reviewing the troops. Not a lot of military interest in what we were doing. 'Their' chief of police came on the scene, a Major, and had a chat with us. Hands behind his back, feet slightly apart, rocking up on his toes, doing the Dixon of Dock Green[58] bit.

---

58. A BBC television series about a fictional London police station, with the emphasis on petty crime.

During the days after the invasion he had personally seen to the collection of all privately owned firearms in the town, given a chitty to the owners, and then locked the whole lot up and kept the key himself.

All seemed to be going well with the drill. Brian and Dave giving instructions on the BA sets. The wrecking, sorry, salvage crew, were checking axes, prise/crow bars and things vital to their needs. Various members of crews were swapping places and duties for experience and versatility. The air bottles would have to be topped up at the end of the day. It would be the responsibility of the leader of their section to get them all four notches up the gauge.

Let's knock off and make up. Not forgetting to flush out the pumps with a quick burst from the hydrants. The pumps were specially ordered for us, gunmetal instead of aluminium to avoid corrosion.

Meanwhile, back at the Ranch, the children had swapped bedrooms during the afternoon. After the initial invasion they had shared the downstairs back bedroom, then Rachel had gone back upstairs. Now Rachel had come down and Wizz had taken the upper room.

The evening news started with a statement by Admiral Woodward (Sandy), that he was declaring an air blockade as well as a sea blockade around the Islands.

There was plenty of radio interference during the 'Calling the Falklands' programme.

Friday, 23 April 1982

Valerie's diary
3pm–11pm.
Flat calm first thing. Then, a light southerly breeze, very unseasonal. The wind blew from n/w during the evening, dropped to 6°C, too cold for 'greenflies'.
Uncle Harold is back in business for legal aspects.

Neville's diary
Turned to at 7.30am, did some jobs round the office. Checked on the machines in the Central Station, all nice and clean after their outing yesterday.

Phil Summers, of the Secretariat, came into the office: would I attend a meeting with the Argy Colonels at 10 o'clock? I was selected as I had a responsible position in the community and being a local citizen, they would appreciate me attending. Malcolm came up and I told him about the invite to the Secretariat. In his opinion should I go.

'Sure, chay,[59] you go. It's the only way to find out what's on their minds.'

I pointed out that 'I'll have to get that pump down to the Jetty today or Bloomer will be touchier than he is.'

10am

To the Secretariat. Showed my driving licence to the guard and walked in. The meeting had been arranged in the conference room. Trust me to be about the first to arrive. Bloomer was already there.

He launched: 'Where's my pump?'

I replied: 'Have you got any stuff from the Brook yet?'

'No.'

'Well, I'll put what we have down on the jetty this afternoon, there's plenty of foam concentrate in the German Camp and hoses too.'

'Good.'

Besides Bloomer there was Captain Hussey,[60] another who spoke perfect English, there on liaison duties. Hussey was the only Argy I saw who got into a jogging suit, mind you he did only break into a fast walk.

Then there was 'their' boss of the post office and communications, 'their' legal beagle and about half a dozen wild looking other blokes. No one appeared to be carrying weapons.

On our side of the table the town's people were represented by members of the community in business, commerce, and trade.

Bloomer opened the proceedings by referring to someone who had told an Argentine Officer to leave the West Store.

'Well,' said Olga, 'I didn't know he was your Governor Menendez. He was just another soldier in a uniform. As we had been instructed by your edicts from Government House not to permit military personnel into the store, he should have known better.'

'He did laugh about it anyway.'

That was an ice breaker. The meeting started. Bloomer welcomed us as representatives of the population, not in any official capacity, but, so that 'they' could explain what the future was to be for the people and the Islands. A few of the laws of the Islands would have to be re-phrased to suit Argentine laws, but most of the laws were good and would remain so as they are unique to the Islands.

The Islands would be Argentine, the people would have all the privileges and freedoms of Argentine citizens. I wondered: what privileges and freedoms are there in a dictatorship?

---

59. Chay is a Falkland Islander word meaning mate or pal.
60. Captain Melbourne Hussey of the Argentine Navy.

All people who married after 2 April 1982 would not be permitted to divorce as that is the Argentine law. (Freedom?)

Children would be taught Spanish at school. The younger the pupil, the more lessons in Spanish. Teachers would be brought over from the mainland as they would be better than teachers from elsewhere (humph). It was hoped that all adults would voluntarily learn the language.

People would learn to drive on the right-hand side of the road. Arrows had already been painted on the roads to help the Islanders. This was done as 'they' felt that the Islanders especially in Stanley (Puerto Argentino) would be able to convert to drive on the right much easier than 5,000 military drivers trying to drive on the left.

They expanded on these points and a few other trivial matters which seemed almost like grovelling. Perhaps it was the soft touch, or else.

When asked about the bombing of the Port William Islands on the 21st, Bloomer said that the air force have to practise their skills and techniques somewhere, and as the wildlife was not nesting at this time of year these Islands had been chosen as the targets. There would be more practising with bombs and big guns and whatever else armed forces did.

One of the business representatives said that he had a lot of Pesos and Pounds tied up in tourism and that he had not been able to fulfil his obligations to clients because of the invasion. He asked if he would get compensation.

'Ah that's not our fault, next question.'

'Will our mail be not interfered with?'

The postal rep jumped up all flustered.

'Do you mean the post has been opened and interfered with?'

'The address and the stamps on the letters have been defaced and have been so for quite some time.'

'Do you mean the letters have been opened?'

'No, just defaced.'

'Ah, if a letter is incorrectly addressed it is corrected, we do not have censorship.'

I wondered to myself if that would be next.

Another asked: 'Your military have brought Alsatian dogs into the Islands. We have strict laws regarding the importing of livestock which includes dogs. We have a problem with hydatid disease which is carried by dogs and infects sheep and humans. Will you do something to control these dogs or send them back?'

A brief rapid conversation in Spanish.

'We know about hydatid disease as we have a sheep industry on the mainland. These dogs are so expensive to keep and train that they will be adequately immunised and the group that brought them will not move anywhere without them.'

I asked: 'Do we have freedom to move within the Islands? I would like to go fishing to the Murrel river and to Mullet Creek.'

'Just at the moment it is a little difficult and we do not recommend that you or anyone else goes to the Murrel as you might catch something that you do not want. When this is all resolved, and we are really in control, things will be back to normal and people will be able to go fishing and shooting as they did before.'

Well! We weren't going to be too well off with that lot.

We were invited to go to Government House on Monday to listen to Argentine governor General Menendez who would be only too pleased to give us more detailed explanations.

That ended that lot of 'rubbish' and, not even an offer of a glass of water.

I told Bloomer that I was off to the German Camp to get the fire-fighting equipment for the jetty. Back at the Dockyard I told Malcolm what had happened, and we agreed that there was no point in my attending Government House on Monday. As it was, I would get a lot of stick from round the town for attending today anyway, but we had to have people there to get a good account of the meeting.

I took 212 up the hill and found one of the Argy officers who I had spoken to before. I asked him about white containers of light water for making foam. He showed me what they had taken from the Nissen hut and how they had stored it. No sign of any white plastic cans, they were about 10-gallon size, so should be quite visible. I went further afield to another group and asked them, they were only too willing to help load hoses onto the truck, but no sign of even an empty container. When asked again, a couple of the blokes did shuffle their feet and look the other way.

I took about a dozen of the metal 5-gallon cans of protein concentrate; they were dated 1960 and I think ex-navy stock. Although out of date, were usable for practice and had to be good enough for the jetty, as we did not have anything else. It was pitiful to see two young lads struggling with a can between them. Whereas I might be a bit larger than some, I picked up a can in each hand. They shouldn't have to puff and blow like that, they should have been in tip top condition being military. I asked was there a problem, yes much upset stomach and sick. That explained the miles of stained toilet paper strewn around and hanging off the fence wires. The whole area did whiff a bit of human what nots. It had been rumoured in town that 'they' had cases of dysentery. That's it, the silly buggers had seen 'water' on the white 10-gallon cans of foam making 'light water' and had drunk it; it's a wonder they weren't dead.

The loading of the truck continued.

'What is in these cans Senor?'

'Protein concentrate, mixture of blood and guts.'

'Que?'

'Sangre y intestino.'

'Oh.'

Don't think that did the morale any good either.

I took the pump and stuff down to the jetty after lunch. Bloomer had told me there would be an interpreter there to assist me. Pat McPhee came along too to help explain the workings; he had had many years associated with the Service. The interpreter turned up, a medium height slim ginger-haired youth. His English was textbook but spoken with a lot of hesitation. I asked him if he had British ancestry as he could have been of Welsh origin.

'No, my parents are German.'

'Kunnen sie Deutsch?'

'No sir, I am sorry, but German is forbidden in my home.'

We got hold of a petty officer and some of his volunteers. They weren't all that interested in the machine and succeeded in soaking some of their own officers while having a squirt with the hose. The petty officer wasn't impressed with the antique foam generating set and said so in no uncertain terms. I told him that it was all that I had to offer in the time, meanwhile hoping that no-one had a nose round the hose laying truck and others of our vital equipment. Just then the suction hose key got kicked overboard, and it reappeared on the jetty just like that, followed by a frogman. A mine clearance team.

There were ten or twelve 40ft shipping containers on the jetty. Some had the yellow triangular explosives sticker on them, while others just had 'munitions' painted on in white paint. I noticed some familiar faces shifting packages and crates; they were usually on the Argentine trading ships which called in from time to time. It seemed that 'they' had brought their own stevedores.

Oh well, it's near enough to 4.30pm, let's go back and knock off.

I went over to the Rose for a pre-supper drink. I ran straight into trouble. A telling off from the landlady for going to the meeting, should have refused to have anything to do with the b*****ds. From round the room came cries of shouldn't have gone, letting the side down. Don't believe the sods, shouldn't have anything to do with them. And the one that did smart a bit: 'Turncoat.'

I wondered who was going to adjust and service their oil burners and gas fires next time or put out their chimney fires? Who would make and repair their dentures for them?

Well, my money wasn't refused, and I didn't get heartburn from the whisky.

I walked over to see Father and had a natter with him. He told me that his younger brother Harold, at the request of Bloomer-Reeve, had been brought back into town by helicopter from the farm they'd been staying at. Bloomer wanted Uncle Harold to assist 'them' in reforming the laws of the Colony, Uncle being the Registrar General and Magistrate of the Islands.

'Humph, we'll have to see about that,' he said.

And so ended yet another imperfect day in the Islands.

Saturday, 24 April 1982

Valerie's diary

7am–3pm.

Light n/w wind, overcast.

The Task Force are blockading South Georgia!

Rachel's birthday party, 3pm–5.30pm. Afterwards Rachel and self walked as far as Government House. First time since invasion for me to go that far west. Rachel has been as far as Racecourse Road to the Peatfields' for school. So many 'Greenflies' everywhere. Unnerving.

We paused to enjoy the glorious sunset. Politics and wars can't take those away from us.

Neville's diary

Valerie was away overnight at the hospital, due home at 3pm-ish.

I did some jobs round the house, which included a bit of cooking for the party. We found it easier to have birthday parties, or any other functions, on the Saturday nearest rather on the day if the occasion fell on a weekday. I didn't normally work on a Saturday thus there would be at least one of us, if not the both, to get things sorted out food wise and to organise any games we might be permitted to assist with.

The children these days seemed to have a liking for savoury things rather than filling up on sticky cakes and buns and other sweet stuff.

The menu would be: sausage rolls, sandwiches, empanadas[61], some winter salad, and I had kept a strip or two of beef ribs in the deep freezer. I would marinade some of these and wind up the oven and barbeque them on the oven bars, with a large meat pan underneath to catch the drips, basting frequently. They went down very well.

The girls set about tidying and cleaning the front room which was in a bit of a state, as they and some of their friends were using it as a classroom.

Valerie arrived home just as the guests were arriving. By the time she had climbed out of her uniform and had a breather, the children had settled in and were swapping yarns of experiences in occupied territory.

The record player was called into action and some shuffling and thumping which passed for dancing took place. Some of the old favourite games were played including the famous hunt the thimble (or slipper or whatever) then some card games and then the food. That's one way to keep children quiet.

We had decided that the party should end at 5.30pm so all could get home while it was still daylight. The old tradition of giving all guests a piece of birthday cake on departing was observed. Some of the children had been collected by their parents who also gave lifts to others. We walked a few of them home, Valerie and Rachel walked on up as far as Government House. Valerie hadn't been that far west since before the Argys arrived.

There was a beautiful sunset, which is so common in the Falklands. We thought of the old saying 'red sky at night, shepherd's delight'. Well, if the fine weather continued, we wouldn't be chased out of our houses to make way for the 'greenflies'.

We listened to the radio for a while and learned that the Task Force had blockaded South Georgia. Something must have happened there already, the Beeb wouldn't be allowed to give out information like that before an action, would they?

Rachel remembers ...

I loved my birthday party: it is a strong, lovely memory from those darkening days. It was all about being with friends, laughing, making a noise, being happy together, eating treats. Doing something totally normal. By then we had learned to cherish everything familiar and enjoy every second of it because we knew that everything could change at a moment's notice.

---

61. Empanadas are the South American answer to the pasty. Just smaller and spicier, usually deep fried.

Sunday, 25 April 1982

Valerie's diary
3pm–11pm.
Frequent rain squalls from s/w and much colder.
British helicopters engaged an Argentine submarine in South Georgia.
Sandbags have been put around the hospital emergency generator shed as protection from military action.
I slept in nurses' accommodation overnight.
There was a build up of Argy army vehicles along front road after 11pm.

Neville's diary
So much for the red sunset. South west wind, much colder than yesterday with rain and snow. We went over to see Father before lunch and had the usual natter. Much comment was made by him regarding the announcement from the Beeb that there was a blockade round South Georgia. Father had heard on the radio that the British had bombarded the island and a helicopter had engaged a submarine, the Sante Fe, and the whole lot had surrendered. A telegram had been sent to Mrs Thatcher asking her to tell Her Majesty that the boys were back on South Georgia Island. Phew.

I suppose there won't be lots of happy, smiling Argy faces round the town now. Best policy will be tunnel vision and not smile at anything, wonder if there will be reprisals.

Valerie went on duty at 3pm and would be staying there overnight.

Weekends are bloody awful now: we can't go for walks, there are notices at the back of the town, 'do not pass this point or the guard will open fire'. Can't go fishing, the guns have been taken away so we're not able to go out and get some geese, they are at their prime just now. The library is closed so we aren't able to change our books, and I've read all we have in the house. The children are fed up with playing Ludo, Monopoly, and other games, so am I.

It's only three days steaming from South Georgia. We'll see the Task Force sail into the harbour next week and it will be all over, and the Argies can go home before they get hurt.

Monday, 26 April 1982

Valerie's diary
7am–3pm.
I watched a quiet sunrise – my favourite part of the day.
Frost, light n/w wind.
There has been a build up of troop activity around town.

The peace talks have broken down.

I bought Rachel some birthday presents in Pink Shop. A t-shirt and a small, framed picture.

Neville's diary

There had been the noise of vehicles and troops moving in the night. I couldn't see much when I looked out, but they seemed to be moving in an orderly confused manner.

Let's get off to work and test the humour of the visitors. I shouted to the girls as I left not to go too far afield in case 'they' weren't too happy about the retake of South Georgia.

There didn't appear to be more anti feeling than usual in the dockyard, perhaps 'they' didn't have access to radios. There were enough aerials popping up around the place to set up a station, could these be the things used for jamming the 'Calling the Falklands' programme frequency?

I had Vladmar, one of the Polish seamen who had jumped ship in January while seeking asylum, working with me. Although we had a bit of a language problem we got along fine. I suppose there is a 'pijin English' dialect to suit all occasions.

With the approach of the Task Force being imminent, I decided it would be best if I checked the fire extinguishers in all Government properties. Well, as far as I could. Vladmar and I went up to the Secretariat and sought out Harold Rowlands, the Financial Secretary and now acting Governor. I told Harold what we were going to do. We checked those extinguishers in the Treasury, then went upstairs to the Chief Secretary's floor. All the gas & water extinguishers were full and there were a few spare charges too. I decided to discharge one of these outside to see what effect it might have on the guards. I pointed the nozzle away from me and hit the red button.

Oh boy!!

There was the 'shunk' sound of the gas leaving the cartridge then a 'crack' which really shouldn't have happened.

No water came out of the hose. The top half of the container lifted up as a split appeared at what would be water level. The gas and water blasted out all round, except for a couple of inches on the side where I was standing, good job too, at 600lbs per square inch pressure, my knees, or something, might have got damaged or damp. Vladmar gave me to understand that I should get the Argies to test the extinguishers!

I would have to dismantle the remains of that casing and see what had happened to cause the mishap.

Inside the water container is a siphon tube with a stainless-steel mesh strainer. The gas, when released, pushes the water down the casing and out through the hose and nozzle via this tube. There was a largish lump of crystals on the mesh blocking the tube preventing the escape of the pressurised water. There obviously had been electrolytic reaction between the different metals and the water. The way to test for this would be to blow into the tube, and if clear there would be a gurgle in the container. I would have to replace that extinguisher with one of the spares and test all the rest by blowing down the tube. Any blockages would necessitate the dismantling of the offending beasts and wire brush the bit of mesh smaller than a golf ball. Not a long job, but multiply that few minutes with the number of jobs wow, at a pound each would be ideal. We found two more in that building and soon had them in tip top condition. It must have been that the building was continually warm to hot with central heating permanently on which caused the problem as we didn't find this trouble in any other building.

Afternoon: I had a chat with Malcolm regarding the so called 'safe houses'. A lot of people had moved their sleeping abode to stone houses down in the town. I felt that it would be better if these houses were supplied with a selection of dry powder and gas water appliances on a loan basis for the duration. He thought it was a reasonable precaution, the dry powder ones were probably the better as we were now having difficulties with the drinking water supplies let alone water to fill extinguishers. He went on then to tell me that a couple of Argies had been looking for me, asking about refilling an extinguisher.

'Where did they come from'?

'Don't know.'

'I'll take a look at the Town Hall and ask there. I want to check the bits and pieces there anyway.'

There was a major standing at the door. I asked him if two men had come from there with a fire extinguisher for refilling.

'Don't know.'

'I will have a look inside at the fire appliances while I am here.'

I opened the door, out popped the barrel of a rifle and a terrible smell. A voice said 'Si?'

'I want to check fire appliances.'

'Que?'

'Mata fuegas.'

Slam went the door.

Back to the office. Two not very tall Argies came in sheepishly, looking round, and carrying a blue dry powder extinguisher.

'Please a new one,' said the one with sergeant stripes.

'You have had a fire, un incendido? No?'

'No. No accidente.'

'Ok.'

I gave them a full one and off they went, obviously relieved. I refilled the one they had brought in. There was a lot of powder in the bottle, which I had to empty out and the charge cap looked as if it had only been dented badly and not hit hard enough to get a full blast. I think there had been a bit of a skylark and the thing had got knocked over, hence the embarrassed expressions of the two lads. They came back several times during the occupation, always apologetically and with a smile.

Valerie said that the noise of troops and trucks in the night had awakened her in the hospital. She had looked out and there were hundreds of men assembled on the roadway outside the Secretariat, and being moved away in trucks; this had gone on for most of the night.

The girls decided to have an earlyish night; this gave us an opportunity to wrap up the parcels for Rachel for the morning. As we applied the wrapping paper and sticky tape, we reminisced over previous birthdays. This would be her first under enemy occupation.

Tuesday, 27 April 1982

Valerie's diary

3pm–11pm.

Fine spell continues but colder and a white frost. Light n/w wind.

Gave Rachel, our birthday girl, a Sonia Paul picture, a shirt and a Thermos lunch box kit.

Faith and Vi Felton are away to UK as are Owen McPhees.

The Argies have imprisoned several local people: the Haynes family were taken away at 4pm with a few others: Velma and George Malcolm, Gerald Cheek, Owen Summers, Stewart Wallace and family.

We are ordered to observe curfew and blackout from 6pm.

Crowds of folk are now looking for safe accommodation in the hospital.

Argentine civilian Dr Mario takes over as Senior Medical Officer.

Neville's diary

Happy Birthday Rachel.

Rachel was pleased with her presents. Valerie had bought her a framed print of a picture of a pair of wrens, the original was painted by Sonia Paul, a local artist of some talent. Also, a t-shirt with a penguin motif. I had got her a pair of unbreakable thermos bottles in a picnic case; this would come in handy when things got back to normal. And, of course, there were presents from Wizz and Grandad, some pencils, rubbers, notebooks, all things which are 'speshul' when you are young.

A good morning to do a bit more renovation on the Central Station. After breakfast, I got my Polish mate and armed with brushes and paint, sallied forth when the sun dried out the iron on the east side of the building. As we worked, we kept a weather eye on the sky as the Task Force could be only one day away. No vapour trails. A few bangs in the distance which would be 'them' trying out their various weapons. 'Their' radio detector vans were dashing about the town. With so many amateur radios and halo aerials about it must look like a town full of transmitters. It was.

The day had clouded over, so no more painting outside. I gave the sign board, which was taking up a lot of bench space in the office, another coat, cleaned the brushes and put them away.

George came into the office; he was the Colonel's driver and body-guard, and the office messenger.

'George what is that thing under your arm, and do you know what it is for?'

'Neville, it is an Uzi gun, I am a fully trained soldier and know all about this gun,' he said, waving it all around.

'Careful George, it might go off.'

'No, it is very safe.'

He was quite right, the magazine had electrician's tape over both ends.

'Neville, er, um, where are the keys for the security cabinet in your union office?'

I didn't think that was an official enquiry.

'Don't know George.' He obviously meant the keys to the safe.

'Vice Comodoro Bloomer-Reeves wants you at the secretariat with your list of firemen.'

'When?'

'Now immediately.'

Off I went. There was a lot of hustle and bustle of troops coming and going from the building. Armed men on the road, looking very serious and armed men on the corners too. Something on here I thought. Bloomer looked at the list.

'I hope this is enough,' he said.

'What do you mean? There are thirty-six of us which are all the available men.'

'You will find out. And by-the-way there is to be a curfew from 6pm and black out from darkness to daylight as from tonight.'

'That's a bit short notice,' I almost gasped.

'Yes, things are getting a little serious.'

I rushed off back to the office. On the way I saw Gerald Cheek in his front porch. I went in and told him about the blackout and curfew, then asked him if he was still ok for driving 212.

'I don't think so,' he replied. 'You see that marine there with the rifle and radio?'

'Yes.'

'He is going to take me on a picnic. Keep talking and see what he does.'

We nattered on for a few minutes, the marine got impatient. Gerald said farewell to his wife and two daughters, picked up his suitcase and went off with the bloke at gunpoint.

I wondered who else had been invited. That's what Bloomer meant then.

I saw Malcolm crossing the dockyard. I called him and he came up to me. I told him of the curfew and blackout, a few Anglo-Saxon words were uttered. I said about Gerald, he said 'bloody hell they're taking hostages now, who else is going?'

I went home to tell the girls about the blackout and asked them to find some thick blankets and any dark material we had. I nipped over to Father's to tell him of the blackout and curfew.

'Huh, they can't keep me in my own home like that, it's a free country.'

'You could get yourself shot if you don't heed the warning. I'm going down to the West Store to get some black poly bags, do you want some too?'

'Yes ok.'

There were a lot of heavily armed men outside the FIDF hall. I was stopped on the hill approaching the Store. An Argy with a rifle was stopping everyone. I said I wanted to get to the store.

'No, wait.'

After a few minutes he said ok, we could go. We did quite swiftly, I got the bags that I wanted and a crate of beer, just in case. I returned home via the front road so as to see a bit more of the picture. In the yard in front of the police station were just about all the youths of the town, lined up and looking quite serious. Major Dowling was much in evidence.

The girls had dug out what they could in the way of heavy material and blankets for the blackouts. To preserve the window frames, I put one fair sized nail in each corner; they would stay until I could find some cup hooks in the shed. That took care of the bedrooms, kitchen, front room, bathroom, back kitchen, pantry and the hall door leading into the front porch which was half glass. By the time I had finished it was quite dusky so I switched on the lights and went outside to check if we had any leaks of light. Although it wasn't full dark, I couldn't spot any beams of light, let's hope 'they' would give us a warning if we were transgressing. Valerie phoned from the hospital: 'did I know about the blackout?'

'Yes, I did.'

'And the curfew?'

'Yes, I did.'

'Had I told father?'

'Yes.'

'Had I heard about the hostages?'

'Gerald Cheek?'

'Well, there's Dr and Mrs Haines plus their children, Stuart Wallace, wife and two children, Brian Summers, Owen Summers, George and Velma Malcolm as well as Gerald. If hear of any more I'll tell you tomorrow.'

'Who is going to be SMO in place of Dr Haines? Alison?'

'No, they have flown in Dr Mario and another Argy civilian doctor. Mario has been here before and is familiar with the place. Alison is to do the R/T in the mornings. We have an armed guard to accompany anyone on house calls. See you tomorrow, cheers.'

The local announcements said that some members of the community had been taken to a place of safety for their own protection. They would be treated well and looked after properly. There was a great spiel about the blackout and curfew which was for our own protection and it was regrettable that circumstances had forced this situation to come about. We had to comply with the edict of Governor Menendez or else.

'Calling the Falklands' was scratchy, but the message came through, 'Keep your chins up, your heads down and hearts high' – how the hell can you do that, or is it a cryptic warning.

I felt quite weary after all that and it's 10.30pm.

Anyway off to the cart, had a read for half an hour as usual and put my light out. There was a knock on the window and a chuckle then the gate shut with a quiet click. Whoever it was missed out on a can of beer. It took a long time to drop off after that. I wonder who it was. I counted a few thousand sheep. I wonder who it was. Bennett, you have an overactive imagination. It was probably some local taking a risk.

The Task Force is pretty close though.

Rachel remembers ...

I was glad that we had my birthday party the week before my birthday because now parties had definitely been cancelled.

Curfew and blackout made us all feel trapped in our homes. My favourite purple blanket had been taken from the foot of my bed and nailed to the window frame. Day and night were now defined as times when we could and couldn't go outside our houses, when we could and couldn't look through our windows. I found it very hard to be locked in my house.

One day I said to mum, 'I just want to see the moon and stars again'. She just nodded her head and said, 'Soon'.

We all lived with the great hope that it would soon all be over.

Wednesday, 28 April 1982

Valerie's diary

7am–3pm.

Drizzle and fog from n/w. Miserable weather all day. Perfect day for 'Greenflies'.

The hospital is rather chaotic. Folks coming and going. Windows being taped with masking tape crosses and blackouts organized. Apparently, deadline for peace talks and shooting etc. starts 8am on Friday.

Neville's diary

The talk in the dockyard was naturally the hostage situation. Keep your nose clean would be the ideal thing now. If the Argies had any sympathy at all locally, they just blew it right away.

Plenty of new Argies ensconced in the dockyard now. Malcolm had been shunted out of his office and had taken space in the old garage just a few paces away. People were coming and going to and from the Central Store, trying to obtain sheets of plywood or hardboard for blackouts, or anything that might do. Some people were putting masking tape, criss-crossed, on their windows to give some form of protection against flying splinters of glass resulting from bomb blasts or shell bursts. The shooting was due to start Friday at 8am. Where did that bit of news come from?

George bounced into the office, he wanted to borrow a screwdriver, and to inform me that the Colonel wanted to see me in the office.

'What for George?'

'Don't know.'

Malcolm stopped me on the way and said that the Colonel had stated that the work force would work until one o'clock and then go home. There would be no loss of pay for the shorter hours, it is not the fault of the people that they must have a curfew and they have chores to do at home and as the days are getting shorter they must have the time to do these jobs before curfew.

I went into the Union Office.

'Good morning Colonel, you wish to see me?'

'Good morning Bennett, yes. Bloomer Reeve says that you want extra equipment from Moody Brook.'

'Yes, there should be spare foam making equipment up there, surplus to their needs, we need them down here for the town and to make up for those I have put on the jetty.'

'Okay, you can go up there and take what you want.'

'What? Just walk up there and walk in and help myself?'

'Well, you can drive in your fire machine.'

'I'm not going up there and poking around like that by myself.'

'Oh, you can have a guard with you. PAGANINI.'

In came Capitan Paganini, one of the Colonel's engineers. The old bloke had a natter with him in Spanish. I received a few dirty looks from the Capitan, he went back into the other office returning a few minutes later with tin hat, heavy jacket, side arms webbing and rifle.

'Ok, we go,' he said.

We walked up to the Central Station and got out the Fly. Paganini sat huddled in the corner of the passenger's side. I did offer him the option of driving while I held his gun, he declined, that was apparently not on.

'Drive steadily,' he ordered.

So, straight up the middle of the road. I pointed out some of the local spots, the Beaver hangar, Felton's stream, the slaughterhouse where sheep and cattle were butchered for mutton and beef. He wasn't impressed one little bit. I pointed to the sand bar where the channel narrows down before running into the stream at Moody Brook bridge. There was a good reason for all this talking, I felt I had to get him to speak.

'I have caught trout here. There is one fish which has broken my line, and the lines of several companions on a few occasions.'

He sat up. 'You have trouts here?'

'Yes.'

'In my home in Bariloche, close to the foothills of the Andes, we have excellent trouts and I like to fish very much.'

Good, now he was taking notice and seemed to have perked up, I should be able to get him to co-operate a bit.

There wasn't a guard on the gates to the camp. The very large, well painted, Royal Marine sign had been removed. At the west end of the

Belsen Block was a very long power cable pole resting on a stack of kerosene drums with a camo net draped over it all. From the air it would look like quite a heavy gun hidden behind the building. Hmmm.

The camp had been built as a naval radio station after the First World War. There had been, and still standing in parts, a wire mesh fence on preformed concrete posts with a barbed wire topping and a triple roll of barbed wire outside this. It did look like a prison camp. About the end of the Second World War some of the lads based there had gone into town on a pass and did whatever young sailors do. They were a little tardy in returning and the chief officer confined everyone to barracks. As a measure of their protest some of the non-offenders had climbed on to the roof and painted in large block letters the word BELSEN in white paint. They had been ordered to paint it over with the same black stuff as the roof. On a frosty morning it was still possible to read the offending word quite clearly. This building had been the generator shed, heavily built with big buttresses supporting the walls. The builders, Cubits, said at the time that it was bomb proof.

I parked the Fly by the red fire point shed in the middle of the camp. The Marines had used this area as a fuel and petrol depot. There were several large containers, which I recognised as having been there before the invasion, close to the main barracks and officers wing. I started to walk towards these.

'Not so fast,' said Paganini.

'You are the soldier, you open them,' I said, from what I thought a safe distance.

There were some familiar faces moving about. I recognised them as some more of the men I had seen on the FIC jetty when the Argie boats had been in before 2 April. Why were they at the Brook humping crates etc about if they were crew of the *Bahia Buen Successo* or the *Islas Del Estado*?

There wasn't anything in the containers, and I suppose any booby traps left behind by the Royal Marines had been dealt with too. A major came out of the galley door and had a natter with Paganini. He had a few looks at me and went back in. I managed a peek in the doorway, there were trays of oven ready chickens on the work surfaces which must have been for lunch. Somebody wasn't starving.

I fancied I had seen this officer before, then realised he had been the one outside the town hall when I was looking for the lads with the extinguisher.

The fire pump parked outside the Officers Block was of little use. I think it had suffered a heavy explosion. There wasn't anything we could use on it, all the accessories had shrapnel holes in them.

I supposed the best place to look was the fire point where I had parked the Fly in the first place. I went to push the door open, the Capitan shouted 'No!'

He called out in Spanish, then slowly opened the door which seemed obstructed by something. A head poked out through the gap and muttered something, then the door opened, and seven men came out. We went in and two more crawled out from under a table, quite a little rabbit warren this eight-foot square shed.

There were lockers round the wall which we had a look in and found four foam branches and siphon tubes. Paganini picked up a breathing set and two spare air bottles and took it out to the truck. I started to examine some foam extinguishers when he said to put the stuff on the truck and let's get out of here.

'Why the hurry?'

'Dowling has just arrived.' I gathered that man wasn't popular with his own side either.

He went up to the galley and was speaking to the Major. I had seen Gary Noote's blue fishing rod in the shed. Gary had been the Royal Marines Commanding Officer at the time of the invasion and we had met a few times fishing at the Murrel River. I wanted to get it, but Paganini was now in a hurry to get away. I started up the Fly, one of the Argies had seen me looking at the rod and passed it to me with a reel. I'd have to get that back to Gary somehow.

Paganini asked me to drive quietly out of the area; while passing the 'gun', I noticed that the fence had a lot of Argie drinks cans tied to it plus one solitary John Smith's best bitter can. I wonder how that got there as that beer hadn't been available locally before.

On the way down the road Paganini explained he wanted the breathing set to make a scuba outfit and could he keep it?

I said, 'Yeah, ok but don't tell the Colonel.'

I put the Fly away and stowed the foam stuff on the hose truck. They would more than likely be more beneficial to the town rather than on the jetty; if that caught fire there wouldn't be time to sneeze.

A quick walk down to the West Store was required before they shut for the day; they too were on short hours. The goods on the shelves were getting less also. I saw Phil Summers looking at some goods and said to him about the power line pole at Moody Brook dressed up as a gun, in a loudish confidential way. There was a stranger on the other side of the shelf we were looking at, he was a bit too clean and wrong complexioned to be an Argy. His ears twitched a bit when I mentioned the 'gun'.

At home I thought it best to have a snack for lunch and a cooked meal with Valerie in the evening. I did some adjustments to the blackout system and had a look around the garden. There wasn't any sign of intruders or vegetables having been removed.

I walked over to Father's to have a drink and a natter. Uncle Harold had been in to see him, they both muttered about the blackout and curfew but did admit that it was for our own good in the circumstances. Valerie came in on the way home and was persuaded to partake of an ale before we retired to our own little castle and pulled up the drawbridge. She said that there was a bit of confusion at the hospital. Dr Mario wasn't happy that he had been dragged away from his lucrative private practice in Buenos Aires without notice and landed in the Islands. As much as he had enjoyed his stay in the Islands some years previously, he didn't want to return to this situation. Valerie remembered him working here before for the simple fact of him wearing his stethoscope round his neck with the metal bit always in his shirt pocket so that his patients wouldn't get that shock of cold metal on flesh when he put the thing into use.

She said that people had been coming and going all day, blackouts improvised, windows taped for anti-shatter, medical and domestic supplies checked. Mario said it was up to the Argentine military to supply anything which ran short. To which I think the answer ran something like, 'Not if I can Pygmalion well help it.'

The off-duty roster would have to be altered to accommodate the curfew hours as staff wouldn't be able to trot round the town as normal. Some of the nurses took up residence in the quarters so as to be on hand. Chris and Les, two local lads, said they would act as Red Cross drivers and do any ferrying which may be necessary. There were two Argy soldiers living in the building who would act as escorts and guards at night.

Thursday, 29 April 1982

Valerie's diary
3pm–11pm.
Clear morning, flat calm, mild.
The political situation worsens, last minute talks going on.
Bronwen kindly worked for me to give me a break. So home I came.
The girls slept over at Grandad's to give him some company.

Neville's diary

I checked a few more extinguishers as far as I could and finished off a couple of other jobs really to keep occupied more than anything else. The Colonel came in all smiles and practised his limited pleasantries, which were getting a bit more extensive.

Where are the lads? A furtive look at the clear sky – no vapour trails. Quite an apprehensive atmosphere in the town, tension from all sides. The morning flag raising bugle chap at Government House tried to liven things up a bit by putting a touch of Tommy Dorsey or Glen Miller into his early morning Colours or whatever it was.

Valerie was due on duty at 3pm. I walked with her and we called in to see Father on the way to the hospital.

He mentioned again the loneliness at night now there was a curfew.

How many visitors did he normally get after dark? Still, when you can't have something that's when you miss it. This is the first time we have been told we don't have the freedom of our own home. But, 'they' assured us, it would be back to normal after the British had seen that Argentina was right.

We decided that the children could stay with Grandad for a couple of nights. If things did break loose and get violent, they would at least be able to raise the alarm if anything did happen to the old chap. His house was a few feet lower down the hill than ours, thus sheltered from the South, but wide open to the West.

Valerie continued on over to the hospital. She wasn't looking at all relaxed and happy any more. I went home and helped the children gather up their sleeping bags plus some other bits including their own special 'Penguin'. They had each been given a toy penguin at birth and despite several new flippers, beaks and some patches later were the same penguins. We had told the children to sleep on the floor, preferably between the two chimneys or under the stairs if any shooting or any big bangs happened. They would stay overnight for a while, coming home in the day for meals.

Rachel remembers ...

Me being forever helpful and compliant, on arrival at Grandad's I totally refused to sleep on the floor and threw my sleeping bag and pillow onto the sofa. I was, however, pleased to be spending time there. He was a lovely man with lots of interesting stories and a well-stocked bowl of sweets.

Neville's diary continues ...

So, back at the ranch I did my usual checks on the property, and then resigned myself to a night of solitude. I could get on with sorting out colour slides, planning the next session of decorating, read a few chapters of a book ... Oh, how bloody monotonous.

The Argentines had shipped in a selection of duty-free Television Sets and offered a hire purchase scheme on these. £10 down and £100 to pay in monthly instalments. They broadcast TV programmes from the Falkland Islands Broadcasting Station studio, but mostly in Spanish, and a good lot of cartoons. We didn't have one.

The door opened, good old brave me gasped and jumped to my feet.

Valerie came in, she was in tears. I had seen her in tears only once in our 15 years together. When she had caught her breath she said that Bronwyn had arrived in the hospital and said she thought Valerie needed a break and [she] would take over the duty and sent her home. She went through to the bedroom to change out of uniform. As the sun was down over the Yard Arm, I thought an anti-malarial draught of Gin & Tonic would be beneficial to both parties. It was nice to have her to myself. Gradually it emerged that she had been bottling things up and it had got all too much. The planning and alterations, the Doctors Haines being taken away as hostage and the uncertainty was just a bit too much for a country midwife.

Friday, 30 April 1982

Valerie's diary
7am–3pm.
Dull, overcast. Light south south east wind. Drizzle.
There is now an air and sea blockade around Falklands.
I had a walk around after 4pm ish with Rachel. We called in to see Mrs Binnie, Susan Binnie and then Mrs Johnson at The Rose.
Back in time to put up the blackouts and observe curfew at 6pm.

Neville's diary
Valerie went over to the hospital for her early shift feeling a lot calmer and happier than yesterday. The break had done a lot of good.

The girls had a key to the house with them at Grandad's, so would be able to let themselves in after I had gone to work. There were instructions left on a pad on the table as what to do about a meal, and a few chores to keep them amused. We would have to sort something out from the deep-freeze to take with them for the evening meal. I didn't think the old chap would have too much extra in the cupboard.

Friday again, did the rounds, all in order nothing had been removed and the motors started first try. Remarkable as some things had stood outside for a few weeks now.

Back in the office I started cleaning the stove parts which the plumbers had passed over to me. I wanted to have a clean assembly to take on the next call so I could replace it immediately rather than go through the time-consuming rigmarole of cleaning on site.

After work, Valerie and Rachel went for a walk round the town, calling in to see some friends before they, like everyone else, were shut up for the night with the curfew. On the way home a visit was paid to the Rose Hotel where Stan and Mrs Johnson were holding the fort since Velma and George had been taken away by the Argys, Mrs Johnson being Velma's Mum. The pub had of course closed like all other public houses, but as the hotel had a wholesale licence as well, Mrs Johnson would sell bottles of wine and spirits as well as cartons of beer.

Nearby stood a rather nice modern bungalow owned by the Government. It had been taken over by the 'Argy Marines' and their Alsatian dogs. Some of the dogs were black, others traditional colours for the breed, a mixture of smooth and some long haired. The handlers seemed a friendly lot and proud of their charges. They used to put on a show while exercising the dogs each afternoon on the playing field in front of our house. One of the parents along our road had complained about the dogs being exercised during the day and on the playing field as it was where the children could play freely. The handlers did wait then until after curfew before starting their games. The dogs then put on a good show, pretty good for a bunch of foreigners.

The girls went over to Father's, we watched them along the road from our gate; it was only 150 yards or so. We had our supper and listened to the BBC news, there was an air and sea blockade around us. The Task Force must be very close now.

On a clear night with the right wind direction you should be able to smell the funny mixture of odours peculiar to the Royal Navy ships: brasso and chips with a bit of stale cabbage and diesel thrown in.

Tomorrow's another day.

MAY 1982

Saturday, 1 May 1982

Valerie's diary
What a way to start the day! Stanley airport was bombed at 4.40am.
Steady rain showers from the s/e.
Malcolm Ashworth still delivers the milk!
Situation worsens. Sea bombardment of Argentine land bases.
Argentines move into the oldies end of the hospital with some of their
wounded.

Neville's diary
'BLOODY HELL!' I had lifted at least 6 inches off the bed, Valerie sat
straight bolt upright.
　'What was that?'
　We could hear the reverberations from a series of heavy explosions and
the distant rumble of large jet engines. I looked at the clock: it was
4.30am. Then came the rattle of anti-aircraft gunfire.
　I said to Valerie: 'I think the boys have passed by and dropped a calling
card.'
　She replied 'Oh goodee!'
　We looked at each other. How silly to have tears of joy in your eyes
when you are being bombed, but it was by our own side.
　I looked out from the front porch, but all I could see were tracer bullets
fading towards the north and anti-aircraft bursts down over the airport.
I went into the kitchen to make a pot of tea.
　Tuppence cat looked a wee bit on edge but calmed down when I
explained that it was ok as it was a British noise, and that there would be a
lot more of them soon.
　We waited for the phone to ring or for the fire alarm to sound, but the
explosions sounded a long way off so must have been at the airport.
Nothing to affect the town. Back to sleep for a couple of hours.
　We went over to see Father and the girls, who were excited about the
noise. Father said that the flag hadn't gone back up yet, by which he meant
the union flag at Government House.
　Malcolm Ashworth was delivering milk as usual and told us there had
been a raid on the airport by heavy bombers, and that there was talk of
Naval shelling some of the Argie bases too. The few Argies we saw looked
a bit startled. No wonder – we were right in the middle of it now.
　We returned to Father's after lunch to see if he had any further news
other than what we already knew. There was a roar of aircraft engines
overhead and a lot of anti-aircraft guns firing, plus a lot of loud cheering.

Dad was shaking me by the arm saying that's not quite the way to behave at the moment. I had run out into the garden and was shouting at the top of my voice: 'Come on Maggie's boys, give them shit.'

What a pity it was wasted effort: the Argies had scored an own goal. The first of a few.

Valerie went over to the hospital and found a bit of a problem. The Argies had shooed all the resident older patients, her 'oldies', out of the old wing of the hospital and put some of 'their' casualties from the airport into their beds. Obviously, these dear old folks had to be relocated in the main hospital wing as there was nowhere else to put them.

We listened to the BBC news in the evening. A Vulcan bomber had flown from Ascension Island and refuelled in the air to enable it to reach the Falklands and bomb the airport at Stanley. I remembered seeing Vulcans on the ground in Hertfordshire some years previously, enormous great triangular things. The payload must have been quite heavy.

Ain't it good to be British.

Rachel remembers . . .
Huge, enormous, ground-shaking, window-rattling, bombs . . . bombs . . . bombs. In the middle of the night – It was dark outside. Loads of anti-aircraft guns were going off. Grandad came into our room to see how we were. I was lying in my sleeping bag hugging it as close as I could. I was staring and scared. Breathing was the thing to concentrate on doing. Isobel and I went into the understairs cupboard and, terrified, sat holding each other and crying. Grandad stood in the doorway, leaning on his walking stick. With us, in our emergency bags, there was some Cadbury's Dairy milk chocolate. We decided that this was certainly an emergency and ate some of the chocolate.

Vehicles were rushing around outside.

The shooting eventually stopped. We dozed and waited for the day to start.

Sometime later in the day: I was at home when there was a huge outburst of anti-aircraft fire. The Argentines had lots of these guns, which sounded like heavy machine guns, pointed at the sky. When we heard this shooting, we all rushed outside to see what was going on. Safety concerns forgotten. Maybe the Vulcans again?

There was a roaring plane flying down the harbour from Moody Brook direction. It flew overhead and across town, so close that we could see the pilot. The anti-aircraft guns hit it. The Argy soldiers were firing their guns at it too. All the locals were standing out on the street and in our gardens cheering and shouting, we could see that it was an Argy plane. We watched as their burning Mirage flew over the back of the town and out of sight.

Sunday, 2 May 1982

Valerie's diary

Day off.

Flat calm first thing, foggy patches. Light n/w wind.

Some islands didn't check in on the R/T roundup – West Point and Saunders plus Port Howard settlement.

Hospital is crowded but the Etheridges and Nigel Summers have a little 'club' going upstairs which is a help.

Bombing at sea during night 2–3 May. General Belgrano damaged, a corvette sunk.

Neville's diary

Some of the outer islands didn't come up on the R/T round up. We wondered if they had visitors for lunch or were celebrating the events of yesterday in town.

It was Valerie's day off so we'd planned as large a Sunday lunch as we could muster from the freezer and a few tins, with fresh vegetables from the garden. Grandad came over with the girls and was persuaded to stay for a drink and a bite to eat, in lieu of a birthday celebration for Valerie tomorrow.

The hospital was crowded: the Argies were in the oldies' end, and the oldies had been moved into wards normally used for acute patients. Some members of staff had taken up residence in the unused rooms in the nurses' quarters above the old wing. This was more convenient for the work rota adjusted because of the curfew. A rather select little 'social club' for off duty staff and others had formed and this helped to reduce the tension and smooth any ruffled nerves.

Well, with the children safely over at Father's, supper over, radio programmes listened to, the only thing left to do was to pace up and down the passageway waiting for the next move.

The wind had risen to quite a strong blow. Wait a minute, there's something wrong, what is it? A bit more pacing. That's it, the corrugated iron fence at Malvina House paddock across the green, it's not squeaking and rattling as it does in the wind. Someone has put some nails in it.

Monday, 3 May 1982

Valerie's diary

Blew all last night from n/w.

No extra military activity in town.

I slept under a bed in Sturdee.[1]

Morning: low cloud base, driving rain from n/w.

Not one of my most exciting birthdays. Better luck next year![2]

Neville's diary

Happy Birthday Valerie.

Celebrations were a bit flat. We would normally have a few guests in for an evening meal and drinks. That would have to be sorted out later. There wouldn't be any cards from overseas, nor a phone call from her Mum. Everyone said that we would be back to normal soon. We gave her what presents we could and some pre-recorded music tapes. The children gave her some bits they thought were necessary.

And she was on night duty.

There were the usual glum faces round town. Malcolm asked me to have a look at the stove in Gilbert House, which was part of the dockyard complex and had always been the home of the superintendent of the Public Works Department – until recently. Now it had been taken over by some Argentine Navy blokes in the charge of Capitano Gafoglio. He had also been one of the camera-clicking, binocular-festooned tourists a few weeks before. His job then seemed to be supervising the berthing of the Argentine cargo ships which came at about three-monthly intervals. Back then, these ships would take about 3 hours to manoeuvre alongside the FIC jetty. After 2 April there seemed to be no problem, no matter what [the] state of the tide or direction of the wind – straight up the harbour and alongside without even having to heave in on a winch, and they were fully laden! Funny wasn't it . . . Anyway, Gafoglio paraded round the town (swaggered) wearing the uniform of an Intelligence Officer (Navy) and carrying an Uzi machine gun.

Also, in the house were a radio team and the crews of the two Coast Guard vessels: nice, white-enamelled, powerful-looking boats with a 20mm cannon mounted aft and a Metzler inflatable craft on chocks inboard. They were German built.

---

1. The hospital ward named after British Vice Admiral Sturdee of the 1914 Battle of the Falklands.

2. 12 months later she added: '1983 – Ha bloody Ha – on nights again.'

The stove was out and cold. I exchanged the burner for a clean one. Gafoglio said that there was water [leaking] leaking in the cupboard alongside the cooker. I had a look in to what was the airing cupboard housing, the hot water cylinder fed by the stove was leaking quite fast. He said that it was ok as they had turned off the water, but the problem was the stove had gone out.

I asked what the weight on the switch at the side of the stove was for.

He said, 'Every time we fire our gun, the stove switches off, so we put this weight on the lever to counteract the vibration.'

Oh boy, I said I couldn't relight the fire in that condition. Being a safety hazard, I took the weight off. I told him I would go and arrange for a replacement cylinder. I picked up my tools and set out to find Malcolm.

Ah, there he is up by the union office chatting to the Colonel. No, he is being spoken to by Colonel Dorrego. No, perhaps being shouted at seemed better. There was much waving of the hands and stamping of the feet by the Colonel. I thought oh dear, Malcolm is getting a dressing down for something. He waved me away, so I melted into the background and waited.

'What was that all about?'

'Well I have just been accused of sabotage, subversion and I can't translate what else he accused me of. I think he wanted to have me shot.'

'What for?' I asked, and Malcolm went on to explain.

'Inside this fence is the Dockyard and it is Army. We are in the dockyard and so we fall under Army. That house is outside the fence and so falls under Navy. The Army don't help the Navy unless they asked the Colonel first, but Gafoglio came straight to me so I did what we usually do. I told the Colonel it is a Falkland Island Government House, which didn't make things any easier, and that we would fix it for our own safety. I think he blew a gasket.'

I told Malcolm of the state of play in Gilbert House, [and] and he went to see Gafoglio who in turn immediately saw the Colonel and said 'Please Sir ...' etc.

Bob Stewart drew a new cylinder from the Central Store and was crossing the yard when there was a roar from Colonel Dorrego.

'Oh shit, he's at it again.'

After more explanations, he was at last convinced that we weren't usurping his authority and trying to wreck the Military operation.

Bob put in the new cylinder and lit the fire. We all said 'phew!'.

'Their' pride and inter-service relations and priorities had been restored, and ruffled feathers put back in place. After all, Menendez said that we should carry on as normal. If that hot water system had not been repaired two things could have happened: 'They' would have piled on all the open fires through the house to get hot water somehow, which would have caused a fire because of the falling embers which would have destroyed the house and surrounding buildings. Or 'they' would have evicted some families who had taken refuge in Malvina House which is a private hotel.

Capt. Gafoglio stayed in this hotel on his previous visits accompanied by his wife, who was not too welcome as she was known to overflow the bath.

Not much change on the home front, mutterings from Valerie about spending her birthday on night duty, and that [she] she would make up for it next year (I can't remember her arranging the off duty to suit herself even at Christmas).

The usual fidgety night at home. I had cleaned all my fishing gear in case we had another season on the Murrel river. 'They' had hinted that some places were not safe to go, we had learned that one of 'them' had walked backwards over the mines he was laying and lost both of his feet. The Royal Marines were blamed for that; strange, the Marines said they didn't have any mines with them.

Quarter to ten, what was that? Gunfire, and close too. I carefully went out to the front porch; there was shooting up and down the front road, our name for Ross Road. The gorse bushes at the Monument were alight and burning quite well. I gave the exchange a ring but no answer, as the line was dead. I had another look out, still shooting and shouting, and tried the phone again, still no go. With this direction of wind no harm would come of the fire as it was blowing out over the harbour and I certainly wasn't going to take out a bunch of blokes just for a gorse bush fire in that lot. Good Night.

Tuesday, 4 May 1982

Valerie's diary
Day off.
Dull, overcast and cold from n/e.
The shops were only open for 2 hours this morning.
Did a load of washing with the help of Mary's washing machine.
Colder evening.
Early this morning there was further bombing of Stanley airport.
People living in the West Store were turned out early and made to stand with their hands against wall for three-quarters of an hour.

HMS *Sheffield* hit by an Argentine missile. Fire couldn't be stopped. Ship abandoned. 30? members missing.

Neville's diary

On the way to work, the Argies looked upset. Yesterday their pride and joy the ship '[General] Belgrano' had been sunk by a British submarine.

They had been warned not to play in the restricted area. We had been repeatedly told by the Argentine forces not to go into restricted areas or we would be shot. Why didn't they take heed of their own preaching? They were warned that there was an exclusion zone round the Falklands, that's a lot of 'them' not going home.

There had been more bombs dropped on the airport in the early morning too.

Trouble at Cable Cottage. I went up there with a good selection of bits and pieces. The stove was filthy inside. They had lifted the hot plate off and turned it round so that the thin end was over the fire box, then they had grilled steaks on this and all the juices and fat had run down into the firebox and burner. Some brighter soul had switched it off before it did some damage like catching the overflow alight. This lot didn't look too cheerful either, not surprising what with the 'Belgrano' and the shooting match up and down the front road just 20 yards away last night, they probably had the 'breeze up'.

The Task Force mightn't have sailed up the harbour yet but certainly it has made its presence known. Someone in the dockyard had muttered that the shooting had been started by a couple of blokes from the SAS letting off a few rounds in each direction. If so, good on them. That's all it wanted and leave the rest to the imagination of nervous young conscripts who shot at each other.

I had just got the stove ticking over nicely when Malcolm came into the kitchen and said that Bloomer-Reeve wanted to see me in the Secretariat pretty sharpish. I said that the stove was functioning again and I would pop over as it was just next door.

Quite a lot of bustle in the building. The Argies were not smiling and all were carrying weapons. Officers and NCOs were wearing side arms and the other ranks had either machine pistols or rifles. Being a dull day, they were muffled up in thick padded jackets.

'Morning commodore.'

'Morning Bennett. Have you seen the Colonel today'?

'No.'

'Go and see him immediately and say you want six men.'

'What on earth for?'

'You have got to train them to use your fire engines. We watched the gorse fire last night. We tried to phone you, but the phones were out of order. Anyway, the wind was taking the flames out into the harbour so it was safe enough to let burn itself out. But, because of the shooting, we decided it would be dangerous for your men to go out after dark. So, you teach some of the colonel's men and they can go out after dark.'

The colonel's door in the Union office was standing open and he was looking at some papers.

'Ah Bennett my friend, come in.'

Blimey ...

'Morning Colonel.'

'My dear chap, have you seen Bloomer-Reeve this morning?'

'Yes, I have,' I replied. 'I am to have six of your men and teach them how to use the fire equipment.'

The Colonel explained, 'Certainly, after last night we have decided that it is a little dangerous for your men to go out in the night. We had a few bullets come close to our house and the phones were out of order.'

'Yes, I know, I tried to phone your house.'

'GEORGE!' the Colonel bellowed.

'Si Colonel?' George appeared.

'Get six men with a sergeant for Bennett to train and go yourself to interpret.'

'Yes sir.'

My, weren't we all polite this morning, and speaking English too. I wonder if it had been rehearsed.

Off George went at a good rate of knots, returning shortly with the required men. They didn't look too pleased and came up to the central station almost grudgingly. I pushed open the doors, there was a mumbled comment about no security and locks.

'Not necessary here,' I said, 'and also, there are several of us involved in the service so it would take a lot of keys and keys get lost. It is more convenient to leave the keys in the ignition and the main doors unlocked. It is quite safe really, no one is going to steal a fire engine and as all our homes rely on this service [there's] no need for locks and bars.' Feet shuffling and mumbles.

'Now, these are the fire appliances. The keys are always left in the ignition switches and are not to be removed. This one is a Land Rover base with pump and tank built on to it, andddd ...'

'Slowly please Neville, as I must translate some unfamiliar words,' said George.

Well about an hour and some good old spanglish later, I thought they had progressed quite well. Shame that Alfonso bloke had beetled off. The corporal spoke up and said they would go now as they hadn't had any sleep and they would be up all night again. They felt sure they knew how to function the machines.

Oh boy, oh boy.

Back down to the dockyard to put my stuff away. Had a natter with Malcolm and put him in the picture regarding the Fire Service and the colonel's instructions.

'Very nice of him,' was the comment.

Valerie had been down to the West Store as the shops had been allowed open for 2 hours this morning. Neil from next door was spending nights down in the West Store with a lot of other FIC employees. He said they had all been turned out in the early hours and stood with their hands against the wall. I wonder what that was all about.

The BBC news was quite startling. HMS *Sheffield* had been hit by an Argentine missile, [and] the burning ship had been abandoned. It was thought that thirty crew members were missing. Oh, dearie me, not nice.

Wednesday, 5 May 1982

Valerie's diary
3pm–11pm.
Fog on the deck. Light n/w wind.
Heavy rain squall 11.30pm-ish, then fog started to lift.
'Greenflies' digging in all over the town.
More proposals being discussed in the United Nations in New York. UK and Argentina have to hopefully reply.
Not quite as many people living in the hospital now.
Met the Governor Menendez and his two aides.

Neville's diary
Another not nice day for the 'tourists'.
Valerie did a load of washing in the hope that it will brighten up later.
I turned-to in the office.
We had been having a spot of bother with the priming of the pump on F55. In the spares cupboard were all sorts of pieces for the Flies (although all basically the same machines, a different year of assembly could mean a modification of parts). I resorted to the spares book and sorted through

the parts we had. There should be a paxolin-type pulley on the primer side of the pump, which wears. This could be the problem – it will still work, but it needs care in handling. If you know it, it's ok. As we had some temporary colleagues who could be called out at night, they might get into a fix and not know how to get themselves out of it without causing some damage. I found all the necessary bearings, but neither shaft nor pulley. I had a natter with Ron Buckett, head of [the] government's Plant and Transport Authority [PATA] in the next building to mine. He said he would have a word with Ted Carey, the supt. of the power station. Perhaps Ted and his blokes, who could usually work miracles with their lathe in the workshops, would be able to turn something up. They were using up quite a few miracles as it was, with the power station generating at full bore all day. They were continually doing overhauls of generators because of the extra load caused by many more people being in the town. I doubted they would have the time to help.

The midday news said that more proposals were being discussed at the United Nations in New York.

We went over to the hospital with Valerie and used the tumble drier in the laundry. There weren't so many people living in the 'bug house' now the initial shock and fear had passed, although an uneasy feeling still existed especially as gun posts and fox holes were appearing on the street corners round the town. On the junction of John Street and Barrack Street, a group had dug two holes and put an empty forty-gallon fuel drum in each with one end cut out. A mound of earth was thrown up round the edge as a gun rest, looked all efficient. In jumped an Argie conscript, as I have said before they were mostly young lads and not very tall, and the inevitable happened – his gun pointed straight up in the air; ok for shooting at low flying slow aircraft but not a lot of good for covering fire along the street.

I took the girls into Father's on the way home and had a short chat with him. Curfew was drawing near, then off for a solitary night. I listened to the radio for a while and looked out the window to see what might be seen in the dark.

Thursday, 6 May 1982

Valerie's diary
7am–3pm.
Cold. Light, dry, n/w wind.
Dr Mario is practically voiceless.

Loads of medication requests from the Camp.

Watched dog show on the playing green again 3pm–4pm.

Much helicopter and troop movement across the harbour on the Camber.

Neville's diary

Rudy Clarke dropped into the office and said that there are spare Firefly pulleys in the PATA garage stores. This is down towards the FIC jetty.

'That's in enemy territory,' I said.

Rudy confirmed. 'Yeah, we don't work there for the duration as that could be taken as helping their war effort.'

'I'll have a word with the colonel.'

'If you get the parts together, I'll put them in for you in the Central Station or a private garage.'

'Thanks Rudy.'

I had a talk with the colonel explaining the position.

'NO PROBLEM,' in his usual dulcet tones. 'We go now in my Land Rover.'

The colonel took the driver's seat and George got in the passenger's side with his ever-present Uzi. I sat in the back, with my hand on the door latch just in case a speedy exit was called for.

The men in the PATA workshop must have been of the colonel's section they were all salutes and offers of coffee.

'No thanks.'

My word! The garage was clean and tidy; perhaps they didn't have much work on. Well, all their trucks looked brand new and the people that had seen the speedo on some of them said they only had low mileage, maybe delivery miles.

It wouldn't be much use looking in the upstairs store as I had put all that stuff up there last year myself when I worked for the Central Store. I couldn't remember any pulleys. The fire engine stuff would have been special-order anyway. I went into the spares section behind the office, but it would be hopeless without the storekeeper's files, which were not available – for some reason. One of the mechanics came with me but as I couldn't explain what I wanted he wasn't much help. We returned to the dockyard with much shaking of heads and repeating: what a silly situation to be in because of some silly politicians.

Well, the weather had become warmer. What a pity.

Valerie came home at 3pm. We watched the Argies exercising their dogs on the children's playing green. I don't think there were any children around to want to play on the swings and roundabout. The dogs looked as if they were enjoying the show, they wouldn't do it if they didn't, and it gave the men a chance to show off as well as the dogs.

The children went back to Father's, but with Valerie at home it wouldn't be a lonely night. She said that General Menendez and two others had visited the injured soldiers in the old end of the hospital, that Dr Mario had been doing the radio duty and had almost lost his voice – he had taken loads of orders for medicines.

There was a lot of helicopter movements towards dusk, they were flying across the harbour and landing troops on the Camber who then deployed all along the ridge, must be training ... too much to expect anything else.

Ah well, put up the blackouts and so for another night at home ...

Rachel remembers ...
Late April/May 1982. We kids were playing on the big swings in the middle of the playing field. Some Argies had taken to parking their lorries on the road beside the playing field, St Mary's Walk. They were somewhat hidden from above by the few trees at the top of Malvina Hotel's garden. These Argies seemed to be living in their vehicles. Several times they'd tried to make conversation with us. Standing right by the fence they would call over. Argies only ever went into the playing field after our curfew.

We weren't friendly back to them. The most we did was to imitate and repeat their poorly pronounced questions.

'What iiz your namey?'

One was called Adolfo. Tall, blond, slim.

Adolfo had a black pistol on his belt. On the afternoon in question he was sitting in his truck holding his pistol and presumably cleaning it. A huge bang from the pistol. He leaped out of his truck and ran to check under the bonnet. His mates laughed. He managed to start the vehicle, nothing crucial had been perforated.

My mum came out of our house and called me in.

Friday, 7 May 1982

Valerie's diary
7am–3pm.
Flat calm 1st thing. Sunshine. Flung open the windows in Cradock[3] etc. All of the Argentine casualties in the old end of the hospital have been taken away.
Onions, fruit and provisions were left behind for use by the hospital.

---

3. Ward named after Rear Admiral Cradock of the Battle of the Falklands 1914.

1982 Friday 3-11 'Disturbed night, 1st shots heard 5am ish, the invasion is on, Argentine warships in Port William, planes on the strip, troops around G.H & Stanley. Dull, overcast & quiet from S/W few spots g rain. Very confused in K.E.M, @ least personnel. Arges & guns in K.E.M, disconcerting'

Valerie's diary, 2 April 1982. Valerie's diary is beautifully handwritten and often in note form, reflecting her medical note-taking style. In the editing of her diaries I have expanded some of her notes to help the reader.

An Argentine soldier with Valerie in the background, photographed on Fitzroy Road. Valerie is getting out of the small white vehicle bearing red crosses. Photograph used with kind permission from Derek Pettersson.

Isobel and Rachel, January 1982. Photograph taken by Valerie Bennett.

Valerie with an 8lb trout she had caught in more peaceful times. Photograph taken by Neville.

Valerie with an elephant seal. Photograph taken by Neville during their honeymoon at Volunteer Point.

Bombero armband. As mentioned in Neville's diary, these armbands were made by Isobel and Rachel and worn by the fire brigade while attending incidents during the war. Photograph taken by Jill Harris.

Rachel's bombardment pillowcase. Rachel used this pillowcase throughout the war, sleeping on her mattress on the floor. When the noise of the shelling became too loud, she would put the pillow over her ears. When she was upset or afraid, she would hug her pillow.

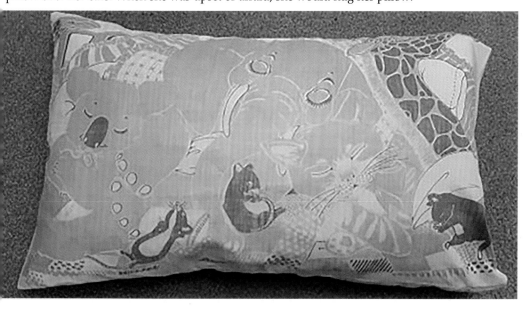

Landing craft from our window. These photographs, mentioned in the diary, were taken by Valerie on 2 April.

The view from the other side of the playing field. Drury Street, including our house, fourth from the left, photographed from an Argentine landing craft on 2 April 1982. These are the same vehicles that Valerie photographed from our window. The editor has been unable to trace the name of the photographer.

Firefly 399 with Corporal Roberto Daniel Curia. This is the airport Firefly that was commandeered by the Argentines. Photographer unknown.

Firefly 212 today. She is no longer in active service but still getting around. Photo used with permission from her current owner, Ralph Harris.

Neville beside Firefly F55, pictured in the doorway of the central fire station. The photographer is not known.

Firefly F55 today. The star of the show! She is currently being renovated. Photograph used with kind permission from her current owner, Nick Pitaluga.

The Argentine flag being raised at Government House. The photographer is not known but several Argentine photographers captured this event.

An Argentine Hercules aircraft at Stanley airport, 7 March 1982. The war diaries begin with the fire brigade attending this landing. Photograph used with permission from Derek Petterson.

An Argentine Pucara aircraft flying down Stanley harbour on 25 May. Photograph used with permission from Tony Chater.

The Argentines distributed anti-British propaganda amongst their troops. This cartoon was picked up by Neville in Stanley.

Fireman first-day cover, received by Neville during the war. The envelope had been altered in transit by the Argentines.

Argentines cooking in the dockyard in 40-gallon fuel drums. This is mentioned several times in Neville's diary. The photographer is not known.

No. 4 Racecourse Road, damaged by a British shell. Weeks earlier, Neville had worked in this property, which is mentioned in his diaries.

The police station after being hit by a British missile. Photographs used with permission from Derek Pettersson.

Argentine weapons abandoned in Stanley. Photograph used with permission from Derek Pettersson.

Argentine graves, with locally made crosses, dug in Stanley cemetery during the war. Photograph used with permission from Derek Pettersson.

Liberation day! We stood and watched as these men, including Major General Jeremy Moore, walked past us and went to meet the Argentines ahead of the signing of the surrender documents. Note the red fire hose on the street heading towards the incident at the power station. Note also the red fire ladder hidden out of sight in the hospital grounds. Photograph used with permission from Rachel Aspögård.

Isobel, Neville and Rachel, 2019.

All four Bennetts had a walk around town. Ended up at the Buckett's for a couple of drinks.

Neville's diary
Valerie was on duty until 3pm. It was one of those days we get in the winter in the Falklands. Flat calm and a bit warmish. The harbour was unruffled and the sun was shining.

Did the usual Friday rounds of the equipment and found all to be in good order despite the changes in weather etc for those bits stored outside. They had been out in the elements for a few weeks now. Nothing happened at work worth a mention, everyone was keeping a low profile, even the Argies.

I saw Rudy and said we had difficulty in finding the parts, he said not to worry he had done the job already.

When Valerie came home, we set out on our usual walk of the boundaries (at least that's what it seemed like). Up Ross Road West this time, see how far we can get. We called in to visit the Bucketts and had a couple of convivial pre-weekend drinks, then returned waiting the start of another unfun, unexciting weekend.

The Argentines had taken away all of their casualties from the hospital. They had graciously left some provisions. Onions, pasta, tinned tomatoes and peppers. Valerie said she had gone round and flung open all the windows for fresh air (a habit of hers even at home), wounded people have an aroma of their own especially if they have a water shortage. Oh well.

Saturday, 8 May 1982

Valerie's diary
3pm–11pm.
Dull, damp, overcast from n/w. Light wind.
More attacks on Argentine military installations during the night. I dived down to x-ray hurriedly, decided it's the strongest room in the hospital.

Neville's diary
Did the usual rounds of garden, water butts, fences and gates. Nothing disturbed, it was good for morale any way. The girls came back home from Father's. No immediate attack had materialised. As the Argies had taken over the night calls for fires, we could be all under one roof again, without the fear of them being left alone in case of a call out. The dear old chap was sorry to see them go; they said that if there were any explosions or gunfire in the night, he would lead them in a prayer and then sing a hymn with them. His Christian faith was very strong.

The weather cleared after lunch. Valerie was to go on duty and earn the crust for the family at 3pm.

I had a call from Pat McPhee – would I bring an appliance up to Davis Street, as there were some fires opposite his house. Apparently some Argy troops had been moved up from the airport and camped in the paddock along the north side of Davis Street. As usual they had made fires to cook their meal and burned anything they could: fence battens, bits of a shed, gates and whatever else. The ground being peat, there was a danger of the fires burning in and spreading underground; there had been many incidents of such in the past. With the liberal use of a spade and some water we put it all out. There, that was that bit of excitement sorted. If we hadn't had to shift the Firefly from the German Camp, Pat would have managed this on his own. I returned the truck to the station after topping up the water and fuel, called in to see Father and then home for a quiet night.

Oh Boy! some bangs and bumps, the British were making sure that Saturday night was a bit lively after all.

Sunday, 9 May 1982

Valerie's diary
7am–3pm.
Cold and wet from n/e. Ever so nasty!
Dull and overcast later.
Walked around town with Neville and girls and Katrina Clarke.

Neville's diary
Same old thing, nothing to do, just wait.
When Valerie came home and had changed, we took our usual stroll round our part of the town. Same faces on guard at the vital points. Katrina and our two just carried on gassing as normal. With all this walking and worrying I had had to pull my belt in another notch.

Nothing new on the Beeb. The usual good wishes at the end of the programme, and 'keep your heads down and hearts high'.

Don't worry, we are, and having a good look around too.

More bangs and bumps in the night.

Monday, 10 May 1982

Valerie's diary
3pm–11pm.
Fog on deck. Heavy rain from n/e.
Few bangs around.

Peace talks going on between the warring nations. Argentines contradictory in statements.

Quiet evening bump-wise. Apparently, the girls counted 49 bumps.[4]

Some vessel or other was fired on in the sound.[5]

Very dark outside.

Neville's diary

For a start there's fog on the deck, what wind there is, is from the nor 'east and someone is making some heavy explosions.

Tom asked me to have a look at the cooker in 4 Racecourse Road. This property had stood vacant for a while as the tenant had gone to England with the exodus. The stove was very dirty and the fuel tank empty. I asked Tom to tell the new occupants to get some fuel in, then I could do something about servicing it.

On the way back to the dockyard, we could see smoke rising from the gorse hedge running along the drive from Government House to the east. George stopped us and said to me to get the fire machine and put it out. I ran to the station collecting Paganini on the way.

'No, no,' he said. 'Bonugli [the Sergeant] has the machine and cannot get it operating.'

By this time we were half way up Barrack Street. There, parked at the side of the road, was a UniMog [Mercedes 4 × 4 lorry] with a canvas back. The driver was asleep in the front. I said to Paganini wake him up and get him to drive us to Government House.

'No,' he said.

'Go on man, he is only a Corporal and you are a Capitan.'

Paganini jumped on the running board. George stood back and I jumped over the tail gate – 'SHIT!' I had landed in a box of mortar bombs.

The truck was a heavy mobile mortar unit. I had seen it parked round the town with the launcher on a trailer, now it was hidden in the back of the truck pointing at me.

We got to Government House. Bonugli, with the aid of his compatriots, had mastered the Firefly and dealt with the fire caused by some poor unfortunate trying to heat his lunch or whatever. I went back to the colonel's office as Bonugli thought he might be in a bit of bother as he hadn't waved the magic wand and put out the fire instantly.

---

4. HMS *Glasgow* bombarding Moody Brook.
5. *Isla de los Estados* was sunk by HMS *Alacrity*.

Colonel Dorrego was a little distraught. Punishment cells were not too far away from his thoughts. I explained to him that due to language difficulties his lads hadn't grasped the ins and outs of the machine immediately.

'Take the big pump and make them practise; put out that fire at the monument.' He said this had burned into the peaty soil and [there was] a potential danger of causing a landslip if not attended to.

I got the visiting team of Argies together and hitched the Godiva pump on to the tow hook at the back of the Firefly. I told Bonugli to drive and set off for the Monument. They complained of being a bit damp and didn't want to get wet through as they didn't have any means of drying off their uniforms. I suppose that dug outs on the sea front are not necessarily equipped with a tumble drier. Halfway along the Front Road, at the triangle paddock by Government House, a fresh outbreak of fire appeared in the gorse hedge. We stopped and backed up the truck to the sea wall. I showed the boys where the waterproofs were kept, they looked a bit happier. The suction [hose] was thrown into the harbour, I showed them how to raise the vacuum and get suction and applied pressure to the hose. This was good fun! The dear little chap soaked the fire all right, then he turned around, still holding the hose, to ask how was he doing, and everyone got soaked for a few yards round him! Surprise, surprise, they all laughed, and no one waved a gun. We loosely packed up the equipment and proceeded to the Monument, some 500 yards to the west. There we redeployed the pump etc. Some suspicious characters were working at something in the water under the sea wall. They were hammering stakes into the sea wall and stringing telephone wires from them. Must have been 'their' signal corps. One young lad had quite an amount of clams and limpets off the rocks; these can be a delicacy if they are not taken from near a source of sewage. These lads were working very close to the Government House outfall.

I laid out two hoses and the chaps really soaked the ground, but a lot of soil was washing away from the root system. I called a halt to the exercise at that point and moved the action to the west side of the monument. There seemed to be some sort of opposition from a group of soldiers on the bank behind the gorse. I think they were afraid of getting damp. So I asked them to help by digging a small trench around the gorse as it was still smouldering at that point, the result being a solid stony silent refusal. I tried again slowly once more.

'No,' definite that time.

At that moment, a vehicle tooted on the road, and there was Bloomer in his runabout.

'What's the trouble?'

I explained what I wanted was a trench dug round the gorse to stop the spread of fire into the made up land, and I thought that as these were soldiers with entrenching tools they would be able to do the job quite rapidly.

'Exactly.' I didn't realise what a powerful voice Bloomer had until then.

'Who is in charge?' or words to that effect in Spanish.

'Me Sir.' Up ran the bloke I had spoken to.

'Tell your men to dig as the Fireman says.'

'Who are you sir?' The reply came in very controlled measured tones.

'Vice Commodore Bloomer-Reeve, Fuerza Area Argentina.'

'Yes sir!'

A ditch was dug in 5 minutes flat. We packed up and departed while our luck held as the visitors in green didn't look too happy with us. Probably they mistook Bonugli and his gang for locals as they had our waterproofs on and were wearing safety hats.

I was glad to get home and into a dry set of clothes. No stirring news on the radio.

A quiet evening at home apart from the fact the girls counted forty-nine explosions. Someone getting softened up no doubt.

Tuesday, 11 May 1982

Valerie's diary

7am–3pm.

Fog on the deck again. Wind from n/e swinging to n/w and gale force with rain during morning.

Delivered Jackie Davies' baby girl.

Quiet evening. What happened to the rum bottle?

Neville's diary

I went up to No. 4 Racecourse Road, they had got some fuel. I cleaned the stove, the smoke box was full of cobwebby soot as was the top of the oven, the burner parts were grotty too. That was a disaster waiting to happen. I had to renew the filters in the line and eventually got the oil flowing and got it lit.

I walked back to the dockyard and cleaned up. George popped in, he is either keeping an eye on me or dodging the colonel. I would have to go back to No. 4 tomorrow to check on the stove.

Home for lunch, then over to see Father and a chat. We are still waiting, something has got to happen soon, all these bumps and bangs in the night are wearing on the nerves.

There are a lot of ruffy tuffy blokes around, carrying assorted weapons and large knives, they tread very carefully as they walk. They are the ones based in the gymnasium. There are a lot of dugout positions in the dockyard. A lot more, with anti-aircraft guns, are ensconced on the slope on the north side of the town hall. Goodness knows what is out beyond the town limits. There were reports of heaps of bodies along the Darwin Road a few weeks ago.

The troops in the town are trigger happy. A youngster had let loose with a heavy-calibre machine gun and sprayed a house opposite the Senior School. No one was hurt, only because the person in the room which was hit badly had just put out his light and laid down.

The houses which were deemed safe due to their strong construction have had some initials in a wreath painted on them. It was the Argentine Civil Defence initials DAP; this puzzled the Argies [as] they didn't know what it meant although authorised by their officialdom. The locals knew exactly what it meant: Damned Argy Pigs.

Valerie was very chirpy; she had delivered a baby. A daughter for Jackie and Taff Davis. Taff had been with NP 8901[6] a couple of years previously and had returned to marry Jackie before all this trouble had started and had a job locally. He had not been able to resist the call to arms on the night of the first of April, being a member of the FIDF.

An Argy Marine was heard to say that he had lived in Portsmouth and had seen the Royal Marines fighting on a Saturday night without weapons, he didn't want to be around when they had guns and ammunition.

There was talk of a ship being sunk in the Falkland sound. The Argies said it was carrying supplies for the locals on the West Falklands. I don't know how much avgas, kerosene and ammunition the people on the West Falklands use, but it was said to be a spectacular discharge of cargo.

What a miserable night weather-wise, we had to resort to an old Falklands remedy: Hot Toddies – consisting of Rum (Dark Navy), hot water, sugar and a smidgeon of butter, as much as you can get on the tip of a hot teaspoon. Administered in sips from a stout glass.

---

6. Naval Party 8901 was the Royal Marines based at Moody Brook, to the west of Stanley.

Wednesday, 12 May 1982

Valerie's diary

Day off.

Fresh, drying wind from west. Almost gale force. Blue patches of sky.

There is a lot of digging going on in Malvina Paddock. Anti-aircraft guns, or something?

Heard a thump far away at 11pm-ish.

Me and the girls do a lot of stores shopping. Misty the visiting cat likes sardines in tomato sauce.

Girls and I watched two Argentine planes shot down about lunch time.

Sunny spells in afternoon – usual walk around town.

Pope starts a visit to Portugal.

Neville's diary

Valerie has a day off, well, she's not at the hospital.

I checked the stove at 4 Racecourse Road, seemed to be going ok. The new occupants were in residence, there was a couple of young lads watching television being broadcast from our FIBS;[7] 'they' had even blocked out the sign over the entrance which says Falkland Islands Broadcasting Station and put up an enormous rosette in blue, white and blue.[8] It looked like a prize rosette from the sports or something. I wonder why there are a couple of military police helmets on the sideboard here as I had also seen down at Cable Cottage. Could be a dodge? Not everyone will stop an MP[9] and ask what's he doing. Perhaps they were being used as messenger boys in emergencies.

After declining yet another cup of coffee, I went up to Ross Road West No. 28. Requested by the Colonel via Malcolm. Good exercise all this walking around. I pounded on the door, which was soon opened by an officer who knew exactly what I wanted. Strange, I was dressed in an oily greasy boiler suit and carrying a tool bag not really much of an ID.

It was a familiar scene in the kitchen: a filthy stove with grease all over it as if there had been a good old barbeque. One little variation, there was water in the burner rings and in the fire box as if the grease had run down inside and someone had poured the kettle over it all. I checked the filters and fuel level in the tank outside, they were in good order and had plenty of fuel. A bunch of blokes were digging in at the rear of the property and

---

7. The Falkland Islands Broadcasting Station, which had previously only broadcast radio.
8. The colours of the Argentine flag.
9. Military Policeman.

in the garden. I cleaned the stove and swapped in a new set of wicks. [At] £2–£3 a set who was paying for them?

When I had finished, the officer offered to share his *maté-yerba* with me. This is a type of herb tea made in a gourd and drunk through a silver straw with a spoon ended filter. This, to the South Americans, is a special social drink, one *maté* is prepared then passed from one to another. I am not partial to the drink at the best of times and was able to refuse.

There was some anti-aircraft gunfire in the late morning, someone must have been having a peep at us from a great height. I wonder if it might help if we were to leave out items of clothing or sheets on the washing line – just to let them know we were still there, if they were doing any snapshots as they passed. Pity we didn't have a few red, white and blue sheets.

Valerie had been out grocery shopping with the girls and had managed to gather in quite a booster for the larder. We were having to think a bit on how to feed all the cats now that fresh meat was not as available as usual. The kitten 'Misty' had decided she too liked sardines in tomato sauce.

We took our constitutional walk around our area of town to let the guards see we hadn't been spirited away in the night. A very pleasant sunny afternoon, reasonable for summer let alone nearly mid-winter.

The BBC reported that all the prisoners captured on South Georgia had been taken up to Uruguay.

Thursday, 13 May 1982

Valerie's diary
Day off.
Fog on the deck, light n/w wind, drizzle.
Fire in the bushes of Stanley House.
Rachel did our laundry in the washing machines at the hospital.
Called in to see the Fowlers during our afternoon walk.
Neville worked on No. 4 Racecourse Road stove.

Neville's diary
Nor'west wind, foggy and drizzly.
Valerie is on another day off, her weekend. We really must get together on this and both have a weekend off at the same time. Park the children with someone and nip off to a hotel and relax for a couple of days by the pool etc. Oh, do wake up, you're in the middle of a war situation and have as much chance of nipping off to a hotel as a celluloid cat has of surviving the furnaces of hell!

Oh! Who is this friendly smiling chap coming through my office door? Why! It's good old Malcolm. I wonder what dastardly deed he wants committed now?!

'Well old son ...'

'Yeees ...'

'You know that the Colonel, (both stand to attention), has had a shower constructed in the block shed to convert cold salt water from the harbour into boiling hot salt water for the troops to shower in?'

'Yes.'

'Well, there's to be an extension built round the outside of the west wall and the north end of the block shed. It will be for the storage of ladders and scaffolding later on, but the colonel calls it his shelter for the lads.'

'Great. I like the bit about the ladder shed ... NO I DON'T, I THINK IT STINKS.' (The penny had dropped!) 'Good morning, the door is behind you.'

'Don't be like that Nev. You have the honour of drawing up the plans for it and estimating the materials needed. It's just a lean-to construction, and then you have the privilege of building it. Remember it's for us, oh, and there will be lots of "their"' troops around, you might hear all sorts of interesting things.'

'Blimey.'

Dental technician, fire chief, drain cleaner, stove servicer, and now architect and construction engineer and linguist, a lot of strings to the bow now.

I pointed out to Malcolm: 'There isn't enough timber in the dockyard for a project like that.'

'The Colonel is arranging all that, get your tape and a notebook, I'll give you someone to help.'

So, a quick measure up: it'll have to be ten feet out from the wall to the west. Six feet out on the north wall which will give the double doors of the block shed room to swing. This part of the block shed was made from the old timber shed. It had a good floor for laying out the freshly made concrete dry mix blocks used for building. I would have to follow the pitch of the roof and have an exterior roof of 6 feet. Roof rafters and all framing 3×4 inch, purlins and noggins 2×3 inch, two doors, cladding of agrilux and corrugated iron probably mixed to give light. I'll get Malcolm to have someone make a few 12-inch spikes to drive through holes in the wall plates to firm up the framing.

I worked all this out in the office and was about to start drawing the plans when Valerie rushed in all out of breath. 'There's a fire at Stanley

House. Mrs Miller [the neighbour] cannot get any one on the phone. The fire is in some bushes at the rear of the building.'

'Ok, sit down and get your breath back, I'll go off.'

I ran up to the hospital and got the Firefly from there, collecting Neil McKay on the way. I saw Bonugli in F55 already on the move.

The rear entrance to Stanley House is via an alleyway or drive off John Street. I turned into this and found that the other Firefly was ready to pump. What a collection of stuff in the gardens: generators, tents, radio masts, an awful lot of armed men. One bloke in particular was tiptoeing around, he had three grenade containers on his back. Looks as if this is the Big Command HQ.

There was no need to panic, it was just a fire in some dead brushwood lodged in a small tree. Some 'greenfly' living in a trench under the tree had lit a rather lively fire to warm his food and up she went.

Bonugli had a whale of a time, ably assisted by Neil, chopping down the offending bush and soaking everything in sight. He had filled the dug out as well; he must have had a nice vicious streak. Everyone was all smiles.

Mr and Mrs Miller nodding encouragement over the fence. One officer was standing chatting to them with a mug of tea in his hand. He remarked to me what a nice day for a spot of fishing. Now, where had I seen him before?

We left the scene, filled the tanks on the appliances and put them away.

I called in to the colonel's office to have a moan about the phone service.

He got his word in first. 'Hello, where are those lovely ladies who used to operate the telephone service? Our men do not understand the system.'

What could I say?

'I will have to organise something,' he said.

Back to the drawing board.

The weather had cleared. I went back to the office after lunch to collect my tools as there had been a call from No. 4 Racecourse Road about their stove. I changed all the filters and cleaned all the parts of the beast and relit it. They had had a top up of fuel and the tank probably had an accumulation of sludge in the bottom. I opened the drain cock and right enough there was quite a lot of water and muck. One of the young lads was digging in the garden, making an air raid shelter. I had the company of Lieutenant Vinelli (Navy) who was 'their' legal bod. I told him about the sludge, he seemed to understand. He spoke of many things, just nattering on. There were the usual thumps and bumps in the hills. He told me that there were 15,000 men in the islands now; I said I hoped they all got home safely. He said that he had visited Moody Brook camp and was surprised to see many original oil paintings on the walls. He went on to say that his armed forces would not be so appreciative as that of art. I asked him if he was familiar with the GCE system in education. Yes, he knew of this. I said that to gain entry to be a Royal Marine it was necessary to have at least four passes at A level. (Is it wrong to slightly stretch the truth to the enemy?)

'Unfortunately, our men are not like that.'

The stove was going well, as it was close to curfew time I went home.

Valerie had taken the girls up as far as John and Veronica Fowler's for a visit and perhaps a post-natal check on the new mum and son.

There must be an awful lot of men dug in in the dockyard that sleep all day and come out at night. When I went to put my stuff in the office there were a lot of faces that I hadn't seen before.

Talks still going on at the UN. The Tory members of Parliament were concerned that Mrs Thatcher might be giving too much away.

There seemed to be a lot of digging happening in Malvina House paddock too. A small mechanical digger was being employed, perhaps they are going to put an AA gun there. That'll rattle our windows.

Friday, 14 May 1982

Valerie's diary
3pm–11pm.
Plenty of rain last night. Morning, strong gale force winds from west–s/w, cold.
Pam Summers cut my and Rachel's hair.

Neville's diary
Plenty of rain in the night with strong to gale-force winds, quite blowy in the morning and cold too.

I did the usual Friday checks as far as I could. The enemy seem to be getting more grip on the town, so I could only check the appliances at the hospital and central station. I had a quick nip up the road to No. 4 Racecourse Road, usual complaint of not enough hot water, oven not cooking. I altered the deflector plate with a pair of pliers to give more flame up the boiler and over the oven. Why don't these supposed superior people realise that these stoves are meant for a family of four or five and not a bloody battalion? Even in their massive blocks of flats, with boilers bigger than a steam ship's, the water runs cool at times.

The two lads were out in the garden chopping an empty forty-gallon drum in half with a stick chopper, must be a barbecue pit in the making.

The plans and material estimate had been submitted to the colonel and met with his approval.

Malcolm asked me to go with Davey Phillips and sort out the boiler in the gymnasium. That's where the big knife-carrying, multi-weaponed professional troops were billeted. We dug out half a cement drum's worth of soot from the furnace – all under the supervision of an officer. I think he didn't want us to make off with one of his super shiny new cross country motor bikes. The crack ruffy-tuffy troops were very cold and miserable. I think one actually had tears in his eyes; poor blokes, there hadn't been any heating for a couple of days and it's a right barn of a place. What would they feel like if they got into the mountains?

Their rations came from the cook in the dockyard. He did a terrific job. All he had to cook in was half a 40-gallon drum on a wood fire. For the duration of the occupation, rain, snow or blow, he had a hot meal each day for the men in that area. It mostly consisted of water with chopped cabbage, carrots, potatoes, some onions, a handful of herbs, an occasional sheep's head. Once he had a forequarter of mutton. The bulk was made up with a couple of kilos of beef dripping, sometimes he had pasta to add to the pot as well. It smelled good ... but?

One unsuspecting member of our work force, having his breakfast outside, put down his sandwich beside him – only to find it stolen along with the piece of buttery greaseproof paper the sandwich was wrapped in. I think they were a mite peckish, anything that resembled food was not safe. Keep everything in your pockets and a hand in on top of it; we developed a hand-in-pocket slouch.

Malcolm would have to get the plumbers to sort out the burner side of the furnace, it was beyond me and looked as if it had had a bit of tender loving care from a willing bayonet or something. The plumbers seemed to be up to their eyes keeping the filtration plant functioning. They were working day and night, perhaps they were taking shifts at the plant. There hadn't been a lot of rain so the stream must be low, the chemical balance would be critical.

We were nabbed by Malcolm on arriving back at the office. He told us the good news. The colonel had obtained a pass for us to go with a gang in a truck to the FIC sheds and get some timber for the building. He had also delegated the Sub Lieutenant in charge of the shower unit to go with us as shotgun guard. He had only a 9mm pistol and a nervous smile. When we arrived at the Works Store building at the FIC, there was a pole barricade across the road, also there was an armed guard with gun ready to repel boarders. The Sub Lieutenant jumped off the truck and amid much fist waving and holster tapping ran off into the main warehouse. He returned with a document. We drove round the corner to the timber shed and grabbed all the 2′ × 3′ and 3′ × 4′ 12–14-foot lengths we could get our hands on. When he thought we had enough he said quick back on the truck and go, go. He stopped when outside the barricade again and disappeared for a few minutes. He came out smiling and asked the driver to move on and stop at another store, where he and some others loaded on cartons of food, coffee, sweets and biscuits. He was a noble sort of a bloke, all heart – he gave us each two toffees and a biscuit.

We arrived in the dockyard with the timber and food. The food bits disappeared quite rapidly into the block shed. I wondered if the colonel knew anything about them, as that part of the operation seemed rather clandestine. Malcolm said that the old bloke himself had drawn nails from the store and Bob Stewart was already making the spikes in the Smithy. We put the timber into the carpenters' shop for security. It was too tempting to leave it out in the sight of the cook who would want to put it on his fire. I had a look at the lengths and separated them into heaps of 2′ × 3′ and 3′ × 4′ and worked out the size of the sections needed to be constructed. All set for the big push in the morning. Malcolm said that any overtime I did on this job would be paid in Falkland Island money and not in Pesos.

Pam had been round and cut Valerie and Rachel's hair, they looked quite trim.

There was still a lot of wind about, nothing to worry the locals though. A good night for an invasion.

Saturday, 15 May 1982

Valerie's diary
7am–3pm.
Moderate s/w wind. Cold, dry.
British Commando attack on Pebble Island during the night. Destroyed some Argentine Pucara planes and an ammunition dump.
Pam and Nigel cooked lunch. Pam cut Isobel's hair.
Karen's birthday tomorrow, get-together in her house after 3. Usuals + Dr Mario and the civilian Argy ship's captain being housed in Admiralty Cottages.

Neville's diary
Turned-to in the dockyard. Arthur Gould and I measured up the timber, cut the sizes we wanted and then the nailing up started. Malcolm came in

at about 8.30am and said that there was a bit of a problem. He waved in the colonel's Polish Argentine aide; he was rather agitated. 'The colonel expects to see you working.'

'We are!'

Malcolm spoke up, 'He expected to see saws flashing and hear hammers banging in front of his window.'

We were working in the Carpenters' shop, using the floor space to lay out the wood on.

The Pole had gone and returned with the Colonel, his holster flapping (again) and looking serious. 'Oh, Oh, humph. This is how it is done, eh?' and he stumped off.

The top brass looked particularly uptight.

Then the news broke.

Those naughty boys wearing funny coloured berets and balaclavas back to front had visited Pebble Island last night. (I had said it was a good night for an invasion!) They had blown up all sorts of aircraft, a radar installation and ammunition dumps. I hoped the civilians there had fared ok.

We worked on til lunch time when we had finished the frames. Arthur and I went over to the site and checked the measurements ready for an early a.m. start on Monday. Perhaps it wasn't prudent to be moving among so many enemy troops who were milling about in the yard waiting for their dose of scalding salt water, but I didn't think the lower ranks would have heard of the Pebble raid.

Pam had come over again from the hospital this time to cut Isobel's hair, usually a traumatic experience. She stayed on with Nigel to cook lunch which was very kind of them. Their own house had been commandeered by the Argies who were storing ammunition there too. They allowed Nigel frequent access to check all was well. Pam was one of Valerie's local nursing staff and because of the takeover of their house she and Nigel were living in the upstairs accommodation in the hospital.

A cheeky Harrier had flown up the Sapper Hill road beside the power station and fired some rockets and things at a missile site by the oil tanks, showing that they could miss vital installations if necessary.

Valerie was on duty until 3pm. I went over to Admiralty Cottage to meet her as there was a birthday party for Karen. Quite a nice gathering; we did the Scottish toast for absent friends, you know, whisky over water.

Dr Mario was there and also another civilian Argentine who was the captain and owner of the Motor Vessel *Yehuin*,[10] an oil rig tender, which

---

10. Later named *Black Pig* by the British.

he had sailed over from the mainland with a cargo of containers. He was then told he was under military rule and would go back for further cargos. To which he replied 'No.' 'They' then took over his vessel and he was subsequently sent home where he hoped to get compensation for his vessel.

The day had deteriorated; it was very dull and cloudy also cold. Walking home we noticed a number of bales of wool had been put into Malvina paddock, presumably to be used as a form of shelter.

We learned that the people of Goose Green had been put in the Hall in the settlement and locked in, either as hostages or for their own safety. We'd had some very pleasant evenings in that hall when we lived at the boarding school. I doubted the Goose Greeners were thinking very much about dancing, singing or playing cards and dice at the moment.

Sunday, 16 May 1982

Valerie's diary
3pm–11pm.
Frost during night, fine morning, blue skies and sunshine.
Two vapor trails across sky 10am-ish. Usual anti-aircraft fire bangs and pops at same – which missed their target by far.
Isobel put her and Rachel's bedding on the washing line for a freshen up.
Plenty of 'fireworks' etc. at head of bay at 11pm ish.

Neville's diary
Not an awful lot we could do so a little lie-in was in order. We had dismantled our bed and stood the bottom half of the divan on its side against the desk in the bay window. This plus sleeping on the mattress on the floor, we hoped would give us some protection from flying glass if things got that close. Goodness knows what turn events might take now that the lads had one successful strike to their credit.

We strolled over to Father's for a catch-up on the news, and a look to the west from his front room window. It appeared as if all the helicopters in the world had assembled on the football field, all shapes and sizes. Of course, the natural protection afforded by the high land behind the football field and the forest (small plantation of trees) behind Government House was what 'they' were seeking, not the aegis of the Red Cross emblem painted on the hospital and Admiralty Cottage. The blue, white and blue flag was still flying.

Father was a little cheered by the happening at Pebble although he too was a little apprehensive. I told him what we were doing in the dockyard, he said that by building the shelter we would at least keep 'them' from throwing people out of their homes and being abusive. Back home for lunch.

I had packed four holdall bags which would be one for each of us. They contained the following items: changes of underwear, a thick woolly pully, a light waterproof, towel, soap and other toilet things, a mending kit, socks, boiled sweets, chocolate, a good knife, string, fishhooks, pencils and note pad, playing cards, a favourite book for the girls and also we would have a copy of all family documents each. I explained that if Mum or I or both of us should be out and a man came to the door and asked them to go with him, they should take their bags and go. We would all meet up later. I also explained that they wouldn't know him, but he would be British, and he would know all about them and us. On the other hand, he could be someone we knew very well. Not to worry. It was something that could happen, we could be evacuated. Ok, so how does one explain to one's wife and young daughters what an SAS or SBS man looks like, in fact who knows? And that we might be moved out from the town so it could be bombed and bombarded to solve the little problem we had.

There were some vapour trails from east to west followed by unsuccessful anti-aircraft gunfire.

Isobel had put her and Rachel's bedding out on the clothesline for an airing. Their bedroom had got musty and stuffy with not being able to open the windows for some time because of the blackouts fixed to them.

We walked over to the hospital with Valerie for on duty at 3 then round the square and home for the night.

Startled at 11pm. What's that noise? I looked out of the blackouts at the front and then upstairs. A nice display of flashes and bangs to the west behind Moody Brook and the hills. Good oh, we'll see the Union Jack in the morning.

Monday, 17 May 1982

Valerie's diary
7am–3pm.
Light n/w wind, warm and sunny.
Plenty of helicopter activity.
TB admitted for repair of hernia.
Betty Ford's freezer started to defrost, contents shared out.

Neville's diary
Off we go then, all available hands in the carpenters' shop. Arthur and I had numbered all the sections and put them in order of precedence. The

gang lifted them up and off we went out through the double doors and round to the block shed. Someone started to whistle the Disney seven dwarfs tune 'Hi Ho, Hi Ho' etc. We stood them in place. I nailed the sections together and put up some spars to support the framing until I had the rafters in place. It worked like magic. The Argies stood open mouthed, the curtains in the Colonel's office twitched. Right, that's the easy bit done. Next, we put a scantling along the wall of the block shed allowing for the thickness of the rafter and the depth of flute in the corrugated iron which would slide under the iron on the shed. I laid out what timber we had and then started to fix from the centre out, nailing to the scantling and bird-mouthing onto the frame. When that was done, I had help to level and plumb the walls. We had to ease out in some places and wedge up in others, then the spikes were driven through holes bored in the bottom plate of the frame. We worked until knock-off time (didn't want it to look too easy).

There had been a lot of helicopters flying around during the morning. I suppose that after last night's whatever it was, someone had to be shifted and the BW&B flag was still flying. The pole outside the secretariat still didn't have a flag on it and we had put up this pole a few weeks ago. Well it's all ready for the boys when they come to town with the correct flag.

Valerie was home at 3.30pm. They had admitted an elderly member of the community for an operation tomorrow. Otherwise not much on.

Tuesday, 18 May 1982

Valerie's diary
3pm–11pm.
Fog, drizzle and cold, light wind from n/e.
Talks still going on!
Suggestion that children should be taken out by a neutral ship, bo—s to that idea.
Two big explosions other side of Camber whilst I was trying to push up Labour Ward window.
Dried onions jumped onto the floor at home.

Neville's diary
Last night's news said that the peace talks were still on. The European Community (Common Market) renewed sanctions against Argentina. Ireland and Italy disagreed but would not break the sanctions.

The mornings were really pulling in now, especially ones like this, cold and miserable. Bad enough for us coming out of a warm house, what must it be like for the poor conscripts dug in up in the mountains or on the coastline.

I carried on with the shelter, cutting lengths of timber and nailing up; was a bit of trial and error. As usual there was a lot of helpful advice shouted both in English and Spanish, everyone had a go at Nev. Some of the troops asked what I was building; they were most grateful and were inclined to have a whip-round for me, but all they managed was a sticky boiled sweet and a badly bent cigarette. I wonder what the colonel's speciality was; he didn't come up with any advice, nor on the other hand any criticism. When I had been in his office last there were lots of maps spread out on the large table in the conference room, they looked like the contours of the Port Howard area. What would he be wanting those for?

At last we were ready for the cladding. I asked Malcolm what was going to be done about that.

'The Colonel has it all in hand but be prepared for another lightning raid.'

Valerie went on duty at 3pm. There was a suggestion on the radio from 'the powers that be' that all the children be taken away in a ship of a neutral power for their own safety. Nobody likes that bloody stupid idea.

The day had improved weather-wise, Isobel gave the windows in the front room a wipe over prior to putting up the blackout.

We decided to have pizza for supper, so Rachel and I made up some milk bread dough and put it to rise in the airing cupboard. As part of the topping, we put some of our very precious dried onion flakes in a cup of hot water to soak. Wizz and I sat on the seat box in the bay window watching the world go by, I was having a pre-supper medicinal tot.

There were two enormous flashes and a cloud of black smoke rising from the back of the Camber ridge. This was followed by the sound of the explosion, then came the noise of anti-aircraft gunfire that really rattled the windows.

Rachel was out in the scullery and asked in a plaintive little voice if I really wanted the onions I had soaking.

'Yes,' I snapped, thinking she wanted to do her own thing with them.

'Well, they have jumped out of the cup and landed on the floor.'

We just had to laugh at that. The vibration from the explosion had caused the problem. It must have been a good one as the place where the flashes were is a good mile and a half away.

I put some more onions in to soak after clearing up the originals. Dried onions are an expensive item and almost a necessity.

We enjoyed our pizza, eventually, and we had another laugh. Valerie rang up from the hospital, a thing she only did in an emergency.

'What's wrong?' I asked.

'I have just been knocked off a chair by the explosions on the Camber!'

'Well, that's not far to fall!'

'I was standing on it trying to shut the bloody window in the Labour Ward, AND, no I'm not hurt, before you so kindly ask.'

Oh dear, the feathers were really ruffled. I told her the saga of our supper which made her feel better. Father rang up and asked if we had seen what had happened. I told him what we had seen and also what had happened to Valerie.

That did it, immediate panic – was she all right, had she been hit by flying glass etc?

There are times when one wishes they hadn't opened their big mouths and said certain things to one's parents; this was another one of those times. I had to calm him down over the phone as I couldn't get over there to him because of the curfew. That took a bit of doing.

Rachel remembers ...

We called it dried onion day. During late afternoon there were two enormous explosions at the other side of the harbour. The force was so huge that Stanley shook. Many people saw the soundwave of the blast coming across the harbour towards us. The noise and shock felt thick, almost as if we were in slow motion and black and white for a few moments. It came through the ground and air. I was in the kitchen making pizza, with the dried onions soaking in a mug of hot water. It was as if the air in the room had turned to jelly, I felt that I could actually see the noise. The force of the blast caused the onions and hot water to jump out of the mug and onto the floor. I watched it happen, but the mug didn't move. It wasn't damaged.

At work in the hospital mum was standing on a stool closing a sash window. The blast knocked her off backwards. She was thankfully unharmed and the window unbroken.

Wednesday, 19 May 1982

Valerie's diary

7am–3pm.

Usual long, dark morning, doesn't get light until 9-ish.

Dull, overcast and calm from n/w, around to n/e at 3.30pm-ish. Fog to top of Camber, cold.

Argentine radio forecasts a British invasion tonight.

Argies keeping talks going, much to everyone's frustration.

Pam gave us some ox kidneys to enjoy now or freeze for later. We had one for supper in sauce, very tender.

Neville's diary

And off to work. What few Argentines were on the road didn't look too happy, the locals weren't too bright either.

The truck was organised for a trip to liberate some sheets of corrugated plastic and corrugated galvanised iron for the roof of the shower block extension.

We went through the same procedure as before at the barricades. Apparently the residents to the east of the FIC buildings have to have a special pass to allow them to walk through the 200 yards of controlled zone. They bypass this by going up the hill to the next street (Fitzroy Road), a bit further, but so what?

We had a bit of a delay while the sub lieutenant (Subby) cleared the permit to remove materials from the Argentine marines' stronghold, we of course were army. Whilst we waited, two really down-at-heel Argies strolled in and began to talk to us, one was a corporal and the other a major. The major said that he was used to the cold as he had trained in Sweden, his companion was a little less fortunate. They, for some reason, had walked in from Goose Green and the corporal had worn through the soles of his boots. His feet were rather large and he had only his dress uniform boots which hadn't stood up to the rigours of Falklands hiking. They offered to exchange cigarettes for sandwiches as the only food they had was a Knorr Chicken Stock cube. We told them that there was a stores depot of theirs nearby – turn left and up the hill 50 metres, it was in the Globe Store, and they departed very rapidly.

I had been sorting out the heaps of iron and Perspex for size, ready to load the required amounts of the various suitable lengths. The go-ahead was given with the instruction to be quick. Well, you just have to count each sheet as it is put on the truck, it's good stores practice; poor Subby, he nearly wet himself with panic – perhaps he had to tell a fib or two. When I was sure we had at least 25% more than we needed, all hands got on the truck. What an embarrassment, the bally thing wouldn't start! Would we have to go and ask the opposition for a tow? No. It started, and the return journey commenced. Phew.

We offloaded the sheets of stuff in a part of the garage by Malcolm's office. A start was made putting up the iron on the walls and roof. I had

Val Berntsen helping me. Thankfully it was a calm day; if a breeze springs up it's quite easy to get injured by a sheet of iron taken by the wind. We began by nailing a few sheets on the west wall, then a couple of runs on the roof. Time was getting on; it seems that the middle of the day is the time for showers so there were lots of bodies pushing round which made things difficult. We would start again in the morning.

All quiet on the home front. Pam had given Valerie some ox kidneys, she cooked one in a marvellous sauce for supper. Cor, smashin'.

There were the usual messages on the 'Calling the Falklands' programme. The Buenos Aires radio forecast an invasion during the night. Either they were a month and a half late or they knew something we didn't.

Thursday, 20 May 1982

Valerie's diary
3pm–11pm.
Gale force wind and rain from n/e all night.
Apparently bombing after midnight 8 miles away – didn't hear it!
Malcolm Ashworth is down to 13 milk cows – but he keeps going.
Wind round to n/w by 11am, fog on the deck and rain.
No-one came up on the R/T at 9.30am – Eileen was transmitting – apparently the cables were cut.
No change in hospital patients except VJ in with pneumonia.

Neville's diary
Gale force winds from the northeast which had backed to nor'west by 11am and left us with fog and rain. We did what we could with the shelter, rain running up our sleeves. I had on a Barbour jacket, which has been a good standby for many years in the Falklands; for some reason we call them Maori jackets or coats, I can't remember why. Maybe the cloth originated in New Zealand.

A rumour buzzed round that there had been some bombing in the night, 8 miles away, we didn't hear it. Mind you, it was rough weather in the night. Valerie said that no one had answered on the R/T during the allotted time. Eileen had been calling but someone had cut the aerial feeders.

This had happened before. One unit would look in through the R/T office window while passing, see a radio transmitter etc and thinking that they were doing the right thing would apply an axe to the wires, thus stopping transmissions. Along would come another patrol, see the damage, think it was sabotage and repair the wiring, and off they all would go again. All the while the detector vans were patrolling round the town, perhaps they thought someone else had transmitting gear. All CB sets and radio ham gear had been called in. Earlier on, I had put up an argument and kept the Pony radio sets used by the fire service. They were line of sight really, although when we last used them, we got interference from some Spanish-speaking station.

Dairyman Malcolm Ashworth was still plodding on with his milk delivery as best he could. All but thirteen of his cows had been taken for slaughter, he had managed to hang on to these through some hard talking with Bloomer-Reeve. Fresh meat was not very forthcoming now. All privately owned cattle on the common had been slaughtered. All owners of horses had been allowed to take their animals out to nearby farms for safety.

Some Argies had been sent in from Fitzroy (26 miles away) driving 400-odd sheep on foot. They arrived in town with about seven animals, which when slaughtered were found to have a great weight of machine gun bullets in them.

Valerie was on duty at 3pm. Another cold miserable night.

The children went off to their beds. I listened to the radio for a while, had a read and a mug of coffee. The water supply had become unreliable and needed boiling before use. We made sure that we always had a couple of buckets of useable water to hand should the supply go off again. The water gathered from the roof was probably better anyway – unless the water butt froze over, which had been known to happen.

I could hear some bangs and bumps so went out into the front porch to have a look. Out over the land to the east, I could see regular pinpoint flashes, then a larger flash from the airport direction. It was a bang and then a pop. How peculiar, the flashes were in the right sequence, but the sounds were reversed due to the distance. First the bang of the explosion, then the pop of the shell being fired from the ship. Some bright individual could no doubt calculate how far off the ship was.

Well, they were making sure that sleep was being lost down at the airport. Keeping them on their toes no doubt.

I had a chat with Taff Davies about the task force, and if there was there anything that could be done to prevent the bloodshed which was now inevitable. In his opinion it was definite there would be a confrontation. He also told me that if I listened to a certain frequency on my radio, I would pick up the task force. Our radio was a rather powerful receiver made by Sony. Of course, they didn't stay on a fixed frequency but jumped about, they must have clever bits of kit to keep up with that, but it was nice to hear the occasional very pukka voice: 'Roger cheps.'

Friday, 21 May 1982

Valerie's diary

7am–3pm.

Talks have broken down.

Commando type raids have started. 6 raids at least by 200 men.

Frost, fine sunny morning, light n/w wind.

Helicopter lost leaving a British ship. 20 lost, 7 rescued.

British flag flying at Port San Carlos[11] (KC) in an early morning raid.

Slept in x-ray room.

Shared cost of a crate of cans of beer with Nigel.

Neville's diary

I put the finishing touches to the shelter and cleared up. It was quite warm inside; the boiler fire was going and with the sun shining in through the perspex stuff it was like a sun lounge. Perhaps the visitors would like to remain inside this rather than go back to the hills. Let's hope that no-one takes the corner off with a truck, it does seem a bit proud but the best that could be managed. The chimney and water tower were a bit of an eyesore, but we didn't have anything to do with that construction.

I put my tools back in the office and thought about having a sharpen up when in walked Malcolm. All smiles, he's got something up his sleeve besides his arm, another nasty job no doubt.

No. All he had to say was that the boys have been at it again.

'Oh yeah?'

'Well, the Flag is flying again at KC and JB!!'[12]

They're here, on dry land.

Oh well, it was probably safer to land out there rather than sail up Stanley Harbour. Last night's shooting was probably a diversionary tactic.

A sad note, a helicopter had been lost in the dark moving between two ships, seven personnel had been rescued but alas twenty had perished.

Valerie said she had made up a bed in the x-ray department, that being her idea of a safe spot.

She had split the cost of a carton of red cans with Nigel for a bit of light refreshment.

---

11. Local names: KC is Port San Carlos. The farm was originally owned by the Camerons.

12. JB is San Carlos, owned by Bonners.

I expect now we will have a lot of new edicts and restrictions issued from Menendez.

Nothing of interest in the local news. The Beeb said that the talks have broken down – there's no need for them to resume – THE BRITISH ARE HERE.

The Falkland Island representatives in the United Nations do not seem to have much support from the rest of the world. All the nations who for years have shouted and screamed for self-determination etc. are anti the Falklands Islanders having their wishes listened to.

Saturday, 22 May 1982

Valerie's diary
Day off.
After all that action yesterday, nothing much happened during the night. Some small arms fire etc., but nothing heavier.
Overcast, light n/w wind, heavy frost first thing.
Morning: I did a deep cleaning blitz in front room/porch.
Visitors: Ramon, Terry Spruce, Neil, Father.
Cup final 1–1 Spurs *v* QPR, replay Thursday.
Cold rain during evening.
Borrowed some music tapes from the Smiths.

Neville's diary
Valerie at home today: she has got an actual weekend off. Looking out of the window first thing there was a heavy frost.

Valerie threatened to do a morning of housework. Discretion being the better part of valour, the girls and I decided to go over and see Father. He was rather excited about the landings at San Carlos.

He told us a couple of his time-worn stories of the visits he made over there to Ajax Bay which was the site of a meat freezer plant in the 1950s. The houses for the staff had been pulled down and brought into Town for the use of the Government. The main freezer buildings were left behind, as the removal of the freezer parts is a specialised job and would cost a lot of money to do. Father being the then Government foreman was in charge of the work force sent out to Ajax Bay to relocate the houses.

He needed some shopping, so we went down the road to Jimmy's at Speedwell Store, on the corner of John Street and Stanley Cottage Hill. We didn't allow the girls to go out in the town on their own any more, just in case there should be any problems. We went back home thinking that the housework coast was clear and had a cup of coffee.

Some visitors arrived. Terry Spruce, an old fishing mate and second in charge of FIC. (Terry had taken his wife Joan and small son Mark out to North Arm at the beginning of the occupation.) Neil from next door popped in, Chilean carpenter Ramón from No. 5 came over, and in walked Father. He thought he needed the exercise. They all sat round having a drink, I thought it nice and cosy – celebrating the landings.

Then Valerie switched on the radio and tuned to the BBC World Service for cup final day. Father and I being the Philistines remained quiet or at least didn't make any untoward remarks about the offside rule. The score at full time was Spurs 1 QPR 1, replay on next Thursday.

The landings at San Carlos had gone ahead initially with little or no opposition, but as the day progressed there had been very harsh attacks by the Argentine air force and their navy planes. Ships were being bombed, the news had been sketchy, definitely one frigate had been sunk, other ships had been damaged [but] the landing was a success. Among the strife there were more than likely acts of heroism, bravery and humour which we would hear of in the future.

There wasn't a great deal of reaction in the town, just some gun fire in the night. Shadow shooting I shouldn't wonder.

We had a domestic evening; the first for a long time. Valerie had been lent some tapes by John Smith at No. 7 which made a pleasant change of music.

Sunday, 23 May 1982

Valerie's diary
Day off.
Rain ++ last night, light n/w wind, sunny spells, some rainsqualls, no frost.
No military activities for 30 hours.
Quiet domestic evening. I skipped through book Battle of the Atlantic which was interesting.
Did a pile of washing with the help of Mary's washing machine.
Bought a pile of potatoes from Stan Johnson.

Neville's diary
There had been some very heavy rain during the night, giving way to sunny spells and squalls with a light nor'west wind during the day.

Valerie did a pile of washing while the lunch cooked.

I walked over to Stan Johnson's, a few yards past Father's house. I had arranged to buy some potatoes from him. He had quite a bit of land which he planted for commercial reasons. I got about a hundredweight, all good-sized taters. Might put a few in the oven later for supper. We haven't had jacket spuds for a while, haven't got any cheese but no doubt we'll find a topping of something.

Terry had stayed for lunch yesterday, after the match he said he had a bit of a problem: he had forgotten to hand in the pony transceivers from his office. These were the radios off the FIC's motorboats used in the harbour for towing etc. No problem, we had walked across the green and hung them up in the central station with the others of the Fire Service.

Another evening in. The local radio groaned on, nothing from the outside world, everybody was waiting ...

We listened to more of John's tapes and off to bed.

We can sleep soundly now the boys are only 50–60 miles away.

Monday, 24 May 1982

Valerie's diary
Day off.
Fine sunny morning. Light n/w wind – able to walk down the road in anorak and skirt.
Harriers had another go at the airport just before 10am.
Sunny afternoon.
Had a go on the roundabout with Alison.
Walked up to McPhees with the girls.

Neville's diary
Queen Victoria's Birthday. No longer a public holiday in the Islands. The May Ball had always taken place on 24th/25th May, up until this year, in the Town Hall. (Give or take a day dependant on whether a weekend came in between as there is no dancing in the Falklands on a Sunday.)

Quite a formal do, men in dress or smart lounge suits and most of the ladies wore evening gowns – and mostly hand-made for the occasion. The first night involved the election of the May Queen or Belle of the Ball [and] a formal air prevailed. On the second night a carnival atmosphere, with a touch of sobriety, and the election (it was felt a bit loaded) of a Prince Charming. Many people used to come in from the farms for their winter holidays at this time. I remember when quite young that it was not unusual to see groups of 12 or so people riding into town on horseback at one time. But with the coming of the land rover and motorbike and the easy way of flying by FIGAS, the horseback travelling faded out, and stabling in Stanley became expensive or difficult to find, as paddocks owned by farms were sold off.

Out in the camp they would have a busy round of social activities, each of the larger farms would have a 'Two Nighter' which comprised two nights of dancing and merrymaking. These great fun weekends were staggered through the winter. Added to this would also be grand slam whist drives and sheepdog trials. At the end of the work season a week's sport events would take place, one on the east and one on the west. Mounted and foot events, gymkhana, and steer riding. People would travel the length and breadth of the Islands visiting old friends and relatives. At Christmas, the Stanley Sports Association held two days of racing in Stanley on the racecourse to the west of Government House. And again, the farm people were on the move coming into town. Quite a good social life really. If one travels from farm to farm now it is still possible to see a heap of empty spirit bottles at gates where tracks merged, and riders met up on the way to town or other venues. It was always polite to 'have one for the track, chay' and not only from one bottle. Really 'hail fellow well met'.

And, back to today!

A fine sunny morning, I decided to work on the central station, but would have to wait for the night damp to burn off the iron in the sunshine. I went down through the dockyard to tell Malcolm of this and ask if he had someone who he wanted kept occupied. I glanced over my shoulder to the east and some black spots danced before my eyes, oh dear, black spots before the eyes, then followed by large flashes and loud bangs.

That was an air raid and in broad daylight, cheeky blighters. A crowd had gathered to watch. Argies and locals, all cheering. Rudy had climbed on to the stair rail outside the Central Store and waved and cheered.

An Argy officer called up to him:

'If you want to see the end of this war, you had better stop that. Some of these soldiers in this dockyard are not as broad minded as I am, most of them have lost friends in that raid and some even relatives.'

Rudy saw the point the officer was making.

I had the assistance of Vladmar the Pole again. We painted the east side of the fire station. The paint went on quite well in the sunshine, and we heard a few bangs but didn't see any vapour trails. The airport had had a pasting this morning. You don't know where those little 'sparrows' are going to peck next.

Valerie and the girls went up to see Grace McPhee on Davis Street after doing some shopping. On the way home she saw Dr Alison on the playing green, she had her children with her and they all had a spin on the round-a-bout. I'm sure Daniel enjoyed it as he was only two years old. Certainly,

Alison and Valerie did, they were in a different world, oblivious of anything for a few minutes.

Tuesday, 25 May 1982

Valerie's diary
Day off.
Cold drizzle from s/w, sunny spells.
Grandad feeling pathetic with cough and cold.
Bought the game of Cluedo for the long evenings.
Watched Argentine planes belting around the harbour, trying to find
somewhere to land.

Neville's diary
It's Argentine National Day. 'Vientecinco de Mayo', a bit like St George's
Day to the English, only the Argentines get a bit more steamed up. They
are not quite so reserved. They were all walking about in clean uniforms,
smiling, with polished boots, some even had nice new shiny holsters for
their pistols.

We had managed to put up the guttering on the west side of the central
station yesterday. As the weather was fair, we tackled the east side. All
went well, I had put up the new guttering brackets which I had made of
wood in an old-fashioned design same as the ones already there. Goodness
knows the age of the guttering, definitely not this year's work. It was made
of wood slotted together in two lengths, each length being sixteen foot or
so. The building looked better for the guttering being back in place.

We gave the double sliding doors an undercoat of salmon pink paint
in preparation for the topcoat. We had at least been lucky weather wise so
far this winter, no bad weather, yet. Due to the present circumstances,
Malcolm had not been able to proceed with any of the planned maintenance. But as he had to keep the workforce occupied and out of mischief,
a lot of the PWD buildings had freshly painted roofs. The Colonel kept an
eye on the costs in this respect, he was watching public expenditure. He
was also heard to say 'You Falklands people work well.'

There was one task being performed in the dockyard which was not
being done in a carefree manner but given the respect it was due. That was
the making of wooden crosses for war graves. Some had already been used
for Argentine military graves in the cemetery. They were of a simple construction, made in the carpenters' shop. Officers had white painted crosses
with the name in black, conscripts, enlisted men and NCOs had plain
wood and the name burned in the wood with a hot iron.

There had been some small arms fire during the night. Someone in the drill hall had got a little nervous and put a few shots into St Mary's house. No one was injured but some of Monsignors' books had rather large holes in them.

Valerie had been down the road to the west store and bought a new board game called Cluedo, we'll have to sort that one out.

We went over to see Father after lunch. He was really down in the dumps, he had a cold and a rather nastier than usual cough. He did cheer up with our company.

We returned home to do some chores before curfew. I had made some new blackouts which were less cumbersome than the previous ones which had got a bit tatty anyway. Several pieces of plywood and hardboard for the windows in the bathroom, pantry and back kitchen. They would be easier to take down in the mornings. The signs of a lack of ventilation were now quite evident. As we had been asked to conserve water, a thorough wash down of the paint work was not possible either.

We could hear the sound of low flying aircraft, not the roar of jets, but a slightly softer note of the Pucará. A twin-engined turbo-prop ground-attack counter-insurgent aircraft assembled in Argentina. There were several men lounging on the playing field and leaning on the telephone pole by our front gate, watching the five planes. They would fly low over Fairy Cove, cross the harbour, flip up their wings to show the underside and the Argentine colours painted there, all patriotic for Independence Day. To get a better view we walked up the garden path, it was 3.30-ish so we had ample time to watch before curfew. The five planes chased round the harbour and out through the narrows and back in over the ridge came four ... Oh, one's hiding somewhere.

Round they went again out through The Narrows and back again came three ...

Out through The Narrows and there was a splash. I looked up and there he was, the dear little Harrier dropping some sort of bombs on the Pucarás as they flew at water level.

Three down, two to go.

And there was Rudy on his peat shed roof jumping up and down cheering.

The troops at the fence were getting a bit fidgety, loosening their holsters, let's get in out of sight. Only one left now, I don't know if he landed at the airport or on a road somewhere.

That was a nice little international airshow.

Now let us have a display by the dog team. They did.

For Independence Day the dogs had their uniform coats on with the corps badge embroidered on the corner, all very smart.

A little snippet of news was that the May Ball had been held in a private house where several families were gathered for the duration of the hostilities, and the dress code was observed.

I wonder what our troops are doing.

Wednesday, 26 May 1982

Valerie's diary
3pm–11pm.
British destroyer HMS *Coventry*, and container vessel *Atlantic Conveyor* (24 died) lost yesterday off the East Falklands.
KC beachhead attacked from the air again.
Cold and overcast from n/w, some drizzle.
The Pope visits UK on Friday, offers to go to the Argentine afterwards.
AS had appendix removed, all Doctors in theatre.
Quiet night bang-wise.
Aston Villa win European Cup.

Neville's diary
Cold from the nor'west and overcast but dry enough to paint the doors of the central station – which we did.

The paint was cold and took a bit of effort to spread smoothly. There was a little local pedestrian traffic and a few well-chosen remarks were directed our way, such as 'Have you got that paint the right way up?'

Some dejected 'greenflies' slouched along the road and not even a smile from them.

The sad news had started to come in now. A British destroyer and a very large container ship had been sunk by Argy aircraft action. The beachhead at San Carlos was again under heavy air attack. Somehow a story emerged that the Argentine planes took off from one base on the mainland and landed at another. Confusing? Well they wouldn't be able to see how many were lost on each raid.

The radio announcer from the BBC said that the troops were preparing to move off from the northwest to attack an important strategic target. The only place they could go was Goose Green. Nice of them to warn the enemy – unless the attack had already begun.

There was a quick flight by an Argy helicopter from Stanley to Green Patch farm 18 miles away. They went to fetch AS, a young lad in need of an appendectomy.

We were instructed by the local radio to stay in our own homes after lunch as members of the armed forces would be calling on us to issue identity cards.

Valerie was due to go on duty at 3pm. As she was changing into her uniform, there was a knock on the front door. I went out quietly to the front porch and there was George from the colonel's office and a captain whom I didn't know. The door opened without a squeak, they were both looking down the harbour.

'Boo!' I couldn't resist it.

'Oh!! Neville don't do that.'

'Hello George, are you here to give us identity cards, or is this a serious visit?'

'This is medical Dr Capitano (some name I didn't catch) we are going to issue cards to you and your family.'

'Come in.'

George had his faithful Uzi with him which he nonchalantly tossed onto the table in the kitchen. Tuppence cat didn't go much on that, he wanted to get out.

'Sorry little black cat,' said George.

It didn't make any difference – he didn't get a friendly look.

Rachel remembers ...

I was sitting at the table drinking a mug of tea and was frightened when the gun was dumped on the table right in front of me. The weapon was so close that I could smell the grease on it.

Neville's diary continues ...

The cards were to be issued to all persons aged between 16 and 65. This seemed to be an anti-infiltration scheme, but one which failed in the onset. George had a nice machine gun and the captain had a nice pistol, but they didn't have a camera.

Valerie came through from the bedroom in her uniform. They both stood and said good afternoon. Tea and coffee were offered and politely refused.

I produced the Argentine white travel card which had been issued to me along with all other travellers to and from the Falklands in 1973. This was not accepted. The new card had to be issued in the Islands and counter-signed by Bloomer-Reeve.

Valerie asked if she could proceed with the formalities as she had to be at the hospital by 3pm.

Rachel remembers . . .
Mum said rather sternly, 'Well get on with it then, I have patients waiting for me.'

Neville's diary continues . . .
George opened a file and took out a form and some cards and dug a pen out of his pocket.

'Your name please?'

'Bennett, Valerie Elizabeth.'

'Date of birth please?'

'3rd May 1936.'

'Height please?'

'5 feet 8 inches.'

Mumble mumble in Spanish '1.73 metres?'

'Cough hmm, weight please?'

'I don't know.'

'Occupation?'

'I'm just a nurse.'

George started to write, the captain tapped the table and said in very clear English: 'No madam, you are not just a nurse, you are the Matron of the hospital.'

She said 'I thought I recognised you doctor.'

'Yes Madam,' he smiled.

The questions continued.

'What skin colour?'

'White.'

'Eyes?'

'Hazel.'

'Hair?'

'Dark, going grey.' (Blimey, so it was!)

'Place of birth?'

'England.'

'Language?'

'Only English.'

'Thank you, Madam, if you will carry your British passport with you as well as this card it will help identification.'

She put on her coat and picked up her bits and pieces and off to work. My turn.

'Name?'

'Bennett, Neville Kenneth.'

'Date of birth?'
'14th October 1937.'
'Height?'
'6 feet 1 inch.'
'Weight?'
'105 kilos.'
'Hair?'
'Blond.'
'Eyes?'
'Blue.'
'Colour?'
'White.'
'Place of birth?'
'Here.'
'Oh! British!' Very nice of them.
'Occupation? Oh, you are the Fireman', so he put down 'Bombero'.

That was it, they apologised for not having a camera, asked me to carry my passport and off they went.

*   *   *

It had turned out to be a pleasant day. I strolled up the garden to have a natter with Ken and Dot who lived opposite on Pioneer Row. There was the rattle of machine gunfire and that of small arms from the monument and also from the other side of the harbour. Ken, former paratrooper, had been at Arnhem in WW2, said they were probably zeroing in their weapons – but did they have to blast hell out of the flock of logger duck young which roost on the beach to the west of the monument?

They shift to the other side of the harbour with the change of wind. It was possible to see a raft of ducks numbering at least 100 floating across the water. They are a harmless flightless bird – larger than a domestic duck; their flesh is unpalatable, but their eggs are delicious. There was one pair of the ducks that had made their home in the gorse bushes for as long as I could remember. The drake develops white feathers on his head with age and this one had feathers the colour of cotton wool. They roosted on a rock just out from the sea wall. Their only enemies were seals, but their chicks (up to seven normally) are vulnerable to Skuas. But by good parentage they very often saved the whole brood. Now they had been shot by a bunch of bloody Argy soldiers.

Thursday, 27 May 1982

Valerie's diary

7am–3pm.

Light n/w wind, beautiful sunrise.

Argentine troops on the move from n/w.

Cold wind.

Air to ground fire other side of the Camber.

Spurs win replay FA cup 2–0.

Water mains being repaired outside Phyllis' house next door.

Neville's diary

Off to work, carrying the brand-new shiny Identity card. Millions of others in the world do this too, but not the British.

What's in store today?

Argentine soldiers are moving westwards in large numbers, both on foot and in vehicles. Now that the whereabouts of 'Maggie's Boys' is known, the troops held in town are being moved to meet them.

Malcolm asked me to go across the road and clean the stove at Tom and Hilda's. He was overnighting there with his wife, mother and a couple of other friends. It was a wise precaution. The cooker would be kept on full heat for longer hours than usual to cater for the food and hot water needs of the extra people now under that roof. The burner wasn't really dirty, just enough to warrant a clean. Hilda made me a nice hot cup of coffee and put in a little something to ward off the cold.

The dockyard buzz was all about the British troops breaking out of San Carlos. Let's hope the people locked in the hall at Goose Green keep their heads down.

By all accounts the people issuing the ID cards yesterday were not all as polite as George and the Dr who came to us.

Public disgust was expressed at the shooting of the Loggerducks, Gulls and Giant Petrels in the monument area yesterday. The odd visitor, in the past, has been forgiven for inadvertently shooting one of these protected birds. This wholesale slaughter really got up our noses.

When I had finished the stove, I returned to the office and had a good clean and tidy up. I also had a good look at the tools and sharpened those in need as they had had a busy time over the past few weeks. I had another read through the handbook on rescuing someone from a crashed plane. Not that the instructions for releasing the canopy of a crashed Lightning would be similar to that of the Harrier, and I shouldn't think any civilian would be allowed to get within half a mile of a downed aircraft.

Someone was showing a great deal of interest in the back of the Camber. Bombs and rockets being dropped from a great height. This is about the third time that they have had a go at that spot, must be a supply dump or a camp. The raid was soon over, and the AA guns were late on parade again.

The plumbers were on overtime, there was a water main leak on the corner of Drury Street, outside Phyllis's house. They repaired the leak with a collar and installed a new easily accessible stop valve.

Valerie was home at three, we went over to Father's. He was not yet 100 per cent but well on the road. He was a little on edge and seemed to have something up his sleeve, he'll tell us when he is ready.

The girls are getting fed up with no school and having to amuse themselves. Not being able to wander outside as they were used to doesn't help.

The library had been open but was difficult to get into as the town hall was being used as a casualty centre. The stench of wounded bodies and the great unwashed was awful. A screen of wood and hardboard panelling had been constructed to let people have access to the library without seeing into the rest of the building. With so many armed men prowling round down there it was uncomfortable to go in, even to exert our rights of freedom.

Rachel remembers ...
Yes, it stank. It was intimidating being watched by armed men as we went about our daily business – even doing something as innocent as visiting the library.

Neville's diary continues ...
Home and pull up the drawbridge again. Somehow it gives a sense of security to be all at home together in the warm and behind closed doors. The food is a bit scratchy at times, but the ones I love are here and no harm can come to us. So, let the explosions go on at night round the town, we're getting used to the noise especially the gun which fires twelve shots at midnight.

Friday, 28 May 1982

Valerie's diary
7am–3pm.
Many big bangs last night around the town, Rachel slept through it!
Mod n/w wind, 8/8ths cloud, steady rain.
Slipped up with my off duty, turned to @12 noon–3pm, never mind!
Pope John starts to visit UK.

Neville's diary
There seemed to be more than the regular pattern of bangs last night, makes me think someone was getting softened up. A cloudy morning, moderate wind from the nor'west with rain.

There was to be a bit of a push on work-wise, I was co-opted on to the navvy gang. A power line pole on the junction of Philomel Hill and Davis Street had suffered some damage and was becoming a hazard to the public. A new pole had already been delivered to the site. A hole was pre-pared, which had filled with water overnight. We were mildly surprised that no one was taking a bath in it. We bailed out the water and tidied up the edges. The new pole was manhandled with brute force and a couple of ropes into position – avoiding the still-standing pole which had the power lines connected but which had been taken out of circuit for a few minutes. A dumper truck of cement came along, we poured the mix over the rocks which had been rammed in round the base of the pole. The whole thing was braced up with lengths of timber and rope to allow the cement to set.

In the middle of the operation, a troop of Argy soldiers ran up Philomel Hill. All were spotlessly dressed in clean lightweight camo suits, shiny new boots, slimline helmets, new rifles but no spare magazines nor webbing or pouches. Must be a training run. If there is a blockade on, how did they get here so nice and clean? They had just got to the rough part of the hill above the Davis Street junction, when there was a shout from the leader who had been running backwards (show off). They all dived into the side of the road and ducked their heads. We looked up, there was a largish vapour trail going westwards followed rapidly by two lesser trails very high in the sky.

When the planes had gone out of sight the, now not so clean and shiny, soldiers moved off again.

A land rover sped past us and screeched to a stop a couple of hundred yards further along the road. Two men jumped out and disappeared into the garage. One came back out and got a rope. Jumbo's rover was pulled out onto the road and tow started. Obviously Jumbo hadn't donated his vehicle to the cause, and the blokes had started it without the keys. This theft was happening all round the town. There was no supply of petrol remaining but there was rather a lot of diesel available, so diesel rovers were being commandeered.

Back down to the dockyard. Being Friday once again, I did the usual checks on the equipment. How wonderful, everything started at first go, even the pumps and Rover which had stood out for over a month now (British workmanship).

Home for lunch.

Well, that's a first: Valerie had had a bit of a mix-up with her off duty. She should have been on duty from 7am–3pm instead of 3pm–11pm as she thought, and she went over at 12 noon.

Saturday, 29 May 1982

Valerie's diary
3pm–11pm.
Cold wind from s/w. Light rain. Squalls.
Water to be off each day from 9am–4pm to ration use.
Curfew now extended 4pm–8:30am. Charming.
Goose Green and Darwin back under British flag. 250 Argentines killed.
Residents at Goose Green have been held prisoner in the hall there for a month.
Boss of Paratroopers killed in action. RIP.

Neville's diary
Cold southwest wind.
The town water supply is to be shut off 9am to 4pm daily. There are more people in the town than were ever envisaged so the essential supplies of water and electricity are being stretched beyond belief.

The plumbers, water filtration plant staff and those at the power station are doing a job above and beyond.

The curfew is now to be from 4pm to 8.30am next day, and that is going to be a looong time indoors.

Valerie would be on duty at 3pm today. She will have to have a good think as to how she could rearrange the off duty lists so that the living out staff wouldn't be on the streets during the curfew hours.

I went over to father's, chewed the fat with him for a while and made sure he understood the new hours of curfew. He had heard the news of Goose Green's liberation but remarked that we hadn't learned of the cost yet. All we knew was that the people of Goose Green had been confined to the Hall for a month.

250 Argentines had been killed in the fighting, and the leader of the Paras plus others there had also been killed. One believes that the members of the parachuting fraternity do get rather upset if something happens to one of their colleagues. So be warned Mr Argentine.

Valerie was a bit put out somewhat, with the lack of news and the dribbly drabbly way in which we did hear anything from the BBC. Her father had been a newspaper printer in Taunton, so from a very early age she had been used to reading newspapers and learning of world events that way rather than the scratchy reception on shortwave radio.

Oh! There we go again, bombs, rockets and things down the harbour with the cacophonic accompaniment of anti-aircraft guns.

The phone rang. 'There's a fire in the ground outside my house,' said WG. 'A rocket or something has burned its way into the ground. Come on down and put it out.' His house was on the outskirts of the town.

I replied: 'Well now, you and I both know that it's long after curfew, and the military have control of the fire service during the hours of curfew.'

He was insistent: 'No, no, you come down.'

I had to, reluctantly, put my foot down. As much as I wanted to help him, I wasn't going to put my men or myself in that much danger.

'No sorry, we would get shot, you phone the military if you are that concerned.'

'Thank you.'

So, in for a long night. Play some games with the children, listen to the radio, look out of the front window.

The nights were really pulling in now. Not having put the clocks back the hour for winter, it was dark until later in the mornings than it would usually be.

That was all overshadowed by the great news: Goose Green had been liberated and the Union Flag was flying once more. How were the people there, how had they fared during their enforced stay in the hall? What damage had been done?

It's Saturday night! I will have to get a little something to celebrate that one with!

Sunday, 30 May 1982

Valerie's diary
7am–3pm.
Frost and hailstones during the night. Fine, sunny, fresh morning.
Naval bombardment of Two Sisters etc. during day.
Paratroopers understandably upset at Goose Green because their boss is killed.
1,400 Argie prisoners were taken at Goose Green.
Curfew 4pm–8.30am has taken some getting used to.
'Calling the Falklands' – reception good.
Water turned off all evening. I was cheesed off!

Neville's diary

Hailstones in the night and a frost, not good conditions for anyone sleeping outside. The morning was bright and sunny.

I prepared and cooked some lunch, we didn't seem to have such large appetites as before, but we couldn't sit still for too long either. I must have worn down the centre of the hall carpet through pacing back and forth, must have covered some miles since 2nd April too.

The Two Sisters (mountains to the west of Stanley) seem to be receiving a lot of attention today from (we hope) the British, in the form of air attacks and shell fire from ships. Could this be the start of something big?

There were already some craters in those hills, mostly grown over now. After the end of the 1939–45 war a certain local contractor was given the task of destroying some explosive material left by the West Yorkshire Regiment. He asked advice from the resident professional armourer and was told to use fifteen packets only each time. Large chunks of rock were blown out of the ground and travelled some distance. Chimneys were cracked in the town and pictures came off the walls. The professional gentleman asked the contractor to show him what he was doing and to see the packets and asked how many.

'Fifteen, Sir.'

The packet was slit open and ten packets were produced from what was actually a carton!

Valerie came home at 3pm.

There was some dribs and drabs of news, about 1,400 Argies had surrendered at Goose Green. A Harrier pilot had been found, he had ejected a few days previously and had taken refuge in an empty shepherd's house southwest of Goose Green at Paragon or 'Trinklyda' (Tranquilidad).

The radio reception was exceptionally good for our 'Calling the Falklands' programme. It would be a bit much to expect the Argies to block every frequency. There had been a message for 'the man playing billiards': 'Keep it up.' I wonder what that meant.

Just to add to the happy atmosphere in the house, the water supply to the town has been shut off all evening. Good job we kept all available buckets and pots filled and a supply of boiled water handy.

We had been advised a week previous to boil all tap water before using it. We did that and also for the roof water which we used for cooking. Tea made from roof water tastes a bit funny. I don't know what anti-aircraft shells are made of, but their fallout rattles on the roof frequently. There is probably shrapnel in the gutters adding to the flavour of our water.

At least the shelling has stopped.

Monday, 31 May 1982

Valerie's diary
4pm–12 midnight.[13]

Frost and frequent hail and snow squalls from s/w.

Argentine Red Cross ship in the harbour.

Everyone (locals) very anti-Argie now. 17 Royal Marines killed in Goose Green on Friday after the Argies showed the white flag and killed the Marines.

Neville's diary
Hail and snow from the southwest.

There are some Argentine soldiers who have never seen snow, don't realise it is slippery, and spend more time on their backsides than on their feet. Maybe their boots are not too good for the job. Some don't even have a warm jacket and wrap themselves up in a blanket and are hunched up with the cold. Many don't even know where the 'Islas Malvinas' are. Now some of them will never go home. There are frequent burial parties in the cemetery and by all accounts the graves are not too deep either.

Tom asked me to accompany him down to his mother's house on John Street close to the cathedral. It was empty and would be vulnerable to frost bursting the water pipes, he didn't want to face a flooded house. No one had forced an entry but there were a lot of footprints in the snow round the house, not local type of boot prints either. Tom told me where to find the stopcock which I did and turned it off. I also took the added precaution of tying up the arm of the ball valve in the supply tank in the loft. Tom went round the house turning on all the taps, hot and cold. He opened the drain cocks on the range and hot water cylinder.

There was a loud bang and a whistling noise outside, very quickly we moved out into the garden and looked up. We saw a long trail of smoke leading from behind the hill to the south and up northwards. There was a blinding flash in a patch of cloud then two small vapour trails going from west to east in a clear blue patch, all was well with the boys.

There is not a shred of sympathy locally for the Argentines. We had heard on the news that a troop of Brits at Goose Green had moved to accept the surrender of a group of Argies waving a white flag when a group of other Argies opened fire from the opposite end of the trench.

Back at the Dockyard, Malcolm said that the main sewerage drain from Rowan House on Stanley Cottage hill was blocked. Would I give him a

---

13. Shift times had to be changed due to the longer hours of curfew. Valerie couldn't walk home after a late shift so would overnight in the hospital.

hand after lunch and blow it through with the Firefly? He had the divine permission from the colonel.

On the way home, I saw that there had been a lot of digging happening in the police cottages gardens by the R/T station.

Valerie said that a large mobile crane had arrived by the fence of the gardens followed closely by a long truck with a large cargo container on the back. A man had climbed onto the top of the container and had attached the hooks from the crane onto each corner. The crane then proceeded to lift the container off the truck and up and over the high-tension power lines with the chap still standing on the thing. They nearly succeeded, but as the man didn't have insulating rubber boots, he suffered when the container swung in the breeze and touched the wires which resulted a heavy belt of electricity going through the poor bloke. The container was dropped down rapidly, and the man was taken off.

The boom of the crane was extended, they tried once more and got the container over the wires and down into the garden where it was covered over with soil and tussock bogs. Presumably it was to be a shelter for the drivers of the trucks which were hidden under the trees along St Mary's Walk at night.

After lunch, I wandered over to the central station and met Malcolm there. We drove to Rowan House in the Firefly. The drains were quite full. A couple of good blasts with the hose and a bit more to clean the system out was all it needed. I topped the tank up with water from the nearby hydrant.[14]

There were quite a few bangs in the night.

---

14. Stanley had a number of fire hydrants supplying non-potable water. The water pressure was not sufficient for sustained pumping for firefighting but could be used for topping up the Fireflys after incidents.

JUNE 1982

Tuesday, 1 June 1982

Valerie's diary

8am–4pm.

Cold, dry day from n/w. No further snow. Cold all day.

British troops continue to consolidate position around Mt Kent.

Apparently, a Harrier was shot down this afternoon and pilot seen to parachute out.

Neville's diary

Cold, miserable nor'west wind, a grey day. The snow had all disappeared yesterday.

We believe the British forces to be grouping around Mount Kent, 11 or so miles from Stanley. It's very easy to look westwards and wonder if I waved my hand or a scarf, would someone be able to see me through his binoculars?

All the residents of Davis Street have been told to move down into the town. They were given short notice to relocate and to take all their valuables with them; there had been some objections all to no avail. The street had to be cleared according to the rules of war – to protect civilians from over-shoots or short-fall shots.

Rod and Lil's house had already been occupied by a family from Callaghan Road, so I wouldn't have to worry about that place for a while. If the shooting gets serious goodness knows what will happen then. Surely that won't happen now. The British have demonstrated their capability at Goose Green and just by landing at San Carlos they must have raised more than a few eyebrows on the other side and elsewhere in the world.

Not much to do in the dockyard on a day like this, I fussed about in the office for a while. I made some long-handled scoops for boiler cleaning, bending up flat iron and attaching them to wooden handles.

The army cook had some lads chopping up wood for his fire, the usual delightful smell of vegetables cooking with herbs was heavy in the air. Propaganda smells. One day a chap had shown me a piece of meat he had found in his ration; it was half the size of a teaspoon, this was the only meat he had had for 1½ months. Their MPs, special forces and other troops milling round in the dockyard at odd times would discreetly and politely ask for a cigarette. Anything which looked like food left unattended disappeared rapidly. The various units close by would send a man into the dockyard to collect a bucket full of whatever the cook had magicked up in his cut-down 40-gallon fuel drums. None of them seemed to be having a square meal, all good stuff for fighting forces. What's that about an army marching on its stomach?

I took a walk down through the dockyard and saw Malcolm talking to a middle-aged Argentine officer. I had noticed these two conversing before. I got the keep off signal so perambulated until the conflab was over.

'What's that all about then?' I inquired.

'He is some sort of medic from the town hall, and a bit of propaganda from either side doesn't do any harm. He told me how good his troops are even though a lot of them have trench foot. I told him about the napalm they had found at Goose Green – that really upset him, he was horrified.'

1 o'clock, knock off time.

There was a bit of excitement after lunch, some shouting outside and the sound of running feet. I looked out through the front windows and saw a young conscript running along the road pursued by a bunch of weapon brandishing soldiers, including one of the blokes who periodically wanted a fire extinguisher refilled. This didn't look like a regimental paper chase. Then heavy AA gunfire. I didn't think they were having a go at the young chap too, must be something of ours about. I popped outside and had a squint upwards to the sou'east and there was a pink parachute drifting down with the nor'west wind and going out of sight behind the hill. A Chinook helicopter lifted up from the football field and flew off in the same direction. A few locals ran towards the football field, among them John Smith with Jeremy and Martin, and their faithful white dog.

The conscript had been caught and was being brought back under close guard. I went along the road to meet Valerie and saw the Chinook land again. Some Argy cameramen were present and some armed men who kept everyone at a distance. A figure descended from the helicopter, that's funny – I didn't think British Royal Navy pilots wore khaki boiler suits with white and blue emblems on their shoulders. Another own goal?[1]

Wednesday, 2 June 1982

Valerie's diary

Day off.

Fog on the deck from the n/e. Drizzle.

Pam and Nigel came for lunch. We enjoyed some of the ox kidneys in sauce.

---

1. We later heard that a British pilot had indeed been shot down as well. He landed in the sea and hung on to the Wolf Rock (3 miles offshore) for some hours until dark, when he was rescued by a Royal Navy rescue team.

'Greenfly' are getting dug into Phyllis's hen run, opposite our houses.
All sorts of rumours about the closeness of our troops.
Pope finishes 6 day visit to UK.

Neville's diary

The Argentine Red Cross hospital ship *Bahia Buen Paraiso* had been in the
harbour yesterday and offloaded a lot of stuff in the hours of darkness.
There are some new troops in evidence in the town, did they come in the
'hospital' ship, and what exactly did a 'hospital' ship carry that warranted
offloading in the dark?

I had the usual morning natter with Malcolm. I asked him: 'What's all
the noise and searchlights in the harbour at all hours of the night?'

'The bloke from the town hall told me they are scared of an SAS raid in
the dark and have the patrol boat going up and down the harbour sweep-
ing with its searchlight and throwing hand grenades into the water to dis-
courage underwater swimmers.'

He also intimated that I would have a boiler to clean in the morning
tomorrow and should get the gear ready: 'Orders from above, you know.'

So, with the aid of David Phillips, I altered and adjusted the shovels and
scoops to suit the case and got the industrial vacuum cleaner from the
plumbers, all ready for the off at first thing.

There's not a lot you can do between the hours of 8.30am and 1pm. We
are still getting paid for an 8 hour day though, and the clocks haven't been
put back either, [so] it gets light very late. The standing finance committee
wouldn't like the hours worked for the hours paid ratio.

Pam and Nigel had come over from the 'Bug House' and cooked some
of their ox kidneys from the deep freezer. Pam had made a wonderful
sauce and with some fresh vegetables it made the meal of the century.

A bunch of young Argy troops were making a great effort at digging in,
in the hen run in front of Phyllis's house, just across the road from us. We
had an excellent view of all goings on there. A large hole had been dug and
the walls reinforced with old drums filled with earth. Bales of wool and
tussock had been piled up to disguise the hide-away. Paths had been dug
to the corner of the property where a section of the fence had been
removed to facilitate access from the house which they had commandeered on the corner of King Street and St Mary's Walk. They were
reputed to be the men from Pebble Island; if so, they were probably air
force.

I had just gone out the front gate to go over and have a word with
Father when there was a great barrage of gunfire. AA and other assorted

guns opened up at the back of the town. The officer in charge of the boys in the hen run ran up across the green from the fire station direction. I indicated the noise and said: 'Geese for dinner!'

He stopped and looked at me and said 'Oh, bloody funny.'

He had words with the sergeant supervising the diggers, who by this time had taken shelter in the hen house, and then they moved off somewhere at a fast rate of knots.

The sergeant had a very interesting sawn off 12 bore shotgun with a pump action, probably not sawn off but a custom made short barrelled riot gun. He had a belt round his waist full of aluminium cased shells. I asked him politely if I could examine his gun, [and] he replied equally politely that I couldn't as his superiors might get the wrong idea.

Father seemed rather chirpy. I remarked on this and his reply caused me to be a little concerned.

'Well, I have had a visitor for a little while each night. This came about when I was listening to my radio in the dark in the front room one night. An officer walked in, he said he oversaw the transport which was parked up in front of the house each night. He said that he had heard voices and no lights so decided to have a look. I said to him it's not the Phantom Operator, he laughed at that. Now he pops in every night after dark to see I'm ok. He knows you can't come over after curfew. He won't have a beer or anything to eat, he says it wouldn't be right.'

Father and the old chap who lived across the road had a little arrangement between them; they would leave their outer door unlocked so that if anything should happen to either one, persons looking for them would not have to break down the door. Father kept up this practice which is how the officer was able to get in.

Valerie was on a day off, so we had a domestic evening, listening to the sound of heavy guns, she was knitting, the girls doing things and I reading the same page for the tenth time.

Rachel remembers ...

With no school, most of my friends gone and not being allowed out alone, I had plenty of time on my hands. One of the things that took up many of my hours was making elaborate dolls' houses out of cardboard boxes. I would divide the box into rooms and cut out windows and doors. The rooms were decorated with pictures of furniture, rugs, curtains, etc., that I had cut out of magazines and catalogues. I made glue from a paste of flour and water. Inspired by the house in 'The Sound of Music', I would dream that I was living in such a beautiful, grand, peaceful, safe house.

Thursday, 3 June 1982

Valerie's diary

Day off.

Fog on the deck again. Light n/w wind. Damp.

Apparently town is surrounded by British troops, yet still the Argentines won't give in.

Leaflets are being dropped by Harriers asking them to surrender and [offering] free passage.

Isobel crocheting a multi-coloured table mat.

Neville spent morning cleaning stoves, he got filthy.

Neville's diary

By the time I got to work the thick fog had lifted sufficiently for Malcolm to find my office.

'Get your gear together old son and give the senior school boiler a clean-up.'

'That's a bit like the lion's den, isn't it?'

'Not at all old chap, just keep smiling and you'll get a cigar and a cup of coffee.'

'I saw Bob with some wooden crosses, I hope that's not an omen?'

'No fears, chay.'

Off we went, Davey and me.

The town wasn't all that busy, just a few trucks and a couple of troops on foot. A lot of activities going on at night no doubt. I hadn't been down John Street this far for a few weeks, so we had a good squint at Mrs Perry's house with all its bullet holes. The road outside the school was all churned up from heavy vehicles turning into the large playground at the front of the wooden building. In the south west corner of the grounds is a long building which normally housed the Headmaster's office and the seniors' classroom. All sorts of punishment were meted out in that office, I'd had to pay for misdemeanours a couple of times myself.

There were lots of forty-gallon drums on end and filled with peat and rubble along the south side of the school. Gun barrels were poking out through holes between the drums, several youngish men in attendance.

I said to Davey that I hoped the safety catches were on.

'Yes, chay.'

The Cathedral is of course on the northern boundary of the school play area. In the yard is situated a science and handicraft block and a building for the camp education office. This has a radio telephone system for its pupils in outlying areas now that the boarding school at Darwin no longer functions. We entered the school yard at the south east corner which was, in my days, called the girls' gate. We checked the fuel level in the tank at this point also.

There were several men ambling round, but they took no notice of us. What a mess the yard was in. All the slabs broken and churned up; we'll never play rounders in there again.

An officer appeared from the elaborate construction around the stoke hole door. He invited us in and pointed to the furnace. I opened the flue doors and had a look with the aid of a hand lamp we'd brought. What a heap of soot, all powdery and black. I asked for some more light and a chap came in with an aldis-type lamp which was like a floodlight. We began to lift out the soot with the scoops. When we had taken out all the loose bulk, I improvised a connection for the vacuum cleaner as all the power points were occupied by things they didn't want touched. While Davey used the cleaner, I pointed out to the officer where a fire had all but destroyed the building and emphasised that naked flames in a wooden building were not ideal and could be fatal. He said that they had that all under control and would we take a cup of coffee? We declined. Our throats were caked up with soot and we would have a job to swallow any liquid for a while. A beer would have been better, but we didn't push our luck.

We told the officer that someone would be along to light the fire as we were cleaners and didn't know about the lighting part. We said farewell and departed quietly out through their blackout curtains and back to the dockyard.

And guess what next. Davey was given other employment for the day. Me, I was off to Cable Cottage. Again.

'Very sorry and all that,' said Malcolm

'I know, the stove's gorn out.'

And off I went along to Cable Cottage.

Now I knew something of what the Red Cross ship had brought into Stanley. Food. The residents of Cable Cottage had had a session of grilling steaks on the hot plate. What a lot of lucky Argentine officers they must be, all that hot fat dripping down into the burner and not a conflagration.

I could hear aircraft engines; a couple of the officers ran out to have a look and came back in shaking their heads. The boys stood round looking glum. There was a different youngster with them, a serious looking chap, he had Hilger's Para cutlass and was taking thin slices off a whole ham. He took the slices and some bread rolls into the front of the house where the sounds of merriment bubbled up. One of the other officers came into the kitchen with two of the largest chickens I have ever seen. He put them in a roasting pan and split them open down the breast bone, filled the cavities with chopped onions and tomatoes with a pinch or two of herbs and seasoning, then demanded to know when the stove was ready and get a move on.

The new chap came back in and spotting the chickens said 'Goody goody, a nice meal.'

'This is officers' food; you are having rice.'

More glum looks from the three boys.

A truck stopped outside; another of the residents poked his head in and said 'Quatro muertes' ('Four dead').

I guess a Harrier had hit some of his men. Hilger came back into the room and asked if all was well with the cooker. He didn't look too happy either. Discretion etc, I said Yes. I was just off away.

As I had exchanged the burner at Cable Cottage, I decided to clean up the one I had brought back while I was still a bit on the mucky side. All the people I passed on the way back to the office either smiled or had a good giggle. I wondered why.

Mrs Bennett wasn't a bit amused when I got home.

'Have you looked in a mirror lately?'

'No dear.'

Oh dear, I was a lot blacker than I thought, no wonder all and sundry were having a laugh.

'And you smell, and don't put those hands near me.'

'Yes/no dear.'

The Harriers have been dropping leaflets as well as other things, urging the Argies to surrender, offering free passage home and warning that they are surrounded by British troops.

Sounds of singing during the night, the diggers in the hen run opposite have taken up residence in the bunker.

A quiet night. I wondered if the morrow would bring a rash of stove cleaning or were the steaks just the perks of the storekeeper/supplies officer (Hilger).

Friday, 4 June 1982

Valerie's diary

4–12.

Fog on the deck. Moderate n/e wind.

Quiet day military and hospital wise.

Wind got up during evening then dropped. Moon almost full.

Neville's diary

Not a lot of noise this morning, but a great feeling of tenseness. I checked the appliances in the central station and the hospital, as per normal Friday routines, but abandoned the idea of trekking down to the east end pump. It was in foreign territory and passes and lengthy explanations would be necessary, even if we have the right to live in liberty, we always have had and will, but proving it may be a little noisy.

Anyway, the pump is a good British one and hopefully will defy any attempts at vandalism and start first go when required.

The colonel had asked if some of the men in the dockyard would undertake some welding jobs for 'them' to which Malcolm gave a definite 'No'; that would be against Geneva Conventions having civilians working on machines of war.

George and another lad from the colonel's office had been seen lugging a whopping big machine gun on a tripod through the dockyard. It was deduced from this that the work requested would be to mount this and other guns on the back of trucks. The order then went out that no one was to be on the dockyard over the weekend. We guessed that 'they' would be doing the job themselves. Malcolm asked if I would give a hand in the Central Store until knock off time. This didn't pose any difficulty as I had worked in the store for four years until I had taken the job in the fire office at new year.

There wasn't much building maintenance going on at the moment, so sales were right down. Just a couple of plumbing items. I wandered into the small office where we had had our coffee breaks. I did what store men do when waiting for customers, I looked out the window. Not a pretty sight, all mud, muck and foreign bodies.

This was one of Stanley's first buildings. Upstairs, on the second floor, is a wealth of historical snippets chalked and pencilled on the beams and boarding of the roof. This building was the barracks and headquarters of the original military settlers. The writings refer to the names of ships and their dates of arrival in the Islands plus other facts of interest.

Oh! Blast, there's a customer, in fact two. Two Argy officers, one with a familiar face and the other I had not seen before. He was not so pleasantly disposed and demanded a radio. To my knowledge the store stocked many things, some of which were strange, but radios did not come to mind. The officer I had seen before said that the radio sets were kept downstairs. The colonel then appeared in the doorway, the stranger though only a Lieu-tenant, did not salute but the other did and told the colonel what was wanted. The colonel said it was ok and to get Tony, then he left. I gave

Tony a ring on the phone, he came up the outer stairs in a few moments and sorted the Argies out. While we had been waiting, I noticed the stranger didn't have a gun holster, but he kept fiddling with his bayonet; not a nice person. The radios were the amateur radio and 2 metre transceiver sets which had been handed in back in April by the general public. I had wondered where they had been stored. I suppose Tony had a list of owners matched with a list of serial numbers. The Argies were obviously taking them for their own use and giving a receipt; legalised stealing some would call it.

On the way home I passed the young chap who had done a runner, being escorted by the marine I had seen at the FIC jetty on 2nd April. They both nodded courteously but looked very dejected, I noticed the prisoner was carrying a spoon and a plate ready for some of the fuel drum stew.

Valerie went over to the hospital for 4 o'clock and would stay overnight as usual. She had taken up residence in the x-ray room as it had some good stout walls and barring a direct hit was pretty secure.

The wind that had risen had driven off the fog during the day and died down. Now the almost full moon made the harbour bright and sparkly. Who else was watching the wavelets?

The radio was full of crackles and a lot of blaah, some of it man-made 'static', but the natural noises could portend a fine day tomorrow. Some American representatives to the United Nations seem to be confusing the issue. We're tired of all this to-ing and fro-ing and changes of attitudes.

Saturday, 5 June 1982

Valerie's diary
8–4.
Fine morning. Light n/w wind.
Helicopters are grounded but a Chinook flew between the football field and their military hospital.[2]
Heavy bombardment during evening/night.
Finished off pink doll's hat. Isobel has the crocheting bug.

Neville's diary
A fine Saturday morning, the static was right.
As the windows [are] covered with the blackouts, we can't open them. The whole house smells musty. We will see what we can do to air the house

---

2. This is a very short distance. The Argentine military hospital was in the unused buildings close to the end of the racecourse.

today. We are really fed up with sleeping on the floor too. A firm mattress is supposed to be beneficial to the posture, but this is ridiculous.

The helicopters, usually so busy, were not flying except for one Chinook lifting off the football field and landing at the military hospital four or five hundred yards away on the hill behind Government House. This 'hospital' is really the hostel built for the children who would have come into town instead of going to Darwin Boarding School. A wonderful modern construction utilising wire mesh sprayed with a mixture of cement and silicone adhesive, a process they called Gunite. The large span flat roof was declared unsafe by the director of public works and the building had not yet been used. The superintendent of education, fearing for the safety of his building when he saw that the Argies had mounted a light rapid fire anti-aircraft gun on this flat roof, went to the senior person at this 'hospital' and complained to him. He was told that there was no problem, the roof was being supported and to come and have a look.

Fair enough they had supported the roof, using cases of ammunition.

Another resident at the west end of the town said that he had watched a group of conscripts being shown how to use a machine gun on a tripod. One of the lads had panicked, causing the gun to gyrate on its tripod spraying bullets everywhere until the instructor had bravely managed to stop the thing in full flood.

I walked down to Jimmy's emporium for some stores. His is a handy place as the West Store is only open for a couple of hours in the morning. As I turned the corner to the shop, three Argies stopped me and produced a shopping list. One proceeded to read out in perfect English: 'Two bottles of Gin, 1 dozen best tonic water and a bottle of whisky. Get this for us, old chap', and he produced a large wad of banknotes.

'Not likely, you're not having any booze.'

Apparently, the conscripts were getting paid daily in cash. The MP at the door of the shop came towards us and the three moved on. This is happening every day outside the shops. Mostly they are asking for food and cigarettes, sometimes weapons are produced to assist matters.

Isobel is busy with her crocheting – she's hooked! Valerie had been making a knitted doll for quite a while; it will measure 3 feet tall when finished. The hat was completed to-night.

Oh! Here we go again, Bang thump wallop all night.

Sunday, 6 June 1982

Valerie's diary

4–12.

Gale force winds from n/w with driving rain.

Gave Les and Chris a bottle of rum with thanks for volunteering their time at the hospital.

All the British troops together at Mt Kent, Gurkhas have landed.

Noisy evening from Sandy and the boys.[3]

Israelis invade Lebanon, big air battles.

Neville's diary

A beautiful Sunday.

Gale force nor'easterly wind and rain. All hatches battened down. I don't think the bunker across the road is in use today.

According to the BBC, all the British troops are supposed to be together on Mt Kent. This is quite a big mountain by local standards, but still it must be pretty crowded.

And the Gurkhas have landed.

Oh dear. Oh dear. Oh dear, the end is in sight.

Another musical night. Heavy on the beat. All verses and choruses by Sandy (Woodward not McPherson) and his boys.

Monday, 7 June 1982

Valerie's diary

8–4.

Woken at 3.15am by Les and Chris playing dice with the MPs – I sorted that one out!

Noisy morning from ground and sea.

Full moon, clear morning, sunny, rapidly became overcast during afternoon. Barometer dropping.

Harrier nobbled a gun on the racecourse in a quick dash.

3 British journalists held in Tierra del Fuego, all appeals seemingly failing.

Neville's diary

'Good news Nev!' Malcolm had sneaked up on me again.

'Oh yeah?'

'You've been itching to see the inside of the police station for a while, go on over and take a squint at their stove – and you do not speak nor understand Spanish, claro?'

---

3. Admiral Sir John Forster 'Sandy' Woodward commanded the Task Force.

'Si!'

I was met at the front door of the police house by an MP just as I was going to ring the front doorbell. He took me round the outside to the rear or kitchen door (tradesman's entrance). Someone had tried to dig an air raid shelter in the grounds. They had struck a sewer and the hole had filled up with something nasty and the poor lad was bailing it out. At the back of the building were scattered bits of rockets and lumps of aircraft, souvenirs no doubt. Or trophies.

I was led into the kitchen, which was not normally a bright well-lit place. Today, with black poly bags at the windows and a 25-watt bulb, it was positively gloomy. The stove was out and cold and had been for a while. I asked to see the fuel tank which proved to be half full of kerosene. The fault must be in the filters or because of a barbecue as in Cable Cottage.

I opened the fire box and took off the hot plate, just plain old dirt. I disconnected the fuel pipe and began to strip down the burner. In came one of the young MPs with a cup of coffee.

'Please sir.'

'Oh, thank you very much.'

I continued. The door leading to the rest of the house and the police station proper opened. An elderly officer whom I had seen on the road before, came in. He looked all around and shut the doors leading off the kitchen.

He then very quietly asked me if I had any children. Was this a sinister overture?

'Yes, two.'

'Ah very good.'

He came closer and popped two paper- wrapped hard boiled sweets into the top pocket of my boiler suit.

'For the children.'

I thanked him.

He went back through the house humming to himself.

I cleaned off the top of the oven and took the hot plate outside to the rubbish bin. I scraped off the caked-up dirt and brushed off the burner. I had started to reassemble the parts when the connecting door opened once again;, another officer came in. He looked as if he had been in the wars sometime. He had a scar on his face from the forehead down through his eyes, the side of his nose and lip to his chin as if he had walked into an upright sword. He went through the same procedure as the previous bloke! Lucky old Wizz and Rachel. Two whole boiled sweets each.

I realised later that they were British ration pack sweets. I was getting on famously with the job when there was a commotion in the back kitchen. Seven or eight heavily armed men came in, they were covered in mud and dirt, they flopped into the hard wood chairs round the table. The young MP came in with a tray of cups of coffee. The leader of the group shouted at him to explain who had given the order to bring the coffee. The young chap said that it was the custom of the house to show hospitality and bring in coffee for visitors.

Well!!!!

The automatic rifles, machine guns, pistols, machetes and big knives dumped on the table didn't bother that lad, he just passed round the cups.

An even older officer came in through the house door. He usually prowled round the town wearing a bright red beret and had lanyards and other things attached to his person. I had seen him in Bloomer's office too.

I noticed then that the door had a Spanish list of the severity of alarms pinned to it: Grey alert was an attack from the sea. Blue, an attack from the air. Green, an attack by land forces.

The visitors were asked to sit and smoke if they wished.

'What about him?' one pointed at me.

'Oh, he is a local and doesn't understand us.'

'Huh?' I don't think I flinched a millimetre.

They proceeded to discuss the list of alarms pinned on the back of the door and what the responses should be. They were getting worried.

By this time, I was checking the depth of the fuel in the burner with my fingers crossed. I was in the middle of a war briefing. Cheeky devils kept shooting questions at me in Spanish. The meeting finished. I was waiting the 20 minutes to make sure the fuel was right. I showed the lads how to regulate the fuel flow and departed having exuded a lot of cold sweat. I guessed Malcolm would be interested in what had been happening during my visit to the *Calabozo*.[4] He was waiting for my report.

Other happenings were that a Harrier had made a mad dash down the valley towards the racecourse and had taken out a gun site at Felton's Stream. I hope everyone had some washing on their lines as it passed in case it was taking photos. The noise of gunfire and explosions of the morning had died away to a sporadic bang.

Valerie came home muttering about Les and Chris who were living in at the hospital, voluntarily driving a land rover day and night for the doctor when called out. She thought that as things were coming to a head, a token

---

4. Spanish for dungeon.

of appreciation would be in order, so she took over a bottle of rum for both of them last night.

She was woken at 3.15am by a rattling and clicking sound which she couldn't place, so donning her duffel coat on top of her nightie she sallied forth in true matronly fashion to investigate. She found Les and Chris teaching the two MP guards how to play poker dice. That rapidly came to a halt. Matron resumed her sleep.

We had a quiet night at home, rations are thinning out.

Tuesday, 8 June 1982

Valerie's diary
4–12.
Light n/w wind, sunny spells.
Few thumps and bumps.
Heavy fighting in Syria and air fights.
On the R/T a British naval captain called up and attempted to speak to General Menendez; their Capt Hussey stood in. These talks are being held off until 10.30am tomorrow.
British troops recaptured Fitzroy, Bluff Cove several days ago and fixed the bridge there.
Monsunen[5] is back in our own hands.
Heavy losses during landings at Fox Point.[6]

Neville's diary
Not a lot to do, checked a few extinguishers and pottered about.
There is some Argy activity in the dockyard each morning now. Four of 'them' appear in a 'borrowed' land rover, and tow away the sludge pump. This is a slow running suction pump used to take away water which has seeped into foundation trenches and suchlike, on building sites. 'They' take it away to lift out the water from their gun sites and dugouts at the back of town. Anyone knows that if you dig a hole in peat it fills with water, and 'they' have put some big guns in some big holes in the peat.

All these 'borrowed' vehicles have made more locals slouch along with their hands further in their pockets. It has long been customary to wave to passing vehicles as the driver passing you is either a relative or a neighbour, not any more though.

Valerie, due to go on duty at 4pm, had a nice meal ready for lunch. How she keeps on coming up with these culinary delights with the food supplies

---

5. *Monsunen* was the FIC coastal freighter, usually based in Stanley.
6. This was the attacks on the *Sir Tristram* and *Sir Galahad*.

as they are beats me. She said there had been a bit of excitement on the Dr's rounds on the R/T. A British officer had called up and wanted to talk to Menendez; Captain Hussey had taken the call and there would be further talks tomorrow.

The FIC vessel *Monsunen* was back in the hands of locals at Goose Green.

The evening news from the Beeb said there had been landings of troops at Fox Point at Bluff Cove/Fitzroy, but unfortunately heavy losses had been sustained.

There are more and more Argies coming into town as the British push eastward. They all seem to be hungry. Empty houses are being broken into, calling cards being left, usually brown jobbies. It's going to take a lot of carbolic soap and disinfectant to clean up when we have a water supply again.

The roof water still tastes bloody awful even when boiled. Some of 'them' are using the lower level water supply reservoir to wash clothes and bathe in.

I wonder how badly off the Argies are for food. The 'Red Cross' ship pops in and offloads at night. They are supposed to be bringing in food. There is a mobile kitchen being towed round the town but would seem to be supplying hot water only.

Wednesday, 9 June 1982

Valerie's diary
8–4.
Frost first thing. Not too severe. Light n/w wind.
Moody Brook bombed with cluster bombs.
Thumps, bangs, small arms fire most of the day.

Neville's diary
Clear frosty morning with a light nor'west wind.
Told the girls to keep their heads down and not to speak to any soldiers. Then I pushed off to work. Several Argies in jolly mood made the remark that there hadn't been any Gurkhas yet and shook their heads from side to side to indicate that their heads were still attached to their bodies.

What can I do at work?

Just fuss about at the central station with a paint brush when the frost lifts. The R/T station next door is in a bit of a mess. The points where the receiver and transmitter aerials pass through the wall have been damaged by choppers. The wires have been cut several times and hasty repairs have been made. There is a long length of cable leading from the garage next door to the half-buried metal shipping container in the garden across the lane. It will provide power for those who use the container as a shelter.

The streets are getting dirtier. Lack of toilet facilities is the explanation, eyes down and watch where you tread.

There's a lot of small arms fire going on as well as the heavier accompaniment in the background. The cheeky Harriers had a go at Moody Brook and did a fair amount of damage to the newer buildings.

Rumour has it that before the Argies surrender, they will all have half an hour firing off their weapons in a token fire fight. Each time a batch of small arms fire happens, all spirits rise in hope.

Meanwhile, the cook in the dockyard still boils up something for the troops in the yard. Bunches of troops march down into the shower house for a hot saltwater shower of heated, unfiltered, harbour water. I wonder how long the feeling of wellbeing that they march out with lasts.

Bonugli had to deal with a chimney fire the other night. He and his companions carried an old lady out of the house where the chimney was on fire and sat her in the Firefly. They proceeded to extinguish the fire by spraying water down the chimney with the light hose on the reel. Very effective but not recommended as the cold water on the hot brick work could cause it to crack, not to mention a huge mess in the house. He did, nevertheless, deal with what could have so easily turned into a major incident. I would not like to have to call out the blokes to a fire during the night under present circumstances, it would be simpler to let the thing burn out. However, a slight breeze could destroy a whole street of our wooden houses quite quickly. There are too many strangers in the town now to be out at night, even with the appropriate guard.

The old lady told me that it was nice of the young man to keep her company in the rover and he spoke such nice English, such a shame he disappeared so quick when the others came back. I wonder ...

We don't see anything of Bloomer now, except when he dashes past in his truck. I haven't been summoned to the Secretariat lately either, they must be too busy to concern themselves with us.

Quite a bit of activity round the hills after dark too.

Peter King and Kathleen Cheesemond are doing a wonderful job on the BBC's 'Calling the Falklands' programme. It is possible now to listen without interference as more frequencies have been opened up to broadcast to us, messages of good luck and keep our chins up, etc.

The detector vans still cruise the town.

What will tomorrow bring?

Thursday, 10 June 1982

Valerie's diary

4–12.

Fine morning. Light N wind. Sunny.

Went down the road to the West Store for some food shopping, very muddy underfoot.

Walked up to Haines house, a few pops and bangs.

Quiet evening, everyone has the knitting bug.

Noisy at 12 midnight ish.

Red Cross ship is in again, unloading during the night.

Neville's diary

Fine morning again. Valerie due to go on duty at 4.

Off to work down the hill, the usual crowd of Argies hanging round looking concerned.

   Malcolm came along.

   'Oh boy! What can I do for you this morning?'

   'Cable Cottage stove, chay.'

   'Ok, Mr Binnie sir!'

I picked up my tool bag and trudged off up the road. Not the usual happy smiling faces in 'their' kitchen. The boys really have a down on, and the atmosphere is very bleak.

   The Cable Cottage temporary residents must have had some supplies in the 'Red Cross ship', the stove is really clouted up with fat again. I started the all too familiar routine of dismantling the burner etc. There is a serving trapdoor from the kitchen to the dining room next door. This was a bit ajar and I could hear a 2-way radio conversation going on. Perhaps they have a communication set in the other room today, dodging about so they can't be pinpointed. Another new thing is the bloke sitting on a chair in the corner of the kitchen. He's the one who always smiles, the one who wears a rolled-up balaclava hat. He only has a bit of smile now and he is continuously stripping down his pistol and reassembling it, must be nervous about something. The burner is far too dirty to clean on the spot and I forgot to bring the spare one in the rush. I nipped off to get the replacement from the office, I didn't fancy being in this atmosphere for very long. On the corner outside the house was standing a sentry, I hadn't seen that before. He did a smart slope arms and then saluted by slapping the butt of his weapon with the flat of his hand, such a nice smile too, lots of teeth.

I found Malcolm in the blacksmiths shop; I needed some wicks from him as my stock had run out. Even my trick of burning off the old ones on the reflector plate did no good with being doused in fat.

The lads who had built a shelter at the rear of the smithy were singing. I asked Malcolm what it was, he said that he couldn't translate it all but it was something to do with home and family. Pretty mournful too.

I returned to Cable Cottage, the weather had deteriorated, and gone cloudy. The little sentry went through the process of saluting again, I returned the honours by lifting my hat.

The radio had stopped, everyone was all smiles. Hilger came in with a white polypropylene tarpaulin which he laid down on the floor, the young driver screamed and stamped on it and was reprimanded severely. But there was still an atmosphere, something had happened in the conversation on the radio. Was it Menendez talking to base? Had the General been in the next room talking? Although the guns were not visible, I don't think they were too far away. I completed the clean up and started the stove, giving it a few minutes to draw up. I told them I would be back in a couple of days to check on it, said cheerio and departed for the dock yard. The sentry was still at his post, really odd how oriental he looked. Be a bit of a laugh if he was a Gurkha.

Some International Red Cross personnel had arrived in the ship which was in the harbour. They had come to check on the establishments being used by the Argies as hospitals for their wounded. I think they were being lodged overnight in the hotel down the road. The three of them came out of the LADE office a few feet away from me. I called out 'Hello, Good Morning,' they looked round down their noses and it was clear that they were not interested in communicating with a local, snooty lot.

The afternoon had really turned grotty and overcast. I went over to see Father. Uncle Harold came out as I went in.

Dad said that Harold was sleeping down at the West Store with some other people; they had told him that if he wasn't in the house all day to put some clothes out on the line to let the Argies know it wasn't an empty house.

I had a look at Moody Brook with the binoculars. What a mess, with mud and craters all round. Strangely the green house was still standing, as was the ever-strong Belsen block.

Back home for curfew. I made some supper for the girls and myself. I can't work up much of an appetite these days for a second meal. I smoke far too much as well.

Listened to the news on the radio. A Vulcan bomber, which had made an emergency landing in Brazil on the way home from a raid, had been permitted to leave after being stripped of its defensive missiles. If Vulcans are still raiding that would explain the really heavy thumps in the night.

The local broadcast by the Argies still churns out the same old guff.

I took a stroll down the passage to the front porch, blimey, there's some sort of a battle going on over at Fairy Cove. Some rather large tracer bullets being fired from the west and smaller returns from the east. The large shots come from a source which is moving rather fast. Do the Brits have tanks? If so, how did they get round the Argy lines and through the swamps behind Courtney Ridge? They are certainly giving somebody hell over there. Let's hope they don't puncture the large fuel tanks at the Camber.

The night wears on now to the familiar sounds of thumps, bangs and crashes.

Friday, 11 June 1982

Valerie's diary
8–12.
Heavy frost, light NW wind, sunny spells.
Red Cross men are staying in the Upland Goose Hotel and are visiting Argie hospitals – the beaver hanger, town hall, school hostel etc.
Intermittent shell and small arms fire all morning.
Police station hit by a missile.
Firing started in earnest during evening, tracer bullets, shells etc. etc.

Neville's diary
Frost, cloudy, bright patches developed later in the day.
Was just waiting for 8.30, having taken down the blackout, ready to go down the hill to work. I could hear some blokes coming down the hill by Uncle Harold's house. A barrage of AA guns and the blokes take shelter. A large black helicopter lifts up over the fairy cove ridge and discharges two rockets straight at me and hovers there. Meanwhile, a Harrier had flown low over Uncle's house then turns on its side and seems to fly between the rockets. A large splash in front of the Red Cross ship and a big explosion from the police station. The girls are a bit concerned as to what is going on. The helicopter is gone now. It looked like the pictures of a Sea King.

Snap decision, phoned Malcolm and said I wouldn't be in today.
'That's ok.'

If there's going to be any reprisals I wanted to be with my children.

What was the object of that exercise? Obviously, the path had been cleared by the tanks or whatever last night. I rather fancy there had been a missile site under the rocks at Fairy Cove. There's plenty of bods running about now. Valerie rang and asked if I was going to stay with the girls, and when it had quietened down to go and do some food shopping.

Later, I popped over to see Father. He was ok, he wanted a few bits and pieces from the store. I walked down John Street, all seemed in order that way. I returned via the front road. The sergeant was outside the police station directing traffic. He had a great big smile on his face, just happy to be alive I expect.

I gave Dad a full report on the damage. The northwest corner of the police station house was missing and also some of the wall. Now comes the speculation. The Argies said it was a cowardly attempt to sink the 'hospital ship'. The locals have it that Menendez was scheduled to have a conference in the town hall and that was the target. Where would the rockets have hit if the Harrier hadn't put them off?

Small arms fire most of the day.

Nothing about the raid on the BBC news. I had a look out of the upstairs window, there's a lot of noise coming from the back of the mountains, I'll see if I can get a recording of this. We didn't have any batteries for the tape recorder so I connected up an extension power lead. I switched off the downstairs lights and crawled a few yards up the garden. I switched on the recorder, it was going nicely, and then came a power cut. Someone at the power station threw the switch whenever anything like an air raid was imminent. Must have played hell with the governors on the generators.

Saturday, 12 June 1982

Valerie's diary

Day Off, worked 8.30–4.

Karen called me to go on duty early. Busy night.

Shell hit John Fowlers' house last night. Sue Whitley, Mary Goodwin and Doreen Bonner killed. RIP.

Several injuries.

Light NW wind. Sunny spells. Black frost. Very icy.

All sorts of thumps. Small arms fire around town.

Uncle Harold's house taken over by the Argies. They're also using the fire station to sleep in.

Quiet evening but Moody Brook razed during evening.

Neville's diary

Valerie was called on duty at 8.30 instead of a day off. Karen had had a busy night. A shell from the naval bombardment had fallen short and burst on Ross Road West in front of the houses behind the Monument. Three women were killed, and several other people injured. Three houses were damaged, but the wounded and fatalities were in the one building

I took the girls and went over to see that Father was ok and tell him not to go out with the roads in the black icy condition they were, due to the heavy frost last night. The ice would all disappear before lunch anyway.

A good opportunity for Rachel and I to have a peep at the mountains with the binoculars. There was a series of flashes along the ridge leading up to the Two Sisters, and a swarm of men came running down the slope towards Benders Farm and Moody Brook. The air strike was repeated, a Unimog truck came towards my point of vision on the Two Sisters track. I could make out three men shapes in the front. It was speeding along a straight stretch in the track then it vanished in a puff of smoke. I blinked but it didn't reappear. It had either hit a large mine or had been struck by a rocket. Maybe it was their mobile mortar unit, if so, that could explain the explosion, I had seen three or maybe more lives blown away.[7] Another run by Harriers, Moody Brook camp hit and well alight. More figures running and falling over. As much as I didn't want the Argentines here, I found it most disconcerting seeing them killed even through a pair of binoculars.

All sorts of thumps and bangs round the town most of the day accompanied by small arms fire.

Uncle Harold had returned to his house after lunch to find that it had been forcibly entered by some Argy officers who told him in no uncertain terms that they intended to stay and he could disappear as he didn't seem to be living in the house anyway.

The central station had also been taken over in a hurry, phone lines had been strung up between Uncle Harold's house, central station and Stan Summers' house. One of the double doors on the station had been lifted off its runners and laid on its side to give a guard clear view along the road. How would we talk our way through that lot if we're called out for a fire?

Valerie came home at 4pm, quite perturbed by the three deaths in the night. She said she'd had the bodies carried out to the mortuary from the hospital where they had lain overnight. All the wounded Argies who were able stood, the others sat upright, and all made signs of the cross as a

---

7. I walked up that piece of road a few months later. All I could see at that spot was a lot of shards of metal and a truck door twisted through the fence.

mark of respect as the bodies passed them. Then she EXPLODED: 'The BLOODY Argy reporters wanted to photograph the bodies. I told them no. I locked the mortuary door and put the key in my pocket. That key is not going back on the keyboard.'

Fusillades of small arms fire lasting for half an hour in the evening, was it nerves or did they have a reason for the shooting?

Went upstairs to have a look out the widow westwards. Gosh it was like the 5th November. Star shells, signal flares, parachute illuminations, tracer bullets. Explosions all round, firing across the valley north to south and south to north. A ship must have been firing large white parachute flares lighting up the whole valley, smaller guns were trying to shoot them down. We watched until it became too cold and went to bed.

At last, it's all happening. The people west of the Monument had all been requested to move down into town, a bit late now though.

Sunday, 13 June 1982

Valerie's diary
Day off.
Fine, sunny day. Quite warm in fact. Light NW wind.
Shell and gunfire increase from 9am ish.
3 Davis Street houses alight, fuel depot set alight on racecourse.
Ramon and Raul made empanadas for us all.
Neville showed the colonel how to put out fires.
Wind around to south. Barometer rose, snowy feeling.

Neville's diary
What a noise. 'They' have moved a gun down into town, not too far along the road from us either. 'They' are firing to the west and the shells crackle as they pass just over our chimneys.

The large gun at the Met Station is firing but it is 17 minutes between rounds.

We should have a good meal today. By the order of the visiting Red Cross people, a consignment of fresh beef has been shared out for the locals from the 'Red Cross' ship in the harbour. Ramón has invited us to his home at no. 5, for empanadas.[8]

There is an explosion seemingly from the Met Station, surely the ammunition dump has been hit, a large black cloud billows up.

---

8. Fried pastry turnovers with a tasty, spicy filling.

Pat McPhee came into Ramón's with the colonel and said would I get the hose truck out and take it away to lay hoses as Pop Newman's house was alight and they wanted water on the neighbours' house to stop the spread of the fire. The exchange must have phoned Pat when I didn't answer at home. The last time I saw him was on the FIC jetty with the pump I put there for the Argies unloading their weapons. Seems like years ago now.

Across the playing field to the central station I went.

Each Friday, I have checked the hose truck, it has always started first swing of the handle. This time it let me down. Not even a bit of a spark in the battery. I think the Argies sleeping in the fire station have been using the battery for lights in the shed. I noticed that our radios were not hanging up either.

Pat and Jumbo drew up in 212 and said not to bother, the house had burned down and there was no danger from fire spreading now. I left the truck as it was and hoped we wouldn't want it before I could get the battery charged. I went back for my lunch. While crossing the playing green I saw that a fuel dump on the racecourse had been hit and was burning furiously.

Can't do anything about that either.

The big gun was still banging away, now at 11 minutes between rounds. Just shows practice makes perfect, let's hope their aim hasn't improved correspondingly. The smaller field guns are barking away too, but not so much coming in from the West. The girls are a bit apprehensive because of the noise.

We can understand a little of how the people of West Beirut must feel. The noise goes on.

The wind had swung round to the southwest, the glass has risen, no wonder it feels a bit snowy, not a good sign at all.

A rattling good noisy night.

Peter King's message on 'Calling the Falklands' as usual: 'heads down, hearts high.' They are, don't worry.

Monday, 14 June 1982

Valerie's diary
Day off.
Light snowfall during night.
Heavy, noisy, bombardment all night.
Navy have been told via R/T that we are still scattered around the town and not just in the Cathedral as reported on the BBC last night.

We evacuated to the hospital, with heavy firing still going on.

By early afternoon it was realized all over bar the shouting, chaps!

Ceasefire not signed 'til 9pm though.

George Butler's house burned to the ground, full of ammo.

Neville's diary

Snowing.

Quite heavy snow squalls. I went off down the hill at 8.30 to work. I met up with some of the other chaps and as we got into the dockyard the snow was so thick that the visibility was about two feet in front. An Argy officer came up to us and said that there would not be any work today. 'It's all over, go home,' he said. We all turned round and went back up the hill. The snow was easing off. There were intermittent bangs and thumps, the sun came out.

We watched as Dr Alison Bleaney and her children went into the R/T station. Valerie switched on the radio and tuned into the R/T frequency saying we might hear something important. Alison spoke out:

'This is Stanley calling anyone listening. I would like to speak to Andrew Windsor, over.'

Bob Fergusson on Weddell Island answered. 'I can't help personally, but I know a man who can.'

With that a proper English accent came on and wanted to know what the bother was. Alison explained that the BBC News had said that the 160 residents remaining in Stanley were sheltering in the West Store or Cathedral. She then went on to say that there were at least 600 people still in the town and were living mainly in their own homes. The real English accent said he hoped that they were in time to stop the bombardment and signed off.

If the bombardment hadn't started, what was all the noise about for the past two days and nights?

We waved to Alison as she walked back along St Mary's Walk towards the hospital.

Dennis Place arrived at the corner and turned off the water mains with the stop valve there. He saw us in our front window and shouted to ask us what we were doing there as we should be in the hospital or West Store. Everybody had been advised to take shelter.

There was a continuous stream of soldiers coming down the hill and along the road. They were throwing down their weapons and emptying satchels into the ditches and onto the road. They took no notice of Alison as she walked along. We debated what to do.

An officer ran out of Stan Summers' house and started shooting at the passing troops and shouting to stand and fight. The answer he got could have been translated as 'Not pygmalion likely!'

That did it. We secured the house. Turned off the electricity, gas, and the fuel to the Rayburn. We locked the cats in then took our bags, hurrying along the road to pick up Father. He didn't need telling twice, I hadn't seen him move so quickly for years, even on the snow. There were soldiers passing us all the way to the hospital, throwing ammunition round like confetti at a wedding, it was impossible to put your feet down without scrunching cartridges.

Rachel remembers ...

As we rushed along Allardyce Street towards Grandad's back gate we were startled by an explosion louder than the rest. Our family were separated as Dad and Isobel ran to Grandad's, while mum and I walked there as fast as we could at my slightly slower speed. There were bullets/shrapnel splashing into the muddy puddles and onto the road beside us.

Standing in the doorway of Grandad's peat shed were two men in military gear who I didn't recognise. They didn't look at all like Argies. One was taller than the other. They had a small radio with a very long aerial. Their calm faces encouraged me on. I asked Grandad who the two men in his peat shed were.

He replied 'Oh, they're the British boys. Elvis and [name forgotten], they have been there for a few nights. They pop in for a smoke and a cup of tea in the evening when they feel cold.'

Grandad was giving shelter to British special forces!

Neville's diary continues ...

There was a load of smoke coming from the direction of racecourse road, something had happened there. The ambulance shed was well alight too. Someone said that a shell had hit it and the fuel stored there had blown up. A heap of fuel drums on the football field was being set alight by a soldier. There were some helicopters abandoned nearby. Above Government House was a Chinook standing under the trees and in front of the cable and wireless office was the big blue and white Super Puma with a camo net draped over it, must have been Menendez' escape vehicle.

It seemed as if the world and his wife were in the hospital. Valerie accompanied by Rachel went off to see about the extra food that would be required. Father found a corner with some of his old buddies. Isobel went into the x-ray room where the children were being kept busy. I couldn't settle so I just kept pacing up and down the corridor quietly, an air of great expectancy pervaded.

Capitan Hussey (Navy) and Colonel Dorrego came into the building and asked where they could find Dr Alison, as they would like her to accompany them to speak with the British forces on the radio. Mike, Alison's husband, asked them to take great care of her. They promised that they would bring her back safe and sound.

On his way out, the colonel said goodbye to me, rather formally I thought. It sounded as if the end was nigh.

Only 11.30am seems as if years have passed since we got up. Les and Chris went out for a spin in their rover to see what was going on. When they returned, they said that the roads were full of men coming down from the hills and off the Common. They also brought me back a bottle of Red Label which might come in handy for medicinal purposes.

The day had turned grey, but the snow was melting off the roads and the gunfire seemed to have stopped.

A lunch was served to everyone. Some mutton stew with mixed vegetables, not a mountain of it but hot and tasty. A few beer cans popped just like a party.

There's quite a fuss and stir. Alison, now safely back, said that Jeremy Moore[9] would be coming into town and no-one was to make a demonstration or things could get out of hand.

A crowd gathered in the windows of the waiting room and on the steps. A helicopter landed on the football field. The generals' group was met by Hussey and Bloomer; they walked down the hill past the hospital, looked up at us and smiled.

Looking out of the window someone said, 'Look, there's a Para behind Government House.' It was just possible to make out the colour of his beret, and he was still carrying his rifle.

'Oh! I'll have to get Father to see this.' I went down through the building and fetched him. 'Come along old chap and take a look at this.'

'Of all the luck, I've been waiting for this since the 2nd of April and I missed it!'

One of the Argy MPs picked up a guitar and played 'God save the Queen'.

THE FLAG WAS BACK AT GOVERNMENT HOUSE.

The major of the MP's came in and took the two lads into the Senior Medical Officer's office. He removed the firing mechanism from their

9. Major General Sir John Jeremy Moore was the commander of the British land forces.

weapons and pocketed the ammunition. His usually immaculate parka was in shreds, I asked him what had happened.

He replied with some pride in his voice: 'A British rocket. It was the first time I was not wearing my coat during the day for a long time. I am glad I wasn't when this happened.'

Obviously the rocket which hit the police station had done the damage to his parka too.

Something happening on the front road. A man walking along the pavement shouting 'I'm British, I'm British!' He certainly must be, no one else would be daft enough to do that under these circumstances. He came up to the hospital, said that his name was Hanrahan and began to interview people. A crowd gathered around him.

A nurse came through the crowd and said there had been a phone call, would I go to the power station as it was on fire.

I gathered the available lads in the hospital and sent them off with the firefly while I went down to the central station. There was a mess of discarded clothing and kit bags. I was looking at the hose laying truck [when] Malcolm came in.

'What's up?'

'Fire at the power station. I'm trying to see if there's anything attached to this truck that shouldn't be.'

'I did a course on explosives with the Marines,' Malcolm said, 'and we covered the general idea of booby traps, so I'll have a look see.'

There wasn't anything there that shouldn't be and the blessed thing started first swing of the handle. The Argies had pushed the pump out on to the road which made coupling up a lot easier. We picked up a few more blokes on the way along the road. I jumped off at the hospital corner and Malcolm took the truck and pump down to the sea wall to deploy the pump and then to lay hoses up the hill to the power station. There were some little helicopters darting about on the Wireless Ridge. The snow had thankfully gone off the hill, but I was still walking on ammunition which had been discarded.

The firefly was in action when I reached the site. Len and Kim were on the roof of the old power station office. The walls were made of blocks and the roof of corrugated iron lined with felt. That was on fire from underneath and was burning well, as were the contents of the office. The door was forced, and things got under control. Mike was soaked through to the skin; he only had a T-shirt and jeans on and was starting to shiver. I told him to hurry back to the hospital, towel down and get something dry on.

He said he felt a lot better for having been out and done something, he wasn't alone with those feelings either.

An Argy sergeant came round the corner of the building and smiled and said 'It is dangerous.'

'Fires usually are,' I said.

'No, at the other end of the building.'

I went round to the part previously used by the Plant and Transport Authority, for maintenance of the large JCBs. I was accompanied by Les and a few others. It was very warm in the building despite it being open-ended, tongues of flame were running along the wooden roof beams and the place was full of smoke. A lump of pipe through the nearest window soon cleared the air. There was an Oxy/acetylene welding set on a trolley and some butane gas cylinders by the wall. I ran the back of my hand along the cylinders – they were warm. I got them outside against a grassy bank.

There were two brown wooden boxes I hadn't seen before, definitely not motor spares. One had 3 or 4-inch diameter 4-foot-long tubes, white in colour and I think they had Browning stencilled on them. The sergeant and the officer who had now appeared, pointed to the other crate and said 'this is dangerous.'

Ha, Ha. They were the warheads for the rockets, the tubes being their motors. They were warm too. I said they should get them out into the puddle which had formed from all the water being sprayed about.

'We don't touch, are dangerous.'

I asked, 'how dangerous?' and picked up a couple and made to go out through them.

They screamed.

I shouted to shift them fast and passed the two over to the sergeant. He said only one at a time, the two Argies carried out sixteen or eighteen of the things. I noticed their holsters were open, so I kept a handy length of one-inch water pipe in my hand.

The fire extinguished, Les said he would stay on and keep an eye on things. The rest of us packed up and set off for the hospital, most of us were a bit damp too.

On the way down the hill I saw a pair of soldiers crawl out from under Bill and Barbara's house, on the curve of Brandon Road, and cross over into George Butler's house. A few minutes later an Argy jeep arrived and hooted. The two blokes came out of Butlers, climbed into the jeep and set off down the road.

On arriving at the hospital, I asked one of the MPs if he would accompany me to my home to get some dry clothes as there were lots of soldiers still milling about. The house was as we had left it. The cats were pleased to see us. It would be a bit much to expect them to stay clean for much longer, so I let them out. The MP lad remarked how nice our home was.

I picked up a couple of cans of beer as well as the clothes and went back to the hospital. The soldiers on the roads were all unarmed but looked as if it wouldn't take much to provoke them into making mischief. A couple of men were doing something to the mobile crane, which was parked alongside a garden fence, probably a bit of sabotage.

We had a hot drink in the hospital kitchen. The general and Menendez, with whatever aides they had, were still talking in the secretariat. A rumour had started that there was to be a shootout east of the town, plus a couple of other silly ideas rattling around too.

The daylight was fading rapidly, let's hope for a quiet night.

A British Parachute Regiment doctor and a sergeant medic came in. They didn't need much persuasion to have some of the lunch stew warmed up for them.

A phone call from the power station, they reported another fire. Right'o lads, lets go for it.

It wasn't the power station on fire, but George Butler's house opposite. Those two bloody Argies must have been setting something before I saw them running for the truck. It was no problem to start up the pump and redirect the hoses. There was a lot of noise from inside the burning build-ing. Explosions, and white flashes. Red and blue things flying out at us. The occasional zzip zzip like wasps flying past your ears. The back of the house was now well alight. Bob Stewart said he would take a branch off the hose and spray water on the back of the house. As he disappeared, an Argy MP came up and asked for Bennett.

'Here.'

'A message from Commodore Bloomer-Reeve: It is dangerous, the buildings are full of explosives you must get your men away.'

'Thank you.'

I shouted to Bob to stop what he was doing. I asked him to come round to the front and play water on the buildings next door to stop the fire from spreading that way. What breeze there had been had died away thank goodness. We were getting quite good at shooting down whatever the red and blue things were. The white flashes which happened when we put water in through the windows was a puzzler.

I nipped down to the hospital and asked the two paratroopers that I'd met in the kitchen what we were up against.

Their reply was a bit of a shocker: 'The red and blue things are anti-personnel mines, the white flashes are white phosphorous grenades. If the phosphorous gets on your skin, it's nasty. Mortar bombs just burn in a fire but don't kick one or they go off. The wasp noises are rifle or other bullets exploding in the fire and are going off at one sixth of their muzzle velocity. Good luck mate!'

'Ta.'

Blimey. I returned to the incident.

Arthur said: 'It's a bit dodgy here Nev and I've only got a thin jacket on.'

'Ok Arthur, I'll take the lead.'

The house was clad all over in galvanised iron, corrugated on the roof and flat iron sheets on the sides. The roof collapsed down onto the body of the fire. We continued to put water on the walls and spraying the house next door. The bangs and flashes had ceased, the walls were falling inward. Sparks from the woodwork were spinning off on the breeze which had come up slightly. Eventually it was safe enough to leave. We put the gear tidy and left it for the morning. The pump and stuff on the sea wall should be ok overnight. I thanked the boys for turning out. We were out of doors nearly five hours later than we had been for quite some weeks.

I went back to the hospital, had a hot drink and waited for the result of the peace conference. Valerie and Bill Etheridge had walked round to the Secretariat but couldn't get in nor see anything going on.

The news came through at 9pm local time that the surrender document had been signed.

More excitement, General Moore had arrived at the door and is coming in. What a welcome, he had been to the west store and spoken to the people there. He had a few blokes with him. One was a major from the Marines with a handheld radio. He was trying to convince his men that the shooting had stopped. Healso wanted to know who had said that they [the Royal Marines] had all gone away in April. There was a Lieutenant Colonel from the Royal Artillery apologising for all the noise his chaps had been making. There was a civilian reporter with them, he looked a bit scruffy, must have been short of the common amenities for a while.

They are here, it's all over. Surely, we can go home now.

No, stay put for the night, there's lots of Argies spread about and it won't be easy to inform them all immediately of the surrender. Although there has been a large white flag flying for most of the day somewhere.

I wonder if it looks like a white tarpaulin. I suppose I could claim to have seen it on Thursday in Cable Cottage.

There had been a lot of rumours floating around, like the shootout idea and the town was to be divided into two. Menendez had hedged for so long because he thought that he was surrendering the whole Argentine forces on the mainland as well.

It had gone ten o'clock, Valerie and the girls had gone to bed in the dental department. I'll have a mug of cocoa and find a corner. A helicopter pilot came in, he had landed on the football field and wanted to see what we natives looked like. He was persuaded to have a hot drink as it was a cold night.

Two more Paras came in: Jock and Scouse. 'Hi, how are you?'

There's another phone call.

'Marvin, can you get a team together and go to Giles Mercer's peat shed; it is reported to be alight. Don't take any risks if you meet with any resistance.'

'Ok.'

Another call. 'There's something on fire in the dockyard.'

'Come on, Steve, Len, who else is with us? Let's go down and have a look.'

We ran down the hill on to the sea wall. It was easy to recognise the plumbers' shed and garage. Quite a lot of noise of explosions and flashes again. They have piled up a lot of stuff in the garage and set light to it. Let's get along and have a closer look. I unlocked my office and then walked down through the dockyard. The fire was fierce. Would it spread to the Central Store and the fuel shed? Was the oil pipeline ok, or had it fractured and was letting burning diesel out into the harbour?

Marvin drove through in the Firefly.

'Everything's under control at the peat shed. We couldn't lay hoses as there was too much stuff in the way.'

'What do you mean it's all under control?'

'It burned down; fuel had been poured all over it.'

'Get the truck out now and I'll tell you why later.'

'I can get a suction down off the jetty.'

'No, just go.'

Bonugli came up to me, he saluted. He had formed his men up in three ranks with all their equipment and arms. He said that another group had come down off the hills and put a lot of explosives and things in the garage and set fire to it, [and] his men felt that it was their duty to help put the fire out.

'Thank you, no, you must get your men away and I want everyone else out as well. There are cylinders of oxygen and acetylene, bottles of butane gas, drums of kerosene, petrol and lubricating oil and lengths of timber. There are some drums of a substance called calcium carbide there also which, when wet, produces acetylene gas, and anything which your troops may have put in there. It is very dangerous and because of the powder we cannot put water on it. That is why I want the yard cleared.'

He dashed off, shouting at some men lounging in the yard to get out. He then turned his men left into file and marched them off, having saluted again and apologised for being a nuisance.

I met Marvin in the office and told him the story.

'What do we do about it?'

'Just wait until it is safe to leave. The acetylene cylinders have a safety plug which will burn out. The other stuff will burn away. The oxygen cylinders don't have a safety plug so will explode. As long as the roof holds and the south wall too there shouldn't be any spread of fire other than by radiated heat. The corrugated is pretty heavy gauge and kept on by hook bolts so no wooden frame to burn away. We will have to keep an eye on the Central Store and look at the oil line, that's all we can do as far as I can see.'

The time was 12.30am.

Tuesday, 15 June 1982

Valerie's diary
Day Off.
Snow and hail showers during night from s/e and fresh winds.
And so the Boys are in town!
Choppers [helicopters] all over the place.
Clean up in the hospital.

Neville's diary
[continued straight on from yesterday]
The time was 12.30am.
The men of the East End pump station had manhandled the large Godiva trailer pump up the front road and were ready to go into action. They were disappointed when I said no go. We would rig up the pump in a hurry if the Store caught or got too hot, but otherwise it was sit tight and wait and watch.

I walked down to the jetty and felt the oil pipe, there wasn't any heat there.

Steve [Whitley] and I walked round to the Dockyard house side of the Yard and had a look at the fire from there; the 'wasps' were zipping about.

[These 'wasps' were bullets going off, having got hot in the fire – see yesterday's entry.]

Bob Stewart nipped over to the Store, felt round the woodwork and said there was no warmth in the wood. It would have been easier to get hit by a bullet than burned by the fire. There was nothing we could do, just wait, and we had been doing a lot of that lately anyway.

The door of the Union Office was standing open. I went in expecting the worst. The Argies had been living and working in there for many weeks. I stopped in my tracks. The Colonel had said that when he left the building it would be as he found it. The floors had been scrubbed right through, the chairs stood on the conference table, no rubbish left lying about, all sparkly clean. Remarkable.

The gang had assembled in my office. We sat and stood round talking about the whole episode. Several strangers looked in.

There was a bit of a commotion outside. The civilian who was with the General's party at the hospital was trying to give some Argies a grey wooden box, but they didn't want to know. He came in and I asked him who he was.

'I'm Robert Fox [journalist]. You're the fireman, take care of these, and they're very nasty.'

I pushed the box under the bench. He asked us a few questions as to how we had got on over the past months and then went away.

The men in the LADE office were clearing out stuff and burning the papers in a rubbish bin. While passing the door, I saw, just inside the door, a pistol in a holster on a belt hanging on a chair. Aha I thought, a souvenir, I'll have that on the way back. Never put off what you can do now ... when I returned there was a bloody Argy putting the thing on.

We periodically checked the Store and other buildings in the Yard. At 2.30am the first Oxy cylinder blew with rather a loud bang which rattled the teeth. The other 2 cylinders did likewise. We had heard the acetylene gas blow off and ignite earlier on, the garage's walls and roof looked a bit mangled now. As far as I knew that was all the dangerous stuff gone and the fire was starting to subside. The men started to go off home. Steve, Len and I waited for a while until we thought it safe to leave and went back to the hospital.

The time was 4.30.

Steve and I maintained a fire watch out over the town from one of the upstairs windows in the old end of the hospital. Chris Spall had phoned and said he would do the same from the loft window at Jem Bayliss' house.

At 7am I gave Steve a nudge and decided we could call it quits. There had been a lot of rapid-fire bangs in the night. We put that down to people putting ammunition into ash drums and setting light to it.

We went down to the kitchen and got a cup of hot tea. We had had a long day. Steve's wife, Sue Whitley, was one of the ladies killed in the house on Ross Road. RIP.

There had been six major incidents in the last 24 hours, only one of which we were able to do anything about under the circumstances.

Well, the British Troops are here now, and we could all relax and go about our business as before. All will be calm and peaceful.

I must have had an hour and a half sleep in a chair. I heard Valerie's cheerful voice saying, 'You look in a bit of a mess! Where was the party? You look as if you have been out all night.'

'I have.'

I told her what had happened since I last saw her.

'Daft' was the kindest thing she said.

We found Father and suggested he stay put in the hospital until we had sorted our house out and then I would get his fire going for him.

Our home was intact. The cats were glad to see us. [Rachel was glad to see them too.]

We soon had the water and electricity on. The stove didn't take too long to heat up, we had a cup of tea using water from the rain barrel. Not using the mains water until we were told the supply was fit to drink.

Father's stove was simple, he still had one of the old Stanley Range stoves, burning peat. There wasn't a good supply in his shed, but he had just enough for the time being. I had got a decent heat up just as he walked through the door. He said he wouldn't stay over in the hospital and be a nuisance; he had enough food in the pantry and could look after himself, there were others needing the space. The stores would be open soon, until then we had some of the meat from the Red Cross ship and he would have some of that and make a stew.

I went down to the sea wall to check on putting the pump away. Rudy was there with the boys. They had already flaked the hoses into the truck and were ready to put it back in the shed. There were two Argy MPs at the corner of Ross Road and Hospital Hill, they were directing traffic as best as they could. Some British troops were trying to obtain souvenirs from them without any success.

A mass of Royal Marines ran down the front road, one called out: 'I've got two Johnson 500s that you can have if you get me a couple of Brownings.'

'Right'o mate.'

I walked up the hill to George Butler's house (where it used to stand at least). All the way there were piles of cartridges on the road and weapons in the ditches, some broken and some as new.

I could see why Bloomer had said the situation in the house was dangerous, there were mortar bombs scattered on the ground in the grass and on the garden. Rifle cartridges lay on the ground like leaves in a forest in the autumn. There was a dugout inside the gate. It had a radio on the roof and the previous tenant's belongings scattered round. An Argy was rooting inside, he came out with a mug, some plates and cutlery. He jumped into a jeep and drove off. Smoke was still rising from the ruins. The roof and walls had collapsed inwards with the roof, this had saved the hot embers from spreading. The only thing left standing was the chimney. The sheds at the back were a bit singed and still packed with boxes – leave those to the experts. I saw a lot of rifle and other cartridges lying on the ground with the sides split open. I put a couple in my pocket. I would find someone to ask later on.

I went down to the dockyard. There were a few faces we hadn't seen for some months. People were rummaging about everywhere. I had a look in one building and 'liberated' a couple of gallon cans of Argy cooking oil. I saw a pair of wire crimpers with Les Harris's initials on them. Funny he worked at the power station. I remembered that hand grenades fit under things.

The part of the block shed where the cook had his store looked interesting.

'Nothing in there, we've had some tents and that's all, there's some live ammo lying about – be careful,' someone said.

I went in, there were some small sacks of fresh carrots on a shelf. They'll do for a start. Off with them up to my office, locking the stuff in, back again. There was a shelf behind the door on which stood three cardboard drums. I pulled one off. Empty. The second was empty too, they'd had powdered milk in them. The third was a different weight, I got it down and there we were, 56lbs dried onion flakes! [Abundant replacement for the dried onions lost during the incident after the huge explosion a few long weeks ago.]

There were masses of large bags of spaghetti in another part of the building, along with other items which would boost our greatly depleted food stocks. I got all the stuff home. The girls were going to experiment for lunch.

And guess what, the Argy cook's half Avgas drum cooking pot was stood in the corner by the block shed door, all cleaned out and shiny.

I had a quick look into what was left of Malcolm's office. The three Acetylene Cylinders were standing upright as were the oxygen ones. On the shoulder of the oxy cylinders was a hole larger than my fist, this is where they had blown.

Nowhere was safe to walk in the Dockyard. Heaps of human excreta in abundance.

Argy soldiers had occupied the post office overnight and filled all the desk drawers with excrement spoiling all the paperwork there.

Louis had a small hose and was cleaning out the whole post office. He had a captive crowd of Argies, he was assisted by a British Paras.

I got a can of disinfectant and splashed it about on the ground floor of the Town Hall, especially in the Council Chambers which had been used as a medical Centre. There were heaps of discarded equipment lying about. Some Red Cap British military police had arrived and were much in evidence. A gang of Royal Marines were shovelling muck out of the public toilets in the Gymnasium, putting it in wheelbarrows then tipping it over the sea wall into the harbour. They were grateful for the offer of the pump and hoses. We had had quite a busy day.

I put the FireFly away. En route I spotted a cardboard box in the middle of the road, St Mary's Walk, close to Central Station. I stopped and reasoned that if it had fallen of the back of a truck and had it been so inclined, it would have exploded by now. On close inspection I decided it could be spoils of war. I put the box on the back of the Firefly and drove round the block to our house. I carried it in and said to the girls that it was not dangerous, they could open it up and I would be back directly.

I got back home and was greeted by screams of laughter. 'All right, what's this all about?'

'Dad, you are now the proud owner of . . . 108 jars of shaving cream!'

The box had contained nine cartons, twelve jars in each, of Max Factor shaving cream, excellent stuff, must have been officers only.

I had noticed that the doors of one of the metal shipping containers on St Mary's Walk were open. We went down to have a look at what had been in them all this time. There were two soldiers sitting on the top of a heap of cardboard cartons.

'What have you found there?' I asked.

One said: 'These are Argy officers ration packs. We're after the cigarettes, help yourselves,' in a wonderful Scottish accent.

I asked: 'Do you have any real English tobacco, please mate?'

'I've got this Old Holborn stuff.'

Easy trade: 'I'll swap you for a couple of cans of McEwans.'

'You're on, laddie!'

I sent the girls home for some beers, I picked out half a dozen cartons from the heap.

I had a delightful smoke from the tobacco while the girls opened the packages. Each box contained several smaller packages which produced tins of meat, spaghetti in sauce, biscuits, chocolate, cigarettes, matches and several other things in the way of toiletries. Also in there was a humorous cartoon of a political nature, and a miniature bottle of Beef Breeders Association whisky – one of the better brands produced in Argentina. As the contents of the boxes were of a better quality than I expected, we went down to the container and rescued a few more.

While I prepared supper, the girls carried two of the cartons over to Fathers. That whole 20-foot container was full with these Boxes. I wonder what was in the other two, still closed, shipping containers.

Valerie came home for a meal, quite worn out from the day's activities of clearing up the mess in the hospital and other such duties.

The Argies had left the Old end fairly tidy. They had stacked the mattresses very kindly out of the way, and then put hand grenades between each layer. (What kind of a person sets booby traps in a hospital?)

Isobel and Rachel had taken down the blackouts. Valerie and I sat in our front room window having a before supper drink, just looking out of our own window at the dark. A soldier ran up the path and shouted to put out the light, there's probably going to be an air raid. Yes, ok. We carried on sipping.

We had heard on the Box that the 'radar' had detected an aircraft approaching from the west, but it had turned off. Here we go.

Edict No. 1 (from the British):

Stay indoors. The British forces are under curfew, and local people are warned that as Argentine soldiers could still be about the town, and showing resistance, it might be a 'shoot first' situation.

Oh boy! Here we go again.

The girls had managed to put out their bedding on the clothesline for a while during the day. As the mattresses had been flat on the floor for a long time, they had developed some black spots. These were soon removed with some fresh air and use of a hard brush and soapy water. We put our bed together again, what luxury.

It will be nice to get into bed without having to memorise the exact position of your clothes in case a night emergency call was made. We don't have to worry about the blackouts any more and can switch on any lights we like.

And there's the phone. Probably Father.

'Hello?'

It was Malcolm. 'Hey, chay, it's me, we've got a problem up here. There's bullets and goodness knows whats going off at the back of the house – get your fire engine and come up.'

'Malcolm, I don't know how to start dealing with a fire like that. It must be the dugouts in Dairy Paddock. I'll try and find someone from the British military and come up.'

'Ok, but don't hang about. We are afraid that there might be a shell or something big explode and go right through the house any minute.'

'Righto.'

I rang the exchange and asked if there was anyone who could help me in this situation. I was advised to go to the Secretariat; there were some Royal Engineers there. I got the FireFly from in front of the Central Station where I had left it as I hadn't had a chance to clear it out yet.

What a cheerful bunch of chaps they were, sleeping where they could. I was offered a sip of tea, which was a bit stronger than usual, while I was explaining myself and the problem.

The Captain, 'Robbie', said: 'Sounds a bit like it's up your street, Jock.'

'Aye Sir.' Another Scots accent. He started to wind up a length of nylon cord with a hook on the end and the Capt. picked up his rifle and checked the magazine.

'Ok, let's go.'[10]

I took them out to the FireFly. From their remarks I don't think they were expecting this sort of vehicle.

'There's room for three in the front.'

'No, sir you go inside, I'll hang on the back.'

'Hang on pretty tight; these roads are not like you get in England.'

I drove up the hill towards the power station then turned left into Brandon Road. This road is very rough at the best of times. The Capt. sat and clutched his rifle, much like Paganini had. He asked me what side of the road we had driven on before the Argies had come.

'Down the middle!'

'And during the occupation?'

'Down the middle!'

'Why do you drive down the middle?'

---

10. And so began a friendship with 'Jock' that continues today.

'Wait until daylight and you will see the potholes I'm dodging!'

We got to Malcolm's front gate. Jock said that any further and he would have been seasick.

There was a big glow behind the ridge over the back fence. Malcolm's wife Susan looked very distressed, the bangs and thumps were real enough. Jock said to keep in the shelter of the house, and he would go and take a look.

He was gone for some time. On his return he had the length of nylon line bunched in his hand and explained: 'I've pulled all the nasty stuff away from the fires with this line. There's a lot of small arms ammunition exploding which won't hurt the houses. But, if in any doubt, evacuate the whole row. It's too dark to see what is all there and too dangerous to fight the fires. Keep an eye on it and we'll have a look tomorrow.'

Malcolm wasn't too happy but saw the logic of it all. He offered us a drink which we declined. I returned the lads to the secretariat. They said that all fires from now on must be treated as if they contained explosives or gas. They would come out and help us as they had had previous experience and training.

I went home, nearly 10.30. I poured a drink and listened to the last few minutes of the local broadcast which no longer came over the Box but only on the radio.

The announcer played a record that he had removed from the studio for safekeeping on 2nd April. I stood up with tears in my eyes, how lovely to finally hear: 'GOD SAVE THE QUEEN.'

Wednesday, 16 June 1982

Valerie's diary

3–11 (hospital shift).

Cold from s/e. Occasional snow showers.

Went down town. Only Co-op open and what a diabolical mess everywhere, filthy.

All the Fox Bay hostages back in Stanley as well.

Busy evening. The [military] medics take over [the operating theatre in the hospital] trying to remove a bullet from a face. And they cleaned up after themselves [unlike the Argies].

Neville's diary

Off to work. A cold and miserable start, southwest wind with wintry showers. I had a nose round in the dockyard, Malcolm had all the gang clearing up. What a mess in the old garage where the fire was. Gas cylinders looking like giant sausages ripped open, a heap of mangled weapons, all the plumbers' tools and spares were mangled and distorted like a Salvador Dali painting. Hand grenades could be found in almost every corner. Two plastic rifle grenade carrying cases were found wedged under the stone crusher. They were removed by the appropriate people and found to be full of sugar, must be a new slant on warfare. The toilets were full and flowing out the doors, a job for the portable pump. We looked into the shelter the youngsters had built behind the smithy. They had an electric urn on a stand, several bits of no interest. Then I spotted three stainless steel oval serving dishes which I pocketed, and a couple of folding entrenching spades; I passed these on to a Royal Engineer walking by. He had a black beret; the blokes I met last night were of 9 Squadron and wore red berets, I must ask Jock about that.

The showers, which had eased off, had turned the dockyard into a mess of muddy slurry, real welly boot conditions. Valerie had been down the road and was disgusted with the condition of the town.

She was going on duty at three. We tried some of the tinned spaghetti stuff from the Argy ration packs for lunch, that was very passable.

I went up to the secretariat to have a chat with the lads from last night's escapade.

There was a Marine guard on the door. 'Sorry you can't come in here.'

'I'm the fireman, I've lived here all my life and always had free access to this building.'

'I don't know you and can't let you in.'

A voice from behind me: 'Hello old chap, having a bit of bother? It's ok Sergeant, I know him.'

I looked round and there was an Officer I had never seen before in my life.

'Very good Sir, pass through.'

I thanked the Officer and explained who I was.

'That's ok, glad to have been of service. These chaps are a bit cagey and are playing it by the rules, it'll all work out shortly.'

The platoon was out. The few blokes in the office said that a gang had been up to the gun site and made safe all the nasties laying about this morning, but there were still some small fires burning. They also said that they would be living in the Tabernacle schoolroom and using the Secretariat for a H.Q.

I went down to the dockyard. Malcolm came up and said to go up behind his house and do something about the fires there. I asked him for some help, but he said everyone was busy and there wasn't any spare blokes. I got the Firefly out, drove it up Dairy Paddock Road and turned off on to the track used by peat carters along the back of Brandon Road. The Argies had built a fair-sized hut of top sod and covered it over with corrugated iron for the roof. The walls were smouldering, some deep holes had burned into the ground. A lot of broken wooden crates were strewn about with broken radios and telephones muddled in. Something whistled past my head, I got down flat and crawled back to the truck. I got a soot rake out of the locker, went back to the hut and began to push the walls in to let the roof settle on the burning peat. Between each layer of sods, rifle cartridges had been pushed, these began to explode.

John Blyth called out from his garden two doors along that it was too dangerous to do anything more and to leave it alone.

Discretion being the better part etc I left the b——d to burn out.

I had a drive round the town, what a mess. Fences pulled down, muck of all sorts everywhere. One of the houses at the start of Davis Street had the door standing open. I stopped the truck and intended to go in and have a look who was at home. Inside the front gate was a pile of rifles, not your usual military issue but super-duper hunting rifles with telescopes fitted and a heap of boxed ammunition marked Remington. Wow, just the job. I stopped in my tracks, hand poised to pick one up . . . I saw a thin piece of wire threaded through the trigger guards and leading up to the outhouse. I followed the wire and it was attached to something I didn't want to look at and left well alone.

I peeped in the house, the table in the kitchen was set for tea, all the cups were on their saucers upside down, side plates and bread and butter knives all proper. I said to Jock about this later (his name was John), his boys had been there. The thing in the shed was very nasty and all the cups had a grenade under them.

Two Paras had opened a shipping container in front of the bakery. They asked, 'What's this stuff mate?'

'The bags are first class baking flour and the grease proof paper packages are dripping, all good quality,' I replied.

'We're going to get a truck and take some for the folks we know.'

I wrestled a couple of the hundredweight sacks into the fly and delivered them home. I topped up the fuel in the truck and put it away. I walked down the hill and told Malcolm what I had done and said there was nothing more we could do.

The children and I got some more cartons from the container and went over to see Father. He was in tip top form. He had some tinned things on his table and was making a stew. I remarked how happy he looked.

'I had a couple of visitors last night and they are coming in again tonight, so I've made this stew and got a few cans of beer. They brought me some tinned stuff.'

'All the troops are under curfew still.'

'These blokes are trained to evade that sort of thing.'

Oh well, nice for him to have some company and I expect the lads enjoyed the visit too.

The hostages were back from Fox Bay; although they were healthy, they had obviously been under great strain. They had had no idea what their destination would be when they were taken away in the helicopter all those weeks ago, execution had been a real fear.

Valerie came home at 11, tired out, she was on again at 7am, so off to bed. I didn't tell her about the afternoon's work, she would have only got upset about it.

Thursday, 17 June 1982

Valerie's diary

7–3 (hospital shift).

Light s/w wind. Overcast.

Helicopters ++ around. Plenty of warships etc. in the harbour.

Globe Store burnt to the ground 5am ish, set alight by Argies.

Busy all day organising the Army end of the hospital.

Heard at 5pm that Galtieri has resigned!

Pam, me and girls walked around town. Smoke ++ from Globe Store ruins.

Curfew again from 4pm, few Argies around town, will be shot on sight.

Jock, a Para, came around for the evening after fighting a fire with Neville.

Neville's diary

There's the bloody phone, what time is it? oh 4 or so.

The operator informed me 'There is a fire at the Globe Store.'

I replied: 'Please alert Rudy Clark, John Smith and whoever you think necessary, I'll be at the Central Station and getting the trucks running.'

There was a thin dusting of snow on the ground.

Philomel Hill was full of Argentines waiting to be processed and sent home in a ship in Port William. The MV Forrest was waiting at the Public Jetty to ferry another batch out. All their kit bags were piled in the middle of the road and some Panhard armoured scout cars were parked alongside the Globe Hotel.

I drove straight up the middle of the road; the boys laid the hoses as best they could. We could only get one pump on the Jetty as the British MPs were searching departing Argies there. We certainly could do with some help. I went up to the Tabernacle where the men from the Secretariat who had helped me yesterday were now staying. I loudly opened the gate and stamped my way up the path whistling. I knocked on the outer door and walked in. Bearing in mind that it was not quite 5am yet, one or two eyes looked at me and I heard the metallic click of safety catches being slid back.

'Hi Nev.'

'Hi, there's a big one down at the end of John Street. Ammo and goodness knows what. It's been one of their stores. There's thousands of Argies about. Can you come and help us please?'

'We'll be there in a few minutes.'

All we could do was put water on the fire. The walls of the building were made of stone. The roof had collapsed in onto the fire. Lots of bangs and flashes from the equipment stored inside.

I went to check the other buildings across the road, to Waverley House which was the dwelling and the admin office belong to the Store. I tripped over a pair of legs in the gateway. It was a British Military Policeman. He must have been half frozen in the snow.

'You all right?' I asked.

'Yes, thank you.'

He had a small machine gun trained on some Argy men in the front porch of the house.

'There's an old officer and his staff in there, they won't come out for me, and they know I can't shoot.'

'Ok, I'll have a go at them.'

I had been a bit miffed with the Argies for quite a while and it was coming out now.

I instructed them: 'Gentlemen, get the hell out of there as fast as you can. Your amigos have set alight to the building opposite and there are explosives all round here and in the sheds. I do not mind if you get killed but I don't want any of my men or the man at the gate to get shot by you. Now GO.'

I turned and walked out through the gate.

The elderly officer caught up with me. He embraced me and said thanks, with tears streaming down his face. His companions still snarled.

We kept losing pressure on the hoses. I walked down the hill. The waiting Argie prisoners were stabbing the hoses with their bayonets.

MPs were trying to search the masses of Argies who suddenly were not trying to impress the world with their knowledge of the English language.

'Would you like a hand Major?' I asked.

'Yes please, if you could.'

There is only one rude expression I know of in Spanish. I don't know what it means but I thought here goes. 'Shut your bloody mouths and wait where you are.' If that is what it meant. It worked and they all quietened down. The half dozen MPs got on with the job of searching and disarming the Argies.

I got back to the fire. All the men waiting on the road parted to let me through. That sounds like shooting. No, it's the Squash Court. Sparks and lumps of building were flying over the houses in the front of the court.

'Everyone: get up to the Squash Court, I'll tidy up here there's nothing more we can do.'

The explosions from the Globe Store had stopped. I cut the motor on the pump but had to leave it there on the jetty. I bundled up the hoses that I could get at and left it all till later.

The squash court was situated in the Junior School playground on John Street. The lads were trying to gain an entry by chopping through the south wall which was a rather solidly constructed piece of woodwork. There were too many explosions and too much smoke on the north side to enter by the door there. The Infants' block, built of wood and covered in tarred felt, stood about 10 feet from the squash court. The Anti-Aircraft gun mounted on its trailer, loaded and ready to go, looked out of place in a school yard. In the main building the classrooms appeared ready to receive the day's pupils. Desks and chairs all tidy. However, there were holes cut in the floor for access to the space under the building, and heaps of ammunition and shells stacked round.[11]

The wall was too much for the lads and the fire and explosions were increasing, with debris being propelled into neighbouring properties.

A quick trip to the Secretariat to ask for help in the form of the excavator tank (a large tank with a bulldozer blade on the front). This was in action by the time I arrived back.

The driver had lifted the whole end off in one movement and stood it against the wall of the neighbouring building. The lads got stuck in removing the cartons of food stuff the building was packed with. They found bits of things which could only be the remains of incendiary devices and timing mechanisms. It had seemed odd that food and ammo should be stacked together like that and have spontaneously combusted.

---

11. One child, when they eventually did return to classes, said that her Spanish exercise book had the last lesson marked and corrected by an Argy soldier.

The fire was eventually extinguished. We packed up the gear and went home at 3.30 p.m. It was time I got out of my pyjamas and dressed properly and had something to eat.

Friday, 18 June 1982

Valerie's diary
7–3 (hospital shift).
Light s/w wind. Warm, sunny day.
Funeral for the 3 blast victims. RIP.
Mary and family back from G.G.[12]
Spoils of war from Drill Hall: Pimientos, cooking oil, peas etc.
Dr Charles came for supper. Pleasant evening.
Prince Andrew interviewed outside Secretariat by F.I.B.S. [local radio].

Neville's diary
Last night: After finishing up after the Squash Court fire, John was asked if he would like to join us for a bite to eat – to try some of the local meat. The mutton wasn't one of our better pieces from the freezer. Being a polite young man [he] made no comment on the quality of the meat but complimented the cook – he was invited to return for another meal.

The girls asked why he had a maroon beret, the same colour as a Para, but with a different badge – that of the Royal Engineers.

'I'm an Airborne Engineer.'

'What does that mean?'

'We fly with the Paras, and if the 'plane develops trouble with the engine or gets a puncture we fix it in flight!'

Friday: Work as usual next day, was a bit humdrum. I was kept busy cleaning the much-used firefighting gear and thinking back over the last few weeks. I hadn't seen Major Dowling nor Gilobert since the British had landed. Had they been 'taken out' or got out?

I was refuelling the trucks from spare cans that I had hidden away at the start of the conflict when a very kind soul came in and said: 'Do you know, there are two drums of petrol fallen off the back of a truck and tucked under some bushes?'

So, I ventured forth and 'liberated' one of the drums and stored it in the Central Station cupboard.

In the evening there was a call. A fire behind the FIC offices. Ok, ask Rudy to meet me at the station. This could be a real nasty. Terry Spruce

---

12. Goose Green.

had told me that the Argies had buried ammunition behind his office. This could be another of their attempts to get rid of another section of the town. I had better call in and ask John if he would come and have a look also. I couldn't have the town sirens sounded as the lines were still cut somewhere, anyway if they were sounded surely panic would kick off. We were all still very jumpy.

I stopped the FireFly on Fitzroy Road, overlooking the space behind Terry's offices. There was a fire there. Some squaddy had lit a bonfire to keep warm. He wasn't too happy when we called out to him to put it out as it was on top of an ammunition dump. John said he spoke the same language and nipped off to have a quiet word with the bloke.

Both John and Rudy were persuaded to come in for a 'medicinal' drink at our house, which was enjoyable.

Saturday, 19 June 1982

Valerie's diary
3–11 (hospital shift).
Cool from n/w. Light ground frost.
Neville was out all morning pumping out Y.P.F [Argentine fuel depot] and Town Hall.
I had a burn up of cardboard boxes in the garden.[13]
Andy and Ian, 2 Royal Marines, came to stay for a few days.[14]

Rachel remembers . . .
Andy and Ian were to sleep on camp beds in the front room/living room. I was keen to show them the eye-holes that I had cut in the curtain lining a couple of months earlier so I that could stand inside the curtains and spy on the Argies. They arrived, dropped off their kit and left again. Their kit was stored in enormous rucksacks which they put in front of a cupboard that Isobel and I soon wanted to access. Between us, using all of our strength, we were unable to move one of the rucksacks even an inch! The cupboard could wait.

Neville's diary
We had a couple of Marines stay for a while until their transport out was available. The young lad would put on full outfit at about mid-day and patrol somewhere. He always returned with something for the pantry, the best was a carton of large tins of stewed steak of Argentine origin. Valerie

---

13. The boxes were from recently 'acquired' Argie food.
14. Captain Andy Cole and Ian Smith of Zulu Company, 45 Commando.

was very good with pastry – a tin of the meat in a large pie dish covered with a crust would feed six people.

The Argy shipping containers round the town were being removed and being used by the army as storage units. The ones which had Argy explosive stickers on them did in fact have explosives in them, even those parked in the middle of the town. The ones with 'mun' or munitions painted on the doors or sides contained food and clothing. One container had more cigarettes in it than a small army needs, while another was chock a block with wellie boots. One particular container had a variety of female and children clothing in it, the story being that this was in preparation for the families of the occupying force or new settlers.

The FIDF drill hall was full of food stuffs as was the FIC warehouse. Cheese, flour, rice, vinegar, cooking oils and powdered milk plus many tins of meat and vegetables. The residents of Stanley were asked to help themselves to what we wanted. The remainder was to be taken out to sea and dumped. A squaddy thought he had found a treasure with some cases marked 'Vinegra de Vino'. 'We'll have a good party with this,' he said.

I had to disillusion him before he came to grief and told him it was a very good class of vinegar and his unit's cook would be pleased with it!

Sunday, 20 June 1982

Valerie's diary
7–3 (hospital shift).
Clocks went back one hour.
MV Elk in the harbour.
Light n/w wind, almost flat calm, turned to drizzle during afternoon.
Walked round town with girls.
Mike and Rikki back from Kepple [Island].
Fritz came for supper.
Nursing staff start week's holiday.[15]

Monday, 21 June 1982

Valerie's diary
Day off.
Plenty of rain during night, light southerly wind. Cold.
Caught up on some hand washing.
Andy left to go on the Canberra. Ian will go tomorrow.
Jess joined us for supper – roast leg of mutton etc.

---

15. The military medics ran the civilian hospital while the staff had a much-needed rest.

Neville called out for a fire on Callaghan Road.

Princess Di has a baby boy.

Neville's diary

A friend of one of Ian's, one of the Marines staying with us, came round and had a meal. He said he had a problem about going home.

We thought 'oh dear'.

He said he didn't know whether to walk up the road to his front door or to go through the service lane and over the garden fence. We asked why, [and] he said his mum was threatening to have a street party to welcome him home and he was a little scared of it.

During the evening another phone call – callout to a fire in a store shed on Callaghan Road. It put up some resistance, but we won.

Rachel remembers …

After the Liberation dad and I went for many walks around the outskirts of Stanley looking at where the Argies had been. They had made a huge mess. They had dug into all of our favourite and familiar places, and left heaps of kit and junk behind.

The first of these walks was to the south east of Stanley and up to the Darwin road. We walked up Dairy Paddock Road, past Mike Butcher's house. Stopped for a catchup chat. Out onto the Common. It was an Argie junkyard. My belly felt winded as I looked around and saw the dugouts, big guns, trashed vehicles, food packets, clothing. Only a couple of months before it had been clean and empty, unpolluted. We stood for ages, just looking, trying to take it all in. It was so quiet but felt like an enormous noise had left only moments before.

Using the tip of his knife, dad removed the Oerlikon name plate and sight prisms from an anti-aircraft gun, its barrel still pointing at the sky. I could have sat in it, but was afraid to go that close. I stood at a safe distance and watched dad work.

Around at the peat banks, there was something too horrible. Again, loads more Argie junk violating the familiar. In the middle of the peat bank, there was the shallow grave of an Argentine soldier. That familiar smell of dead bodies. His boots had surfaced, and the flies had found him. I can remember the two pieces of wood tied together with a plastic rosary that made his cross. Something poked into the beads too. A piece of paper.

Next stop, the huge, previously distressingly noisy, 155mm gun at the bottom of Sapper Hill. Still pointing at Wireless Ridge. More mess.

Back home down the Darwin Road, looking at the ships in the harbour and out in Port William. Stepping aside as military vehicles rattled past.

Tuesday, 22 June 1982

Valerie's diary

Day off.

Left at 9.00 for a Gazelle [helicopter] flight to Kepple and Pebble Islands. Foggy in patches.

Landed at Kepple. CM was over at Pebble. Spent 4 hours there.

Jock called in. He is poorly with the flu. Temp: 101.2°f.

Neville's diary

Valerie was asked to go by helicopter to conduct a medical checkup visit to the folks on Keppel and Pebble Islands. She was a little anxious about this as she was not a fan of travelling in small aircraft like the Beaver or Islander. The people of Pebble had suffered the occupation of a group of Argies, and also the attentions of our special forces with their own brand of fireworks they use as a visiting card.

Valerie returned in the evening and astounded us by saying she wanted one of those little helicopters for Christmas, she had thoroughly enjoyed her day flying!

Wednesday, 23 June 1982

Valerie's diary

Day off.

Dull drizzle from the n/w.

Helicopters busy as usual.

Deep cleaned the bathroom, condensation ++ [The after-effects of black-outs and poor ventilation during the war.]

We have to queue up to get into the West Store.

Fred Clarke came to interview Neville for U.P.A. [Press Association]

Jumbo brought 2 cylinders of gas. [For use in our two-ring hob and wall heater.]

Neville's diary

Steve McKay and I had been friends for a long time; he and his mother had been our neighbours when we were first married. His job involved supervising the animals grazing on the common, tending to the dosing of dogs with worming pills and inspecting the twice weekly killing of mutton at the slaughterhouse for hydatid disease in the sheep.

Steve asked me if I would drive him up to the Agricultural Dept. stables at the back of the Sullivan House garden. This is a stone building with a corral/stable yard in front. He had worked as what was called a Common

Ranger for the Agric. Dept. for a number of years. The area round the stable had been cleaned up. Inside the building all the horse harnesses were hanging neatly on the hooks provided. Steve had a closer look and nearly broke down; all the buckles and rings had been cut off each strap and piece of gear. All the gear, which would have been the collection of working items for three or four men, was all destroyed. Pointless destruction of items essential to our Falklands way of life.

We proceeded around the town with our inspection. The extinguishers had not only been allocated by me but were also taken from our supplies by the Argies where they felt the need. Some of the appliances were intact, some, where they could be recognised, were in a sorry state. Others, although refillable, had been discarded on a use-once basis and were on the rubbish tip. None of those were repairable, especially those cut about with shrapnel.

Some of the houses were in a sorry state too. Some of the houses on the outskirts of town had been shot up by the retreating Argies. No. 4 Racecourse Road was not there at all. We looked through the windows of No. 1 Racecourse Road; it looked as if the original occupant had left in a hurry. All sorts of clothes and linen strewn about. I said to Steve, 'I'll just ring the front doorbell in case there's someone home.'

'No, don't be daft, there's no one in – can't you see by the look of the place?'

'Not even a little ding?'

'No' – but it got a laugh out of him!

We had a look round the back of the house, decaying food and goodness knows what. There was a funny thing in the shed, a battery charger connected to a battery which had wires running to the house; that's the second one I had seen like that– oh, leave it alone.

* * *

A while later, Valerie and I took the girls up round Racecourse Road for a stroll; it was the first time away from the routine Ross Road walk. While we were passing No. 1, a man came out and asked: 'Hi Matron, would you like a cup of tea?'

'Oh! Hello, how are you now, are you back at work?'

'Thank you, Matron, a lot better but still on light duties. I'm housekeeping for the fire fighters using this house. Come on in.'

Valerie said the chap was from the airport, a cook, and had suffered severe burns; she had helped to nurse him in the KEM.

I asked him about the fire extinguishers that were in the house and said that we had been unable to gain entry and look for them.

'Oh no, we've dumped them and treated everything with suspicion. The front doorbell was wired up to enough explosives in the loft, via a battery charger in the garage, to take out the whole area and Government House if anyone had rung the bell.'

Oh! Dearie me.

I said nothing, she would only have worried.

Thursday, 24 June 1982

Valerie's diary

Day off.

Cold and dry from N n/e. Sunny spells during a.m.

Jock turned up for a bath. Much better from his bug.

Still catching up on washing with 2 machines in operation.

Stanley airport re-opens after a mammoth rebuild by Royal Engineers, etc., first British Hercules lands!

Jock turned up later with rations – bacon and eggs, etc. too. Treasures.

Still fierce fighting in Syria.

OCTOBER 1982

Sunday, 10 October 1982

Valerie's diary
Day off.
Cold all day from s/w. Frequent snow squalls which didn't lay.
Half marathon run, 500 entries, won by a soldier in 1hr 5min.
Honours list broadcast in BBC 'Calling The Falklands'.
I got an MBE.

Neville's diary
The 'Calling the Falklands' programme came on, with no interference. The list of awards for the conflict was to be read out. Before the announcer, Peter King, got into his stride Valerie said quietly, 'I've been asked to accept one of those.'

'You've what?'

'Shhhh!'

Peter King announced many awards, then got to one very special person: 'And for the biggest Florence of them all, Val, the MBE.'

'Oh, hooray!'

Moist eyes again.

The phone rang: it was Father, 'Congratulations!'

Rod and Lily called, 'Well done', and many others phoned too.

The very often asked question 'Are you going to go to England to be awarded your medal?' was met with a simple, heartfelt reply,

'No, I've been awarded this for my service here and I would like to have it presented here by Sir Rex Hunt.'

Postscript

by Neville Bennett

Another landmark incident happened in January 1983, when the local broadcast was interrupted with the announcement that an aircraft carrying Mrs Thatcher and her husband had landed at the airport, the couple were in transport and would be in town in a matter of minutes. As the cavalcade motored slowly along St Mary's Walk, Uncle Harold sprang out into the road, doors flew open, Mrs Thatcher looked out and Uncle Harold presented her with a rose from his conservatory.

The house next door, now that Mary and Neil were away, was rented to the Royal Engineers. They came into our house and had many meals with us and became somewhat addicted to Falkland Island mutton. One of these lads returned to set up the floating hotels, with a civilian maintenance crew. They became known to us as Uncle Peter, Uncle Bob, Jeff and Doug, and their quarters at that time were so crowded they would walk the 3 or so miles just to sit in a quiet room with us and have a cup of tea. They had also formed a liking for local mutton after being lectured about the stuff during the 9,000-mile journey by sea.

After staffing changes at the hospital, Valerie was again the Matron, this time not acting but the real thing – including all the headaches of seniority. Father's health had deteriorated and he spent a lot of time in the hospital. The military staff made a fuss of him as well as the local girls. The army nurses asked Valerie if they could attend the delivery of babies as well, as they said they didn't get much practice with elderly patients or childbirth in a field hospital unit. Father passed away late in March 1984; he was buried next to my mother.

I made a trip to Goose Green on Union business a week later. I had a pleasant stay with some old friends, but what a shock to see the place after the war. The school had been hit by a missile from both ends. Tony said it had taken 45 minutes to burn down. The engine shed had been burned down some time before the occupation and that was a heap of rusty engine parts. Plenty of barbed wire and minefields, and wrecked aircraft. I was taken towards Teal Creek by Tony, and he showed me the cemetery for the Argentine dead. The bodies had all been moved there by a firm of morticians out from England. A nice white rail and paling fence surrounded the area; the graves all had a cross at the head, with the name on and rank, but sadly on many were the words 'An Argentine Soldier Known to God Alone'.

The Union Delegates from the East Falklands met at Goose Green a week later during a Two Nighter. We learned sadly that there had been a house fire and that one of our long-standing members had perished in the fire.

I sorted through father's house. Some of his books I took to the library, and his sporting trophies I gave to someone who was interested in creating a Museum of Sport in the Islands. There were a lot of family photos which I kept, and some of the crew of HMS Exeter on her return from the Battle with the Graf Spee.

I had installed a new Rayburn and plumbed in the new hot water system for him to make life a little easier before he finally went into hospital. The house was still in quite good condition. Aunt Grace bought it for her daughter.

We were wakened by the fire siren at 4.45am on 10th April. The noise of the fire seemed close; I couldn't see in the dark so called the exchange and learned it was the hospital. We quickly dressed; Valerie went to the hospital, which was well alight at the oldies end, as was part of Syd Lyse's house next door. All our equipment was there, as well as a large machine from the airport which had arrived in about 4 minutes. The whole east end of the KEM and the new military wing, only a few weeks old, were completely destroyed. I prowled round in father's property watching for flying embers. We were informed that seven patients and one civilian member of staff had perished in the fire. Valerie was very distraught, she told me that the nurse who had died had swapped duties with her. Valerie had lost not only two staff members in the fire, but all the patients were old friends too.

The rehousing of the patients and relocation of everything kept Valerie occupied for some time. The military patients were housed in the complex close to the floating hotels, while the civilians were put up in some large buildings and private houses in town.

It was a situation we had all feared – a large wooden building so vulnerable to fire hazard, difficulty in deploying equipment. The local brigade, along with trained men from the Royal Air Force, had done all they could, and they saved lives, but with the building being so dry they hadn't stood a chance.

How did it start? Was the fire door shut or open? Was it still there at that time? Was it carelessness by someone? We may never learn or be told the truth. An enquiry was set up with investigators from England, and legal advisers. Valerie seemed to feel the blame as she was in charge; she had spent so much effort keeping the connecting door shut during the Argy occupation of the Old End, but was this continued? She couldn't answer for 24 hours a day now. She became depressed. The situation of her patients was not ideal, but it was all that could be managed under the circumstances. Four nurses from hospitals in the UK arrived and were accommodated in one of the new houses being constructed for the government. The winter dragged on. Valerie couldn't shake off the shadows of depression.

'Father's gone now, I am not happy with the way things are, I lost some dear old friends in that fire. There's nothing to keep us here now, the girls are growing up and need something better than they can get here at the moment for their future.'

'Yes dear, let's go and see your Mum. She hasn't seen the girls for 11 years. If I can get back into the dental trade well and good, I should be able to earn a living. I'm a bit rusty after this time but I'm willing to have a go.'

We sailed on 26th August on SS Uganda, calling in at San Carlos Water (Bomb Alley) for fuel, and then away north up the Atlantic to Ascension Island.

After a nine-day cruise which was wonderful, we relaxed, no stresses, no call-outs, just the swish of the sea. We didn't see any whales, but did see many flying fish and albatross and other birds not seen from the land. We arrived at Ascension and transferred to the airport by helicopter, an experience I have no desire to repeat. Then it was on to a military plane sitting facing aft and 8 hours to a base in Oxfordshire. We stayed in a hotel on the base overnight. Had a pint of draught bitter, the first for 11 years, wow. Next morning, I asked the receptionist to get us a taxi, or hire car, as lugging round suitcases on railway stations would be a bit much. A few hours later we arrived in Taunton.

Saturday, 8 September

What a fuss, the girls were all grown up since Granny had seen them last, and their Uncle was suitably impressed too. Valerie visited various neighbours and friends in the area; the girls went down to the corner shop and bought something which had really been a dream: a pound of bananas each. Fresh fruit was not one of the things readily available in the Falklands.

We visited Valerie's friends, Charlie and Joan, in Bovey Tracey; Joan and Valerie had trained together. We drove over Dartmoor, walked here and there; it was wonderful to walk on grass and beaches without the fear of losing a limb. We did some shopping in Plymouth and generally relaxed. I was on my way to an appointment with a hairdresser in the shopping centre, when crossing a road I bumped into our Royal Marine friend Andy MacDonald. I told him where the family was and would see him later; to have a haircut with the trimmings after nearly 12 years was a treat. Andy came back in the evening for a meal with us and took Valerie and myself to the General Moore pub for a drink; there were a lot of Falklands Campaign trophies on the walls.

I started looking at adverts and getting names from the phone book, and after nineteen calls I found a laboratory owner willing to give an out-of-touch technician with a bit of maturity a trial. I think he wanted to see what a Falkland Islander looked like. I was given a trade test and passed muster; I could start work on 1st December. Rachel started school in Exeter and Valerie easily found a nursing job.

Valerie began to lose weight. She suggested I went on a diet, implying that she was. She started to skip meals, saying she was not hungry, or had something at work, until she told me she had a pain in her abdomen and a lump under her ribs. She'd been for a scan and a smear test which were clear. Our doctor got her into hospital in pretty short order, and, after several blood transfusions, an operation was performed, removing a kidney with a nasty large lump attached. She was discharged from the hospital in the care of her friend Joan at Bovey, and came back to us full of beans. Our doctor said that if she continued to progress slowly, all should be well.

Unfortunately, that was not to be the case. The cancer spread rapidly, and she returned to hospital where it was found to be in a very advanced condition. Valerie passed away on 8th June 1986.

We three pulled ourselves up by our own bootstraps, as they say. Isobel went to college and passed enough exams to gain entry to nursing training, following in her mum's footsteps. Rachel finished school and went to college; she went on to university in North Wales, from where she graduated with honours and went on to qualify as a schoolteacher. They both married and I have four grandsons.

Neville Bennett
Exeter, 1987 and 2007

'Liberation Day'

by Rachel Simons

Heavy air.
Parents stare.
Dennis shouts, 'get to your safe place,
You're not safe there.'

Noisy air.
Officer barks and shoots
over the fleeing conscripts' heads.
Parents hastily prepare.

Dangerous air.
Scurrying in bullet dodging fear.
Secret hiding men give us hope.
Liberators are near.

Safe air.
Hospital shelter.
Busy staff.
Concern about street fighting. Prepare.

Staring at air.
White helicopter lands.
Peace men walk by,
all hope . . .

Joyful air.
Hospital filled with long awaited relief.
They're here! We're Free.
Brave military men, an answered prayer.

Appendix 1

Fires in Stanley during the occupation

5 April 1982 – Chimney fire, James Street. Len Reives' home.

11 April 1982 – Ash drum fire, adjacent to fuel storage tank. Home of Dr Haines, Ross Road West.

13 April 1982 – Rayburn cooker fire. Flooding fuel. Cable Cottage.

4 May 1982 – Argentine soldiers from the Dockyard were trained to use the fire appliances. It was deemed too dangerous for the locals to go out in the hours of darkness and curfew.

During the occupation, the trained Argentines attended a gorse bush fire at the Monument, fire in the hedge of Government House drive, some chimney fires, and a fire in the trees around Stanley House.

8 May 1982 – Davis street to the east of Philomel Hill. Fire burning into the peat in the ground caused by Argentines cooking outside. Fire extinguished by cutting it our of the ground and applying much water.

13 June 1982 – House fire at 80 Davis Street. It was hit by a British shell, the house burned to the ground. No damage to the neighboring houses.

14 June 1982 – No. 4 Racecourse Road. Total loss of house to fire during bombardment. No attendance by fire service.

Ambulance shed containing helicopter fuel. Total loss.

(3.00pm) Office at the old part of the Power Station. Much damage by fire and water. Fire brought under control.

(5.00pm) House fire at G. Butlers house on Moody Street. Arson by Argentines. Total loss of house which burned until 8.30pm. Much ammunition in the house and on the ground.

(9.30pm) Peat shed fire at G. Mercer's house. Argentine arson. The peat had been soaked with liquid fuels and ammunition scattered on it. The fire was allowed to burn out observed from a safe distance.

(11.00pm) Dockyard garage fire. Argentines in the dockyard reported that Argentines from the mountains had thrown their kit into the garage and had set fire to it. They offered to put the fire out. They were sent away, no one could put water on that fire because of the contents of the next shed. Safe to leave it at 04.45am

15 June 1982 – (8.30pm) Explosions at rear of 3 Brandon Road. Fire service attended accompanied by some members of 9 SQN RE who assessed the situation to be dangerous, that it should be left until daylight. Evacuate the street if necessary. This was not deemed necessary.

17 June 1982 – (4.30am) Globe Store total loss. Argentine arson. Used as a store for many items by the Argies. Fire brigade were assisted by many members of the Task Force.

(7.30am) Squash Court. Argentine arson. Timing devices set among ammunition and food packs. Fire extinguished, building beyond repair. Fire brigade were assisted by many members of the Task Force.

18 June 1982 – Fire behind the FIC offices. Accidentally caused by the British army.

19 June 1982 - Chimney fire at Alice Duncans on Pioneer Row. Also at Keenlysides next door.

21 June 1982 – Fire in Timmy Dobbyns store shed. Complete loss.

22 June 1982 – (1.00pm) Chimney fire at Sullivan House.

(4.00pm) Chimney fire at Billy Lang's house.

26 June 1982 – (8.30pm) Fire at the ESRO Station at the head of the bay accommodating British military. Total loss of the building.

Stanley Fire Brigade during the Falklands War

People who served with the Falkland Islands Fire Service during the war:

Jim Alazia
Gem Bayliss
Neville Bennett
Terry Betts
Les Biggs
Graham Bound
Richard Cain
Gerald Cheek
Marvin Clarke
Mickey Clarke
Rudy Clarke
Lewis Clifton
Charlie Coutts
Peter Coutts
Taff Davies
Dave Eynon
Jim Fairfield
Arthur Gould

Chris Harris
Les Harris
Derek Howatt
Robert Kiddle (Fluff)
James Lee
Les Lee
Anton Livermore
Chris McCallum
Len McGill
Neil McKay
Owen McPhee
Pat McPhee
Phil Middleton
Father Monaghan
Billy Morrison
Brian Paul
Derek Petterson
Tony Petterson

Billy Porter
Glen Ross
Gavin Short
Philip Short
Jeremy Smith
John Smith
Martin Smith
Zach Stephenson
Bob Stewart
Bobby Stewart (Ned Kelly)
Brian Summers
Kim Summers
Owen Summers
Fraser Wallace
Steve Whitley
Susan Whitney
William Whitney (Jumbo)

The hospital staff during the war

Senior Medical Officer (SMO) Daniel Haines (27 April: he and his wife and family were taken prisoner)

Dr Hilary Haines, Dr Alison Bleaney, Dr Mary Elphinstone, Robert Watson (Dentist)

Matron – Valerie Bennett

Nursing sisters – Bronwyn Williams, Karen Timberlake

Nurses –Xenia Barnes, Candy Blakeley, Debbie Bleaney, Gladys Carey, Alice Etheridge, Rhoda Felton, Maud McKenzie, Daisy Rowlands, Ana Smith, Diane Stewart, Pam Summers

Elderly care in the hospital – Ramon Miranda (Boy), Anja Smith

Lab Technician – Teresa McGill

Ambulance drivers – Brian Paul, Abbey Alazia

Cooks – Winnie Miranda, Keva Smith, Claire Peak, Phyllis Macbeth

Clerk – Lawrence Blizzard

Secretary – Shelley Livermore

Gardners – Abby Alazia, Ernie Rieve

Maids – Eve Alazia, Mary Lou Hobman, Anita Munoz, Mally Coutts, Sonia Paul

Elderly care in the community – Ron and Nij Bucket